Unravelling Gramsci

Reading Gramsci

General Editor: Joseph A. Buttigieg

Also available

Gramsci, Culture and Anthropology
Kate Crehan

Language and Hegemony in Gramsci
Peter Ives

Unravelling Gramsci

Hegemony and Passive Revolution in the Global Political Economy

Adam David Morton

Pluto Press
LONDON • ANN ARBOR, MI

First published 2007 by Pluto Press
345 Archway Road, London N6 5AA
and 839 Greene Street, Ann Arbor, MI 48106

www.plutobooks.com

British Library Cataloguing in Publication Data
A catalogue record for this book is available from the British Library

Hardback
ISBN-13   978 0 7453 2385 5
ISBN-10   0 7453 2385 5

Paperback
ISBN-13   978 0 7453 2384 8
ISBN-10   0 7453 2384 7

Library of Congress Cataloging in Publication Data applied for

10   9   8   7   6   5   4   3   2   1

Designed and produced for Pluto Press by
Chase Publishing Services Ltd, Fortescue, Sidmouth, EX10 9QG, England
Typeset from disk by Stanford DTP Services, Northampton, England
Printed and bound in the European Union by
Antony Rowe Ltd, Chippenham and Eastbourne, England

Contents

PART II GRAMSCI, WORLD ORDER, AND RESISTANCE

List of Figures

Reading Gramsci

General Editor: Joseph A. Buttigieg

Antonio Gramsci (1891–1937), little known outside communist circles at the time of his death, is now one of the most frequently cited and widely translated political theorists and cultural critics of the twentieth century. The first wave of interest in Gramsci was triggered by the publication, in Italy, of his prison writings, starting with the letters, which appeared in 1947, and continuing with the six volumes of the thematic edition of the notebooks, the last of which was brought out in 1951. Within the space of a few years, hundreds of articles and books were written explicating, analysing and debating Gramsci's concept of hegemony, his revisionist views on the history of Italy's unification, his anti-economistic and antidogmatic version of Marxist philosophy, his theory of the state and civil society, his anti-Crocean literary criticism, his novel approach to the study of popular culture, his extensive observations on the role of intellectuals in society, along with other aspects of his thought. Although long dead, Gramsci became more than an object of dispassionate study; the intensity of the discussions surrounding his work and the often heated struggle over his legacy had, and continue to have, a profound effect on the political culture and cultural politics of postwar Italy.

During the late 1960s and the 1970s Gramsci's name and ideas started circulating with increasing frequency throughout Europe, Latin America, and North America (and, to a lesser extent, elsewhere too). The various currents associated with Eurocommunism and the 'New Left' that accompanied the swell of interest in what came to be known as 'western Marxism' contributed immensely to Gramsci's rise to prominence during this period. In the anglophone world, the publication, in 1971, of Quintin Hoare and Geoffrey Nowell Smith's superbly edited *Selections from the Prison Notebooks* made it possible for scholars to move from vague and general allusions to Gramsci to serious study and analysis of his work. Gramscian studies were further bolstered by various editions in diverse languages of the pre-prison writings – which, among other things, drew attention to the valuable essay on the Southern Question – and by the publication, in Italy, of Valentino Gerratana's complete critical edition of the *Quaderni del carcere* (1975).

Gramsci's influence became even more pronounced in the 1980s with the spread of cultural studies, the growing fascination with the question of 'power', and the greater attention that scholars from different disciplines were devoting to the relations among culture, society, and politics. The rapid decline of interest in Marxist thought following the events of 1989 had no effect on Gramsci's 'fortunes'. By that time, as Stuart Hall was among the first to point out, Gramsci had already 'radically displaced some of the inheritances of Marxism in cultural studies'. Indeed, Gramsci's ideas have come to occupy a very special position in the best known of post-Marxist theories and strategies by the political left. Furthermore, the ubiquitous concern with the concept of civil society during the past 15 years has rekindled interest in Gramsci's reflections on the subject. Likewise, many of the issues and topics that currently preoccupy a broad spectrum of academic intellectuals – subaltern studies, postcolonialism and North–South relations, modernity and postmodernity, the relation between theory and praxis, the genealogy of Fascism, the socio-political dimensions of popular culture, hegemony and the manufacturing of consent, etc. – have motivated many a reading and rereading of Gramsci's texts.

In the 50 years since Gramsci first became an 'object' of study, his theories and concepts have left their mark on virtually every field in the humanities and the social sciences. His writings have been interpreted, appropriated, and even instrumentalised in many different and often conflicting ways. The amount of published material that now surrounds his work – John Cammett's updated *Bibliografia gramsciana* comprises over 10,000 items in 30 languages – threatens to overwhelm even the trained scholar and to paralyse or utterly confuse the uninitiated reader. Yet the sheer size of the Gramscian bibliography is also an important indication of the richness of Gramsci's legacy, the continuing relevance of his ideas, and the immensity of his contribution to contemporary thought. In many respects, Gramsci has become a 'classic' that demands to be read. Reading Gramsci, however, is not quite an easy undertaking; his most important writings are open-ended, fragmented, multidirectional explorations, reflections, and sketches. His prison notebooks have the character of a cluttered, seemingly disorganised intellectual laboratory. The well-trained scholar, no less than the first-time reader, would welcome an expert guide who could point to the salient features of Gramsci's work and bring into relief the basic designs underlying the surface complexity of different parts of his massive oeuvre. Similarly, a critical exposition of the most important existing treatments of Gramsci's works, together with a discussion of the potential usefulness of his insights to certain current lines of inquiry in the humanities and social sciences, would enable readers of Gramsci to appreciate better why (and in what ways) his ideas have a bearing on discussions about some of the most pressing social, cultural, and political issues of our time.

The multifaceted character of Gramsci's writing and the rich diversity of critical and theoretical work it has inspired cannot be treated effectively in a single, comprehensive study. A series of monographs, each dealing with a specific aspect of his work (but also cognisant of the many threads that link its various parts), would be a much more useful companion to the reader who is seeking to become better acquainted with Gramsci's legacy. Each volume in the 'Reading Gramsci' series is devoted to a theme that is especially prominent in Gramsci's work or to a field of study that has been strongly influenced by his ideas.

Acknowledgements

This book would not have come to fruition without the support and advice of a number of people who merit acknowledgement for the influence they have brought to bear on the content that follows. The responsibility for the contents is of course mine.

The book itself took form across my time at the University of Wales, Aberystwyth; Lancaster University; and the University of Nottingham. During my period at Aberystwyth, I would like to acknowledge the financial support of the Economic and Social Research Council (ESRC) for both a Ph.D. studentship (reference: R0042963410) and a postdoctoral fellowship (reference: T026271041). More importantly, I thank both Pinar Bilgin and Steve Hobden for carrying me through a great period with their personal friendships that have continued ever since. At Lancaster, I would particularly like to thank Bob Jessop for the influential discussions I had with him. He remains a strong inspiration and influence despite my institutional and geographical relocation or different 'spatio-temporal fix'. Similarly the friendship of Graham Smith was a mainstay of support at Lancaster, despite the fact that we never managed to agree on the history of ideas. One could say that our conversations on political theory and indeed our amity were all the more productive precisely because of our intellectual divergences. Among my new colleagues at Nottingham, Andrew Robinson deserves many thanks for providing me with extensive written comments on a draft version of the manuscript. I owe my biggest intellectual debt, though, to Andreas Bieler who also provided detailed comments and feedback on the whole text and with whom I have worked closely over recent years. His exhortations to 'finish the book' and, at the same time, his continued counsel to contest the incipient slide towards liberal pluralism within Gramsci studies, were much welcomed. As always, it is his friendship, good humour, and insight that have sustained me through the usual challenges of academic life.

Conversations and communications that shaped various parts of the book were also shared with Richard Bellamy, Robert Cox, Randall Germain, Stephen Gill, Barry Gills, Marcus Green, Peter Ives, Mark

Rupert, Bill Robinson, Anne Showstack Sassoon, Stuart Shields and Benno Teschke. I would particularly like to thank Joe Buttigieg for his role in drawing my attention to the 'Reading Gramsci Series' and supporting the book ever since our meeting at Manchester's Royal Exchange on St. Anne's Square, a building that always reminds me of Gramsci's insights on capillary power and the role of architecture as one social condensate of the 'material structure of ideology'.

At Pluto Press, Roger van Zwanenberg, the chairman, provided unstinting support and patience throughout the entire project. The assistance of Helen Griffiths (publicist) and Melanie Patrick (head of marketing) was also gratefully received. Lawrence & Wishart granted permission to quote from the selected anthologies of Antonio Gramsci's writings.

Finally, I would like to thank Julie Morton, my first reader, for her support and unflagging faith in me throughout this project, in academic life, and the world beyond. It was her initial encouragement to take up study that set me off on this path and it is to her that the biggest appreciation is always reserved.

Abbreviations

BIP	Border Industrialisation Programme
CANACINTRA	National Chamber of Manufacturing Industries
CAP	Permanent Agrarian Congress
CCE	Business Co-ordinating Council
CGL	General Confederation of Labour
CMHN	Mexican Businessmen's Council
CND	National Democratic Convention
CNTE	National Coordinating Committee of Educational Workers
COCOPA	Commission of Concord and Pacification
Comintern	Communist International
CONAI	National Mediation Commission
CONCAMIN	Confederation of Chambers of Industry
CONCANACO	Confederation of National Chambers of Commerce, Services and Tourism
Confindustria	General Confederation of Italian Industry
COPARMEX	Employers' Confederation of the Republic of Mexico
CNI	National Indigenous Congress
EMU	Economic and Monetary Union
ESF	European Social Forum
EU	European Union
EZLN	Zapatista Army of National Liberation
FAO	Food and Agriculture Organization
FDI	Foreign Direct Investment
FESEBES	Federation of Goods and Services
FIOM	Italian Federation of Metal–Mechanical Workers
FSCSP	Labour, Peasant, Social, and Popular Front
FSM	Mexican Union Front
FTAA	Free Trade Area of the Americas
FZLN	Zapatista National Liberation Front
GATT	General Agreement on Tariffs and Trade
ICRC	International Committee for the Red Cross
IMF	International Monetary Fund
INMECAFÉ	Mexican Coffee Institute

IPE	International Political Economy
IR	International Relations
ISI	Import Substitution Industrialisation
LOPEE	Law on Political Organisations and Electoral Processes
MSN	Mexico Solidarity Network
MST	Landless Rural Workers' Movement
NAFTA	North American Free Trade Agreement
NED	National Endowment for Democracy
NGOs	Non-Governmental Organisations
NIEO	New International Economic Order
NTAE	Non-Traditional Agricultural Exports
OPEC	Organization of Petroleum Exporting Countries
PAN	National Action Party
PCd'I	Communist Party of Italy
PCI	Italian Communist Party
PCM	Mexican Communist Party
PDS	Party of the Democratic Left
PEMEX	Mexican Petroleum Company
PRD	Party of the Democratic Revolution
PRI	Institutional Revolutionary Party
PRM	Party of the Mexican Revolution
PROCAMPO	Direct Rural Support Programme
PRONASOL	National Solidarity Programme
PSE	Economic Solidarity Pact
PSI	Italian Socialist Party
PSUM	Unified Socialist Party of Mexico
SAM	Mexican Food System
SECOFI	Secretariat of Commerce and Industrial Development
SEDESOL	Ministry of Social Development
SPP	Ministry of Programming and Budget
SHCP	Ministry of the Treasury and Public Credit
STRM	Mexican Telephone Workers' Union
SNTE	National Education Workers' Union
TELMEX	Mexican Telephone Company
TNCs	Transnational Corporations
UN	United Nations
UNDP	United Nations Development Programme
UNT	National Union of Workers
US	United States

USAID	United States Agency for International Development
WEF	World Economic Forum
WTO	World Trade Organization
YMCA	Young Men's Christian Association

1 Introduction: the North/ South Question of Uneven Development

Capitalism is a world historical phenomenon and its uneven development means that individual nations cannot be at the same level of economic development at the same time.
— Antonio Gramsci, 'The Return to Freedom . . .', *Avanti!*
(26 June 1919)

The purpose of this book is to 'unravel' the historical and contemporary relevance of the thought and practice of Antonio Gramsci to factors of hegemony and passive revolution to the global political economy. Its central premise is that Gramsci's approach to *uneven development* reveals pertinent concerns about the conditions of hegemony and passive revolution relevant to alternative processes of state formation elsewhere in the modern world. The aim of the book is therefore to provide readers with a detailed analysis of subject matter linked to the practical and theoretical constructions of hegemony and passive revolution. As a result, the book will provide a novel entrance point for readers into concerns about uneven development, conditions of state formation, and the role of international factors shaping hegemony and passive revolution in the global political economy.

Unravelling Gramsci in such a way will promote a detailed consideration of his theory and practice that can add to an understanding of the uneven development of capitalism. The task of excursus and interpretation is crucial because it is a necessary moment of concept formation. Once this task has been completed it is then possible to appropriate and develop concepts in a different context from that in which they were originally formed (Nield and Seed 1981: 218). As we shall see, Part I of the book embarks on an excursus and interpretation of Gramsci's writings by drawing from as wide a reading as possible of his texts, including the pre-prison writings, the *Prison Notebooks*, and the prison letters. Once such concepts and issues are raised it will then be possible to illustrate their explanatory value. Confronting theory and practice and bringing the concepts to bear on concrete empirical examples in Part II of the book will achieve this objective. However, in accord with Keith Nield and John Seed (1981: 226), 'actively to engage with Gramsci requires more than a web of empirical illustration; it demands a theoretical engagement with and against Gramsci.' Unravelling Gramsci therefore takes on a second meaning. It becomes imperative to consider also what might be historically *limited* in a theoretical and practical translation of Gramsci's writings to alternative social and political circumstances of hegemony and passive revolution in the global political economy.[1] This task will be undertaken in the concluding chapter to the book, which will entail generating conclusions *against* the *Prison Notebooks*. Unravelling Gramsci in this second sense, in terms of considering themes that might work against the efficacy of his contemporary relevance, will also assist in developing pointers for future research.

It is hoped that, by recovering facets of older debates and introducing new elements, this approach to 'unravelling Gramsci' will contribute to understanding uneven development, conditions of state formation, and the role of international factors shaping hegemony and passive revolution in the global political economy. To concur with Stuart Hall (1991b: 125), Gramsci 'saw the pluralisation of modern cultural identities, emerging between the lines of uneven historical development, and asked the question: what are the political forms through which a new cultural order could be constructed?' It is to these issues that the next section will now turn before providing a more detailed overview of the organisation of the book.

The 'North/South' Question of Uneven Development

On the eve of a meeting between an Italian delegation and key members of the Comintern leadership in Moscow, the Italian Marxist Antonio Gramsci wrote a letter, dated 18 May 1923, to Palmiro Togliatti, a colleague and co-founder of the Communist Party of Italy (PCd'I). In the letter, Gramsci (1978: 140) declared, 'We are in the flow of the historical current and will succeed, provided we "row" well and keep a firm grasp on the rudder.' Beyond the struggles within the PCd'I and other left parties in Italy, to which Gramsci refers, he also reflected in this letter on the changes wrought at the time by the rise of Fascism and the crisis of capitalism in the context both of Italy and of the world. It was within this context that Gramsci was embroiled in activity that combined militant organisational and intellectual struggle.

This practical and intellectual odyssey began with Gramsci devoting his energy to journalism through columns in *Il Grido del Popolo*, *Avanti!*, and *La Città Futura* between 1914 and 1918. Among other issues, this journalism analysed the concrete phenomena of the nature of state formation in Italy, the reorganisation of society and capitalism through periods of crisis, the introduction of new techniques of management into the productive sphere, the Russian Revolution, and the attempt to build socialism in Italy. Activity subsequently centred on the Factory Council movement in Turin and editorship of the journal *L'Ordine Nuovo* (1919–20) with the aim of realising a vision of revolution from below based on the occupation of factories. The role of the political party later became paramount during the founding and leadership of the PCd'I, whilst Gramsci also further dwelled on the organic crisis of capitalism in Italy in the paper *L'Unità* (1924–26). By 1926 Gramsci had drafted his essay 'Some Aspects of the Southern Question' which analysed class and territorial relations between workers and peasants in the north and south of Italy and the strategic dilemma of forging links between these groups as a prelude to national transformation. Just after this, Gramsci was arrested along with other Communist Party deputies, despite parliamentary immunity, and began an incarceration that was to last almost until his death in 1937. During the show trial against Gramsci, the prosecutor Michele Isgrò enunciated the infamous statement, 'We must prevent this brain from functioning for 20 years.' Yet Gramsci's ambition to concentrate on something *für ewig* (for always or eternity), according to a pre-established programme, began in 1929, when he started penning the *Prison Notebooks* (Gramsci 1994a: 82–5).[2] Within these writings a prolonged reflection unfolded on issues spanning the formation, development and social function of intellectuals; theatre, literary criticism and the role of popular taste in literature; nineteenth-century Italian history; the theory of history and historiography; and the rise of Americanism and Fordism, which all contributed to a major reworking of historical materialism. Although Gramsci's sentence ended on 21 April 1937, he suffered a fatal cerebral haemorrhage that finally ended his struggle against ill health on the morning of 27 April 1937 at the Quisisana clinic (Rome). Almost immediately his posthumous patrimony was fought over and constructed; something that has continued ever since. On Gramsci's heritage, one commentator has pronounced him as, 'the greatest Marxist Western Europe has produced . . . and the one from whom there is most to be learned' (Hoare 1978: xxiv).

Ultimately, then, despite intense social struggle, the 'flow of the historical current' that Gramsci referred to in his letter to Togliatti of 1923 was to sweep him away along with many others in Italy during the rise of Fascism. Yet, since his time, the changing nature of capitalism has been no less threatening to those carried by, and fighting against, the tides of social and political upheaval. To develop the analogy, one can add that Gramsci's thought and action might still be of assistance in charting some kind of course through the stormy waters of capitalism, even if at times he proves to be a little more rudderless or less helpful than one would like.

In his own time, Gramsci appreciated the early stages of development of the modern state in a peripheral region of capitalism. This involved focusing on the Italian situation as part of world history, which included appreciating those relations between capitalist states, seen as the cornerstone of the 'bourgeois' system, and those that represented the periphery of the capitalist world (Gramsci 1978: 400–11). One can recall here an earlier insight from the *Communist Manifesto* that, just as the bourgeoisie created the dependency of the countryside on the towns, it has made 'dependent' and 'semi-dependent' countries, 'dependent on the civilised ones, nations of peasants on nations of bourgeois, the East on the West' (Marx and Engels 1848/1998: 40). As Gramsci (1985: 181, Q29§2)[3] subsequently stated, 'the historical fact . . . cannot have strictly defined national boundaries, history is always "world history" and particular histories only exist within the frame of world history'. It is thus possible to note a spatial awareness in Gramsci's writings that includes a focus on the uneven development of social powers at national, regional, and international levels. 'Moreover', as James Joll (1977: 67) proffers, 'the unevenness of economic development in Italy meant, Gramsci believed, that capitalism might be more easily overthrown than in the other advanced industrial economies of western Europe.'

As mentioned earlier, this is evident in his writings on the strategic problem of uniting the north and south of Italy, especially in the essay 'Some Aspects of the Southern Question' (Gramsci 1978: 441–62). It is also evident in his lesser-known focus on aspects of colonialism and imperialism within 'the global politico-economic system' of Anglo-Saxon capitalism and his focus on dimensions of 'Anglo-Saxon world hegemony' (Gramsci 1977: 79–82, 89–93). To quote one indicative passage – where questions are raised about the lagging effect of hegemony within world order trends, how hegemony might be discernible but recessive, and how imperialism could stand as an explanandum of such trends – Gramsci asks:

> Is the cultural hegemony by one nation over another still possible? Or is the world already so united in its economic and social structure that a country, if it can have 'chronologically' the initiative in an innovation, cannot keep its 'political' monopoly and so use such a monopoly as the basis of hegemony? What significance therefore can nationalism have today? Is this not possible as economico-financial imperialism but not as civil 'primacy' or politico-intellectual hegemony? (Gramsci 2001, vol.5: 64–5, Q13§26)[4]

Such writings are important but are scattered (spanning pre-prison and prison writings) and as a result have been much overlooked. These writings are crucial because they display what Gramsci meant by the 'national' point of departure, i.e. the intertwined relationship between 'international' forces and 'national' relations within a society which react both passively and actively to the mediations of global and regional forces. One of the central objectives of the book, then, is to tease out this articulation of capitalism across different scales, with the argument drawing on Gramsci's understanding of the positioning of both 'national' relations within the conditioning of 'the international' to reveal a theory of hegemony and passive revolution cognisant of the spatial divisions of geopolitics (see especially Chapter 6).

Failure to recognise this spatial awareness could result in an overemphasis on the national limits of Gramsci's problematic; for example, by equating Gramsci's emphasis on the 'national' point of departure with relations purely within the state. This flawed assumption is most starkly evident in Randall Germain and Michael Kenny's claims that Gramsci was 'above all a theorist who grappled with the discourses and realities of "statism"' and that 'the historical nature of his concepts means that they receive their meaning and explanatory power primarily from their grounding in national social formations' within which they were 'used exclusively' (Germain and Kenny 1998: 4, 20). Similarly, it is mistaken to assert that attention to national conditions 'led Gramsci to refuse the international dimension any constitutive status in his guide to action' and that he 'rejected the international dimension' as a causal factor of social transformation (Shilliam 2004: 72, 73). These issues will be discussed and challenged in more detail in subsequent chapters, specifically when a historicised and engaged reading of Gramsci is undertaken (see Part I). The point to make here, though, is that an overly rigid interpretation of Gramsci's outlook on the 'national' point of departure can be avoided. Taking this a step further, some commentators have emphasised how Gramsci draws our attention to spatial differentiation and to the uneven development of social powers in regional spaces, linked to the failures of state formation and hegemony in the Italian peninsula, and how this might even provide a powerful stimulus to understanding non-European settings experiencing uneven development (Roseberry 1994: 359–60; Jessop 2006a: 38). This has given rise to commentary on new kinds of the 'North/South' question within Gramsci's writings, albeit without much detailed consideration or exegesis.[5] Stating it in the most provocative manner, Stuart Hall (1986: 9) claims that '[t]he preoccupation with the question of regional specificity, social alliances and the social foundations of the state . . . directly links Gramsci's work with what we might think of today as "North/South", as well as "East/West", questions'. This is probably no surprise to anybody familiar, generally, with the work undertaken in postcolonial studies and, specifically, with scholarship commonly recognised as subaltern studies.[6] Yet, whilst I have refrained from entering explicitly the domain of postcolonial theory in this book, it has been argued clearly by one informed observer that such theorists' relation to Gramsci has meant that they have frequently 'deferred to his authority while at the same time declining to wrestle with his writing in any sustained or original way' (Brennan 2001: 144; Brennan 2006: 261–4). On a broader plane it has been commented similarly that all too often there is a 'soft focusing of Gramsci' within commentaries on his legacy, obscuring the pivotal role he attributed to class struggle that simultaneously dilutes his primary concern with transcending the capitalist order (Lester 2000: 143). Too frequently, commentators have strived to search for what Zygmunt Bauman has claimed as 'an honourable discharge from Marxism' through the turn to Gramsci.[7] In contrast to such moves, then, this book holds to the importance of analysing Gramsci's writings within the purview of Marxism rather than as a corrective to it (see Brennan 2001: 169). There is much in Gramsci that can help us to think through the particular issues of hegemony and passive revolution in the global political economy, and the aim of this book is to unravel how these are embedded *within* a historical materialist problematic linked to conditions of uneven development, processes of state formation, and the role of 'the international' in shaping the 'national' dimension.

Organisation of the Book

Part I of the book begins with a thoroughly historicised and engaged reading of Gramsci before advancing an understanding of hegemonic processes. Chapter 2 sets about 'unravelling Gramsci' by addressing the concern to historicise his thought and practice and demonstrating how Gramsci's own writings help in the endeavour to read his work and thus situate ideas in and beyond their context. The argument of this chapter therefore delves into issues germane to the history of ideas that are crucial to laying the necessary inter-pretative groundwork for subsequent chapters. The foregrounding of any such interpretative and analytical framework is pivotal to the subsequent task of critically analysing Gramsci's work (Finocchiaro 1992/2005: 214). Having established an approach to the history of ideas, consisting of identifying Gramsci's method of thinking, the third chapter considers his historical and contemporary relevance to understanding the international history of state formation and the rise of the modern capitalist states-system.

Such a task begins by outlining Niccolò Machiavelli's interpretation of the rapidly changing social and political conditions of Italy and Europe in his time, marked by the collapse of feudalism, the rise of absolutist states, the dilemmas facing Christianity, the altering power relationships within Italian principalities, and republican attempts to overcome the division of Italy by the occupation of France, Spain, and Austria. Within Chapter 3, this acts as a platform from which to consider Gramsci's own historical reflections on Machiavelli and the inherent structural weaknesses of Italian state formation, the parochialism of both Papal and mercantile interests, and the insertion of such developments within a European system of states. The link between Machiavelli and Gramsci is important, for 'the regional, economic, and religious cleavages of Machiavelli's time not only persisted into the twentieth century but were intensified and compounded by the peculiarly uneven development of Italian capitalism' (Boggs 1976: 109). The third chapter thus reveals Gramsci's historical sociological approach to analysing 'national' and 'international' factors inscribed within the fragmented processes of Italian state formation, uneven development, and the wider dynamics of European history. The theory of passive revolution is here regarded as pivotal in revealing what has been expressed as 'Italy's faltering entrance into modernity' (Martin 2006: 137). To refer to the statement of the character Tancredi in Giuseppe Tomasi di Lampedusa's (1996: 21) famous representation in *The Leopard* of the contradictions marking Italian state formation, 'If we want things to stay as they are, things will have to change.' The theory of passive revolution thus indicates how 'restoration becomes the first policy whereby social struggles find sufficiently elastic frameworks to allow the bourgeoisie to gain power without dramatic upheavals' (Gramsci 1971: 115, Q10II§61). Focusing on these insights linked to the specificities that fashioned late-medieval Italian and European state formation is a necessary prelude to considering Gramsci's more extensive theorisation of the politics of hegemony within capitalist modernity. Unravelling Gramsci's relevance to understanding processes of state formation within late-medieval and early modern Europe is an often-neglected aspect of debates in historical sociology on the relationship between territoriality and capitalism. As Carlos Nelson Cortinho (as cited in Burgos 2002: 13–14) admits, 'We did not embrace the Gramsci . . . who researched the "nonclassical" forms of the transition to capitalist modernity (the problematic of the "passive revolution").' As Gramsci himself indicated, 'the conceptions of the world, of the state and of life against which the bourgeois spirit had to struggle in Italy are not like those that existed in France' (Gramsci 1985: 249, Q8§3).

The theory of passive revolution is therefore presented as a prelude to consideration of the politics of hegemony in modern capitalism, which is examined in Chapter 4. 'The political development of the concept of hegemony represents', Gramsci reasoned, 'a great philosophical advance as well as a politico-practical one' (Gramsci 1971: 333, Q8§169). Chapter 4 thus elaborates the 'moment of hegemony' as a dynamic process constantly constructed and contested through the expanded role of the state in modern politics. Whilst this involved the key mediating function of intellectuals organically tied to particular social classes it also entailed analysing specific 'relations of force'. The unravelling of Gramsci here details the linkages between the relations of force and the political relation of hegemony, whilst drawing distinctions between the social basis of hegemony and conditions of passive revolution. Linking Chapters 3 and 4, it is instructive to note how the rise of 'capitalist civilisation' led Gramsci to associate the spread of the Enlightenment with changes in historical development across Europe, in the following manner:

> In Italy, France and Germany, the same topics, the same institutions and same principles were being discussed. Each new comedy by Voltaire, each new pamphlet moved like a spark along the lines that were already stretched between state and state, between region and region, and found the same supporters and the same opponents everywhere and every time. The bayonets of Napoleon's armies found their road already smoothed by an invisible army of books and pamphlets that had swarmed out of Paris from the first half of the eighteenth century and had prepared both men and institutions for the necessary renewal. Later, after the French events had welded a unified consciousness, a demonstration in Paris was enough to provoke similar disturbances in Milan, Vienna and the smaller centres. (Gramsci 1977: 12)

Whether we agree with the historical accuracy of this realisation, such features of the transition to modernity that absorbed Gramsci are comprehensively unravelled across the first part of the book.

The three chapters constituting Part II further the engagement with Gramsci through a focus on theoretical and empirical aspects of world order and resistance. The aim of the second part of the book is to deploy the approach established earlier, by indicating how Gramsci's method of thinking can be internalised when reflecting on alternative conditions of globalising capitalism, relations of power, and political resistance within conditions of uneven development. Chapter 5 presents an overview of various neo-Gramscian perspectives that have contributed to thinking in a Gramscian way about the contemporary constitution of hegemony and world order. Central to the argument of this chapter is that the theory and practice of hegemony are still relevant to understanding the changing spatial and territorial structure of power in the global political economy. It will be shown how the conceptual framework developed by Robert Cox in international political economy (IPE) debates links back to Gramsci's own work on the 'relations of force', in order to trace contemporary features of hegemony within world order. This undertaking then acts as a necessary backdrop to the discussion in Chapter 6 that further addresses the scale of uneven development within the global political economy.

This chapter teases out Gramsci's contribution to understanding the geopolitics of globalisation, with specific reference to debates on uneven development. It does so by contesting certain assumptions about globalisation and the rise of transnational capital to assert that Gramsci's theory of passive revolution enables an appreciation of the reciprocal influence of specific spatial scales in understanding the dynamics of global capitalism that encompasses the 'national' and 'the international'. This involves accepting *neither* the dominant fixity of state-centrism *nor* the dominant merger of transnational practices within a transnational state. The fabric of such relations, however, is not analysed solely at the level of theory but also through a concrete analysis of the peculiarities of history and cultural conditions. 'On the contrary', Gramsci states, 'it is necessary to attract attention violently towards the present as it is, if transformation is wanted' (Gramsci 2001, vol.4: 1131, Q9§60).[8] Hence a concentration in Chapter 6 on an empirical context of passive revolution in the history of modern Mexico, a state specifically shaped by the conditions of uneven development elaborated earlier in the book.

The case study of Mexico is important given that this state has experienced many of the classical features of social formations of peripheral capitalism in Latin America. It has been marked by the stratifications Samir Amin (1974: 378–90) associated with underdevelopment in a peripheral formation involving agrarian capitalism; the creation of a local bourgeoisie in the wake of dominant foreign capital; and the tendency to assume statist forms of development characteristic of the periphery induced by the demands of accelerated capitalist production for the world market. The focus on the form of state in Mexico will ensure that the argument not only remains actively engaged with unravelling Gramsci but that it is also attentive to a concrete 'earthliness of thought' through empirical analysis (Gramsci 1971: 465, Q11§27). The context of passive revolution in Mexico covers the constitution and reproduction of neoliberalism within the conditions of uneven development. Chapter 7 then continues the focus on the rise of neoliberalism in Mexico but through analysis of the dynamics of resistance against the passive revolution of capital. Linking with the book as a whole, this chapter unravels Gramsci's own methodological criteria in understanding subaltern classes and resistance. What Gramsci recognised as the 'anxious defence' (1996: 21, Q3§14; see also Crehan 2002) of subaltern classes is tracked through a focus on the case of the Ejército Zapatista de Liberación Nacional (EZLN) in Mexico. How this movement articulated antagonistic strategies of resistance against the circumstances of passive revolution is thus traced, to provide an appreciation of processes of agency in contesting capitalist social relations.

In the final chapter an effort to circumscribe and go beyond the anachronisms in Gramsci's thought and action is undertaken. By 'unravelling Gramsci' according to the second dimension outlined earlier, four principal themes are considered: (1) whether there is a need to go beyond Gramsci's conception of uneven development and raise broader reflections about the sociology of development; (2) whether a faith in the guiding role of the 'Modern Prince' – the Communist Party – is fundamentally misplaced in light of present political realities; (3) whether Gramsci's analysis remains trapped within a Leninist bias toward statism; and (4) whether one needs to be reticent about the primary role attributed by Gramsci to social classes as the agents of political change. Chapter 8 will thus tackle to what extent there is a predetermined essentialist perception of human nature underpinning Gramsci's analysis, which overrides the variety of identities that form the consciousness of individual and collective actors. Raising these issues demonstrates the merits of the book's arrangement in terms of unravelling Gramsci's approach to hegemony and passive revolution that might unravel (i.e. undo) his efficacy as an explainer of the contemporary conditions of uneven development in the global political economy.

Part I

Engaging Gramsci

2 Historicising Gramsci: Situating Ideas in and Beyond their Context

The ashes of Gramsci . . . Between hope and my old distrust, I approach you . . . before your tomb, before your spirit, still alive down here among the free.
— Pier Paolo Pasolini, *Le ceneri di Gramsci* (1957)

Broadly within international theory, attention has been directed to the contested history of concepts and categories and the range of marginalised problems linked to issues of historical interpretation. This has led some to affirm the priority of history and approaches that stress interpretation, practice and the critique of reification (Walker 1993). Elsewhere, historicist epistemological issues have come to the fore within international political economy (IPE) in an endeavour to further open up enquiry to the historically specific constitution of institutional social action within the global political economy (Amoore et al., 2000). Most recently, a strident historicist critique of diverse but related perspectives within IPE, which drew inspiration from the writings of Antonio Gramsci, has also been particularly advanced. This critique has raised complex ontological, epistemo-logical, and methodological concerns about the neo-Gramscian perspectives. Whilst key works have displayed nuanced readings of Gramsci (see e.g. Augelli and Murphy 1988; Cox 1983, 1987; Gill 1993a; Rupert 1995a), such scholarship was reproached for a lack of engagement with the historical contextual theory and practice of the Italian Marxist Antonio Gramsci as well as a neglect of the commentaries, debates, and contending interpretations surrounding his legacy (see Germain and Kenny 1998). Immediate and brief responses to this charge have rather predominantly concentrated on the methodological aspects of the critique (Murphy 1998a; Rupert 1998). Yet little attention has hitherto been accorded to the substantive ontological and historicist epistemological reproof raised by Germain and Kenny related to issues of philosophical meaning, interpretation, and appropriation. Namely, the need to historicise

Gramsci and display 'greater sensitivity to the general problems of meaning and understanding in the history of ideas' as well as to pay 'far greater attention to the problems of meaning and interpretation embedded in his ideas' (Germain and Kenny 1998: 13).[1]

This chapter aims to address the above concerns by displaying how Gramsci's own writings help in the endeavour to read his work and thus situate ideas in and beyond their context. This is an important initial task to undertake for the purpose of this book, given that any contemporary usage of Gramsci's frame of reference has to be cognisant of wider issues embedded within the history of ideas. On that basis, the argument of the chapter is that any 'reading' of Gramsci based on a self-reflexive purpose, rather than a representative interpretation, cannot objectively reveal a 'true' or 'real' Gramsci; thus no 'correct' reading can be produced. After all, any understanding of Gramsci's writings is circumscribed by specific interests and purposes whilst also, particularly in this case, relying on the interpretative injunctions of translated texts, no matter how rigorously they may be compiled. Yet it is also argued that a reading of Gramsci does not simply draw from an open text, nor is any reading as provisional and acceptable as the next interpretation.

> Certainly, 'appropriating Gramsci' has never licensed us to read him any way that suits us, uncontrolled by a respect for the distinctive grain and formation of his thought. Our 'reading' is neither willful nor arbitrary – precisely because that would be contrary to the very lessons we learned from him. It is, after all, Gramsci himself who first taught us how to 'read Gramsci'. (Hall 1991a: 7)

The argument of the chapter will therefore chart a path that avoids reducing issues of interpretation to the extremes either of simply studying Gramsci's texts themselves or of solely concentrating on the social context of such texts. This foray into debates germane to the history of ideas is important for the remainder of the book; it lays the necessary interpretative groundwork for approaching both Gramsci's historical and his contemporary relevance. The present chapter has two main sections shaping the discussion.

First, the notion that any interpretation of a text is limitless, or that any reading is equal to the next, is criticised. If it is accepted that Gramsci can be submitted to an infinity of readings then there is a risk of completely annulling those principles to which he adhered. This seems to be the case with those interpretations that have divested

Gramsci's view of historical development of any Marxist dialectic, to situate him within a liberal, or even 'post-liberal', approach to theory and practice (see Golding 1992).[2] Instead, a dual approach is developed that certainly promotes treating texts as vehicles for the exercise of present preoccupations. However, any engagement with Gramsci also has to avoid exegetical mistakes or the outright distortion and disregard for historical circumstances. These two positions will be developed within a consideration of interpretative controversies by detailing a series of 'autobiographical' issues evident in Gramsci's own writings, which help us to tackle a reading of his work. The discussion therefore draws upon some of the interpretative controversies and methodological criteria that Gramsci himself considered important when reading texts.

Second, despite the diversity of issues raised across debates in political theory and IPE, it is noted that similar arguments have been made concerning the issue of historicising Gramsci. Put simply, historicists reject any claim to absolute or transhistorical values by demanding that ideas must be analysed in relation to historical circumstances and assessed in terms of the particular context within which they derive. Yet, when demanding a historicist treatment of Gramsci's writings, an overly extreme emphasis on contextual issues is sometimes evident in arguments across political theory and IPE. This is recognised as an *austere historicism* that seemingly stymies any attempt to appreciate the contemporary resonance of Gramsci's work. These similar demands are therefore discussed, whilst arguing that, despite the call to historicise Gramsci, there is rarely further consideration of what exactly a historicist treatment of Gramsci's writings would entail. Beyond the need to understand the practical and theoretical context of Gramsci's work, what does it mean to historicise Gramsci? How far does one take the historicising of Gramsci? If historicity is important, does this mean relegating ideas and the social conditions that provoked such issues to the past with no relevance to the present? It is then argued that the assumptions of *austere historicism* are not consistent with Gramsci's own method of *absolute historicism*, which seems to offer an approach to the history of ideas useful to the present by locating ideas both in and beyond their context.

Within this second section, importance is therefore placed on the conditions of the *present* and what is rendered significant in Gramsci's work by *present* practical intentions and understandings of transformative politics (Davidson 1974: 142). Following Stuart

Hall (1988: 161–2), this entails *thinking in a Gramscian way* about the history of ideas and present-day problems rather than simplistically believing that Gramsci has the answers or holds the key to particular problems.[3] Thinking in a Gramscian way also requires one to do one's own work when asking questions about different social conditions. It also pushes one to consider what might be historically *limited* in a theoretical and practical translation of a Gramscian way of thinking about alternative conditions. This aspect of the argument will become all the more important as the book progresses, but particularly in relation to the consideration of a number of themes in the conclusion, which address various possible anachronisms in Gramsci's thought and action that place certain limitations on his relevance to present social conditions (see Chapter 8).

Overall, then, this chapter will engage with and critique some of the central historicist positions in Gramsci debates across political and international theory (see also Bieler and Morton 2006). This will be carried forward here in the style of an immanent critique, by tackling specific demands to historicise Gramsci, on their own terms and according to their own criteria, whilst also revealing some of the weaknesses of such claims. By delving into issues of interpretation and historicism and developing an excursus of Gramsci's texts, it will thus be possible to avoid reifying concepts and locating essential meanings within Gramsci's ideas. Rather than literally or mechanically applying Gramsci's concepts (*pace* Tooze 1990), questions can then be promoted about hegemony and the complexity of state–civil society relations, in a Gramscian way, about different circumstances from that in which they were formed (see Chapters 6 and 7). Hence this book hopefully contributes to a study of politics that, citing Gramsci (1971: 175–6, Q13§2), is 'understood as a body of practical rules for research and of detailed observations useful for awakening an interest in effective reality and for stimulating more rigorous and more vigorous political insights'.

Interpretative Controversies

Whilst writing in prison, Gramsci displayed an acute awareness of how his thoughts might have importance beyond the context of his confinement. On the one hand this is clearly displayed in his prison letters, which 'help the reader gain a precise understanding of the genesis and development of the intellectual projects Gramsci undertook in prison' (Rosengarten 1994: 2). On the other hand, this tendency of intellectual autobiography is also evident in the *Prison Notebooks* themselves.

It was in the prison letters, in 1927, that Gramsci initially outlined his ambition to concentrate on something *für ewig* (for always or eternity), according to a pre-established programme. This plan initially included the study of intellectuals in Italy, their origins and grouping according to cultural currents; the study of comparative linguistics; a study of the theatre of the Sicilian writer Luigi Pirandello (1867–1936) and the potential his plays offered for transforming Italian culture and society; and an essay on the role of the serialised novel and popular taste in literature (Gramsci 1994a: 82–5). This was later to develop into a wider 'intellectual plan' or 'cultural framework' chiefly focusing on Italian history in the nineteenth century, with special attention directed to the formation and development of intellectual groups; the theory of history and historiography; and the expansion of assembly plant production techniques beyond the United States under the rubric of 'Americanism and Fordism' (Gramsci 1994a: 233, 244, 245, 256–9, 360–1, 369).

Gramsci also made self-conscious comments in his letters about his pre-prison journalism and indeed about the letters themselves, acknowledging to Giulia Schucht, his wife, that, 'my letters are "public", not restricted to the two of us, and the awareness of this inevitably forces me to curb the explosion of my feelings insofar as they are expressed by the words written in these letters' (Gramsci 1994b: 111).[4] When referring to his voluminous journalistic writings he also stated that they 'were written for the day and were supposed to die with the day', despite endeavours to publish them during and after his lifetime (Gramsci 1994b: 66). Indeed, newspaper articles were generally regarded as hurried and improvised responses to immediate events that rarely left a mark of lasting importance (Gramsci 1985: 380–5, Q16§21). These 'autobiographical' comments have importance for anyone attempting to interpret Gramsci's writings. They also need to be related to the following passage from the *Prison Notebooks*, quoted at length because of its importance.

If one wants to study a conception of the world that has never been systematically expounded by its author–thinker, detailed work is required, and it has to be conducted with the most scrupulous accuracy and scientific honesty. It is necessary, first of all, to trace the process of the thinker's intellectual development in order to reconstruct it in accordance with those elements that become stable and permanent – that is, those elements really adopted by the author as his [*sic*, as throughout] own thought, distinct and superior to the 'material' that he had studied earlier and that, at a certain time, he may have found attractive, even to the point of having accepted it provisionally and used it in his critical work or in his work of historical or scientific reconstruction. This precaution is essential, particularly when dealing with a nonsystematic thinker, with a personality in whom theoretical and practical activity are indissolubly intertwined, and with an intellect that is therefore in continuous creation and perpetual movement. Hence: (1) biography in great detail, and (2) exposition of all the works, even the most negligible, in chronological order, sorted according to the different phases: intellectual formation, maturity, the grasp of a new way of thinking, and its confident application. *The search for the leitmotiv, the rhythm of thought, more important than single, isolated quotations.*

This initial research should be the foundation of one's work. Moreover, among the works of the same author, one must distinguish those that he himself completed and published from those that were not published because unfinished. The content of the latter must be treated with great discretion and caution: it must be regarded as not definitive, at least in that given form; it must be regarded as material still in the process of elaboration, still provisional. (Gramsci 1996: 137, Q4§1 emphasis added)

Whilst this passage is followed by a reference to studying the writings of Karl Marx, it would be reckless to dismiss the 'autobiographical' relevance of this note. Importantly, Gramsci goes on to distinguish between the use of writings that had an immediate function (letters, circulars, manifestos, and presumably journalism) and unpublished works that are posthumously edited and published by others. He also warns that correspondence should be dealt with cautiously, as well as advising that the support of other contributions or commentaries on a particular thinker should be taken up (Gramsci 1996: 138, Q4§1). Additionally, with reference to the idealist philosopher Benedetto Croce (1866–1952), who will be discussed in more detail shortly, Gramsci outlined similar methodological criteria to assist in the study of political theorists. This involved a systematic study of 'organic' works as well as 'minor' writings in helping to define the terms of a 'philosophical biography' (Gramsci 1995: 366–7, Q10II [Preface]).

Rather than a mechanical application of ideas, then, the aim of this book is to follow Gramsci's own advice and grasp the *leitmotiv* or *rhythm of thought*, within what he also called a 'strangely composite' approach (Gramsci 1971: 324, Q11§12), by drawing from a whole variety of volumes available to the English-speaking reader. Consequently, as wide a reading as possible of Gramsci's writings will be conducted. After all, a theory of historical materialism should not aim to become a total or rigid doctrine that is beyond question. Indeed, just as Gramsci rejected any perception of Karl Marx as a 'shepherd wielding a crook', or 'some Messiah who left us a string of parables laden with categorical imperatives and absolute, unchallengeable norms, lying outside the categories of time and space' (Gramsci 1994c: 54–8), so Gramsci himself should be treated. The aim, instead of developing a total conception of the world, is to concentrate on a theory that can progress as a practical canon of historical study (Gramsci 1994a: 311), thereby overcoming any attachment to universal truths and avoiding a philosophical position similar to medieval theologism: making an 'unknown god' of the economic structure (Gramsci 1994a: 365).

A further series of issues, evident in Gramsci's writings, which are useful for considering his own work relevant to this book are the methodological criteria that he considered to be important when developing interpretative readings of texts. Most notable in this respect is the critique of representation that emerges from Gramsci's reading of Canto X of the *Inferno* by Dante Alighieri (1265–1321).[5] In bringing his own interpretation to particular texts, such as Dante's, Gramsci displayed a clear awareness that any interpretation develops observations that are 'unexpressed' or that may lie inert in the text. The active process of interpretation might thus involve a reader developing certain observations, intentions or traces that might be concealed within the actual structure of the text. Clearly, objections against this interpretative method are possible and Gramsci recognised that they would have a 'semblance of truth' (Gramsci 1985: 153–4, Q4§79). Such objections would be especially warranted because a 'richness of expression', involving equivocal or ambiguous assertions within a text, could become 'mutilated by a lack of understanding' by a reader (Gramsci 1985: 267–9, Q23§39). Yet, despite these possible objections, Gramsci pondered whether a text is reconstructed by its reader in any other way than in the 'world of concrete expression', meaning in the historical moment in which it is received (Gramsci 1985: 153, Q4§79).

By contrast, Gramsci also stepped back from arguing that the interpretation of a text is limitless, that any reading is as valid as any other. For instance, with regard to texts of Georges Sorel (1847–1922), French theorist of revolutionary syndicalism, Gramsci recommended establishing what was of a permanent and essential nature in such work following 'the parasitic incrustations that intellectuals and dilettante admirers have deposited on his thought' (Gramsci 1995: 459, Q11§66). This vitriol was particularly directed at Mario Missiroli (1886–1974), a liberal journalist in Italy influenced by Sorel and then a supporter of Fascism after 1922, who made large editorial injunctions when posthumously publishing some of Sorel's work. As a result, in keeping with the methodological advice noted above, Gramsci advised a return to studying Sorel's texts, to distinguish between what was brilliant, superficial, accessory, or bound to 'extemporary polemics' and what was the substantial 'real meat' (Gramsci 1995: 454–60, Q11§66). Notably, in relation to Dante, he also condemned attempts to go 'beyond what is conveyed by the letter of the text' by making 'bizarre additions' that glide over the text (Gramsci 1985: 156–61, Q4§83). Again his recommendation was instead to reread the text in an attempt to ascertain its meaning(s) whilst also warning that the prose of commentators should not strive to alter such meaning(s) (Gramsci 1985: 119–21, Q6§62; 372, Q21§13; 375, Q21§14). In characteristically somewhat equivocal fashion, Gramsci (1992: 128–9, Q1§43) states, 'Finding the real identity underneath the apparent differentiation and contradiction and finding the substantial diversity underneath the apparent identity is the most essential quality of the critic of ideas and of the historian of social development.'

These twin positions of interpretative method come together in Gramsci's writings notably when dealing with issues of theatre criticism and in his analysis of the cultural and political role of the plays of Luigi Pirandello.[6] A Shakespearean tragedy as much as a play by Pirandello, argued Gramsci, can be given various theatrical interpretations, leading to varying forms of originality, but there is nevertheless the 'printed' book form, which exists independently of the theatrical performance (Gramsci 1985: 140–2, Q14§15). Therefore, different readers can generate alternative readings of a text according to changing circumstances, but the text itself – the 'printed' book form – has an independent existence separate from its readership. These points are interestingly brought together in exactly this manner by Edward Said on the worldliness of a text and the relationship between text and context (Said 1984). All texts have a certain 'worldliness', a situation in the world, that entails restraints upon what can be done with them interpretively. The example of Shakespeare is also invoked by Said, who states (1985: 3): 'Each age . . . re-interprets Shakespeare, not because Shakespeare changes, but because, despite the existence of numerous reliable editions of Shakespeare, there is no such fixed and non-trivial object as Shakespeare independent of his editors, . . . the translators who put him in other languages, [and] the hundreds of millions who have read him.' However, despite this emphasis, Said then goes on to lend credence to Gramsci's position, stating that 'on the other hand, it is too much to say that Shakespeare has no independent existence at all, and that he is completely reconstituted every time someone reads . . . or writes about him.' Instead, 'even so relatively inert an object as a literary text is commonly supposed to gain some identity from its historical moment interacting with the intentions, judgements, scholarship and performances of its readers' (Said 1985: 3–4). This method can be called an 'immanent' reading of Gramsci. Rather than attempting to uphold a representative interpretation of texts, based on revealing an essential meaning, the reader instead acknowledges their fragmentary and open nature. As a result, a reading in favour of a particular purpose can be developed, which concentrates on the relationship between author, text and context, and which adheres to exegetical rigour and accuracy, whilst acknowledging that certain elements are immanent in the text and need to be related to the changing 'concrete terrain of history' (Gramsci 1971: 450, Q11§28).

When developing an immanent reading, the very fragmentary nature of Gramsci's writings may even play a positive role in the overall process. They do display, after all, a distinctively dialectical way of thinking that develops, not in a linear fashion, but as a 'network' or 'web' with a coherence established through 'multiple branchings out', rather than sequentially. 'They', therefore, 'require a different sort of suspended attention, an openness of reading to match their openness of writing' (Forgacs and Nowell-Smith 1985: 10). An immanent reading provides such openness. Despite the apparent disorder and incongruities evident in Gramsci's writings, a rich vein of novel ideas and insights may be traced which contains themes indicative of a consistent intellectual project (Femia 1979: 472). As Gramsci (1985: 131, Q3§155) stated:

an architect can be judged a great artist on the basis of his plans even without having materially built anything. The relation between the project and the material building is the same as that between the 'manuscript' and the printed book. The building is the social objectification of the art, its 'diffusion', the chance given to the public to participate in its beauty (when it is such), just like the printed book . . . [but] the architect does not need the building to 'remember', but the plan.

It can be further argued that this approach to the interpretation of texts is also consistent with the historicist method developed by Gramsci. This was referred to as an *absolute historicism*, an approach to philosophy and concrete political activity that conceived the historical process as a synthesis of past and present, which is contrasted in the following section with an *austere historicism* present in more recent arguments on the history of ideas.

Historicising Gramsci

In attempting to grapple with the complex problems of interpreting the fragmentary and elliptical nature of Gramsci's writings, common emphases have emerged within many of the commentaries. For example, Geoff Eley (1984) has called for the historicising or contextualising of Gramsci's thought and action, whilst also distilling elements useful for the present. This involves going beyond the privileged texts of the notebooks in order to promote an understanding of Gramsci's 'national–popular' or Italianate elements, but without confining such features to a 'historicist prison'. Similarly, Alastair Davidson (1972) has emphasised the importance of going beyond the exclusively textual approach in an effort to display an awareness of the real problems in which Gramsci lived, whilst also extending the focus to look at aspects of his intellectual formation.[7] Elsewhere, calls have been made for additional attention to be paid to the context of Gramsci's writings, although in some cases these demands have been made in a rather anecdotal or tokenist way (see Diggins 1988; Phillips and Bedeian 1990; Walzer 1988).

Diverging emphases on the issue of historicising Gramsci particularly emerged following the production by the Royal Shakespeare Company of Trevor Griffiths' play *Occupations* at the Place Theatre (London) in 1971 (see Griffiths 1996). This play is specifically interesting because it has Gramsci as one of the central characters and bases its theme around the Factory Councils movement in Turin during the *biennio rosso* or two red years (1919–20). Following the production, a weekly journal called *7 Days* carried a critique by Tom Nairn combining aesthetic and sociological concerns not too dissimilar to Gramsci's own theatre criticism. Griffiths then disagreed with Nairn's critical approach and provided a response (see Griffiths 1971; Nairn 1971).[8] In both pieces arguments about the importance of historical context arise. According to Nairn the play was mined with historical contradictions and inaccuracies to the extent that it exhibited a 'non-documentary freedom with history', a 'historical wildness', and succumbed to 'ahistorical speculations' that remove Gramsci from history altogether (Nairn 1971: 18–19). In response, Griffiths argued that Nairn's approach to the play was too restrictive to the extent that he was overzealous in his pursuit of historical accuracy. 'Nairn's it's-either-historically-"accurate"-or-it's-purely-and-only-"symbolic" is just too crude and unfruitful a measure of the value of a play (or, indeed, of anything else)' (Griffiths 1971: 22).

Whilst this debate is interesting in itself it also has wider significance for the present discussion because these different positions on historicising Gramsci can be traced within key debates on the history of ideas. In particular it is possible to highlight how comparable demands to return Gramsci to his historical context can result in a similarly restrictive or *austere historicism*. The following will outline in more detail such demands and show how, in contrast, an alternative historicist approach may be developed that seems to be consistent with the *absolute historicism* evident in Gramsci's own writings; thereby furthering an appreciation of ideas in and beyond their context that is central to the argument of this book and its aim of 'unravelling Gramsci'.

An Outline of Austere Historicism

Richard Bellamy has developed some of the most important arguments on the issue of historicising Gramsci to emphasise that thinkers of the past are constrained by *their* contemporary definition and understanding of politics and that this then limits the contemporary relevance of past thinkers situated in specific historical contexts. In this sense he explicitly acknowledges a debt to the methodological writings of Quentin Skinner (Bellamy 1987: 2, 174n.6). Skinner's approach rejects a focus on what can be termed 'perennial problems' or 'timeless questions' in the history of ideas. Rather than such 'universal truths' an emphasis is placed on the particular intention, occasion, or problem specific to a situation that can only be naively transcended. Consequently, 'the classic texts cannot be concerned with our questions and answers, but only with their own' (Skinner 1969: 50; see also Skinner 1974a, 1974b).

Similarly, Bellamy criticises commentators for applying Gramsci's 'ideas to events and movements that he neither knew about nor could have anticipated' (Bellamy 1992: 5). Therefore, Bellamy argues, by returning Gramsci to his historical context it is possible to appreciate that Gramsci was more of a national thinker than a general theorist and that he did not generate a series of 'timeless ruminations' on certain political problems but reflected on a particular agenda within the constraints of a given social and political tradition. As a consequence, to continue the argument, it becomes imperative to have fairly detailed knowledge of Italian history and culture as well as Gramsci's pre-prison activity in order to appreciate the distinctively Italian dimension and political tradition of his thought (Bellamy 1992: 5). Whilst Bellamy does acknowledge that Gramsci may possibly have some relevance to contemporary peripheral capitalist states – due to concern about an early stage of modern state formation, conditions of uneven development, and the illiberal and fragile nature of democracy in a peripheral region of capitalism – this potential is negated (Bellamy 1994: ix-x, xxviii). Restrictions are ultimately imposed on this possibility because of the particular historicist conception employed by Bellamy and his tendency to reduce Gramsci to a distinctive Italian political tradition.

Elsewhere, Ernesto Laclau and Chantal Mouffe argue that 'the era of normative epistemologies has come to an end' and that rereading Marxist theory itself deserves no more than deconstructing its central categories of analysis, abandoning the conception of subjectivity and social classes it offers, and its world-historical understanding of the consequences of uneven and combined development (Laclau and Mouffe 2001: 3, 4). The effect of this reading is that Laclau and Mouffe stop, indeed prevent, the texts of historical materialism (such as the *Prison Notebooks*) from generating new meanings in different contexts. It is then on this basis that they reject historical materialism and falsely assert a difference from the past. 'It is no longer possible to maintain the conception of subjectivity and classes elaborated by Marxism, nor its vision of the historical course of capitalist development' (Laclau and Mouffe 2001: 4). Within the history of ideas they succumb to the approach of particularism, which views the past as marked by an otherness that does not have purchase on the present to uphold 'a universal, non-contextual recommendation which claims to be true, but the possibility of whose truth is eliminated by virtue of its claim being non-contextual, both in space and time' (King 2000: 5, 301–2). It is this reading of Gramsci that permits a reduction of his concepts to undefined social and political spaces that are unified by discursive formations within an irreducible pluralism (see Ives 2004b: 144–60; Morton 2005a: 439–53).

Weaving these strands of critique together, the point that Gramsci has to be related to his historical context is readily accepted but this should not mean that his concepts are simply an expression of these conditions. Yet, in demanding a historicist treatment of Gramsci's writings, an overly extreme emphasis on contextual issues is often developed (cf. Ghosh 2001: 42–3). In particular Gramsci is often invoked as a member of an 'Italian political tradition' to the extent that:

> Gramsci has to be regarded as an Italian thinker, addressing a peculiar set of social and political problems and arguing within a distinctive cultural tradition which can be neither totally assimilated to Marxism nor satisfactorily extended to the analysis of contemporary . . . societies. (Bellamy 1990: 313)

Yet this reification of political theory within a particular 'tradition' belies the point that the history of political theory should be a history of events taking place within a social and historical world of reflection and conceptualisation, rather than a 'tradition' representing the history of political theory in terms of a movement from the philosophically 'true' to the historically 'actual' (Maclean 1981: 114–15). Bellamy's restrictive historicist treatment and appeal to an 'Italian political tradition' is also somewhat dismissive of the contemporary relevance in Gramsci, because the Italian 'addresses problems which do not concern us and employs assumptions we cannot share' (Bellamy 1990: 337; see also Bellamy and Schecter 1993: 165–7). This results in an *austere historicism* that reduces past forms of thought to their precise historical context and tends to relegate Gramsci to history. The danger is that by elevating the Italianate dimension of Gramsci's activity to centre stage an austere historicist treatment of his works might actually smother a concrete sense of how his thought and action might help us to understand alternative historical and present-day conditions of uneven development.

Traces of this vein of austere historicism can also be found in additional arguments in and beyond political theory. Once again

Nairn stresses the large degree to which Gramsci was irremediably bound up with problems linked to the peculiarities and contingencies of Italian politics; although, linking with Chapter 1, it is noted that Gramsci's situation in Italy is analogous to issues of 'North/ South' development subsequently (Nairn 1980a, 1980b, 1982). A reluctance to work through the contemporary theoretical and practical efficacy of Gramsci's philosophy can also be found in James Martin's (1998: 2–3, 166–72) more recent examination of Gramsci's political analysis. The tendency here is to concentrate overwhelmingly on the *problems* rather than the possible *potentialities* of any contemporary relevance. Similarly, whilst offering a critique *against* something, the call by Germain and Kenny for greater sensitivity to be displayed by arguments within IPE to the general problems of meaning and understanding in the history of ideas and to the task of historicising Gramsci fails to argue *for* any positive substantive positions on the history of ideas (Germain and Kenny 1998: 4, 13–14, 20–1). At best, all they offer is the rather impoverished and highly vague assertion that as long as Gramsci's insights and ideas are 'understood rigorously albeit flexibly' they 'can be applied in very different contexts to his own' (Germain and Kenny 1998: 14). This differs very little from Robert Cox's own position that Gramsci's concepts, albeit stemming from a particular historical context, can be flexibly considered in relation to alternative situations (Cox 1983). Beyond a call to historicise Gramsci and attend to debates within the history of ideas, Germain and Kenny fail to develop what historicising a thinker means or what this might entail.

It is also open to question to what extent an antipathy toward Gramsci surfaces in some of these arguments as a result of an attachment to liberal principles of political theory rather than developing a historical materialist critique of capitalism and a stress on political transformation. For instance, the underlying purpose of much of Bellamy's engagement with Gramsci seems to derive more from an interest in promoting liberal political views (Bellamy 1995, 2001). This is especially evident in his critique of Gramsci on the role of the intellectual, where particular liberal preferences surface. In Bellamy's (1997: 41) view intellectuals need to act as upholders of universal values and perform the role of legislators 'concerned with the legal framework that makes both politics and culture possible . . . with intellectuals playing their part alongside their fellow citizens'. In a similar sense, Laclau and Mouffe (2001: 176) aim not 'to renounce liberal-democratic ideology, but on the contrary, to deepen and expand it'. Finally, Mark Neufeld (2002: 7) has also criticised the liberal–reformist assumptions and commitments of Germain and Kenny that do not flow from radical concerns about emancipatory change. As a whole, all these theorists of *austere historicism* can be revealed as 'conceptive ideologists', those 'who make the formation of the illusions of the class about itself their chief source of livelihood', by attempting to conjure the 'trick of proving the hegemony of the spirit in history' (Marx and Engels 1845–46/1976: 60, 62; see Morton 2005a; 2007).

However, once demands to engage with Gramsci's work are taken seriously, it becomes possible to develop an alternative historicist reading of his work. It is argued in the following part of this section that this alternative not only offers the basis for articulating an approach to the history of ideas useful to the present but that it is also consistent with the *absolute historicism* elaborated by Gramsci himself.

An Outline of Absolute Historicism

A dialectical understanding of historicism is one of the hallmarks of Gramsci's philosophical thinking. Yet to pluck a floating citation as an example of this understanding precludes an appropriate appreciation of the complexity of such an approach to the history of ideas. For instance, in one of the few direct citations on this issue Gramsci (1971: 465, Q11§27) stated: 'The philosophy of praxis is absolute "historicism", the absolute secularisation of thought, an absolute humanism of history. It is along this line that one must trace the thread of the new conception of the world.'

Yet this absolute historicism was not so 'absolute' and may even have been a polemical cover (Morera 1990: 130; Poulantzas 1973: 201). To explain, in the prison letters Gramsci argued – 'in a realistic and historicist sense' – that there was a 'certain lucidity' to the position that the soul has a degree of immortality, 'as a necessary survival of our useful and necessary actions and their becoming incorporated, beyond our will, with the universal historical process' (Gramsci 1994b: 314). This kind of emphasis becomes apparent when a wider reading of Gramsci's writings is undertaken; thereby following Gramsci's own recommendation to return to and reread texts to ascertain different meanings, as outlined earlier in this chapter.

One of the impressions throughout a (re)reading of the *Prison Notebooks* is that the writings are suffused with subtitled references to 'Past and Present', for example:

> How the present is a *criticism* of the past, besides [and because of] 'surpassing' it. But should the past be discarded for this reason? What should be discarded is that which the present 'intrinsically' criticised and that part of ourselves which corresponds to it. What does this mean? That we must have an exact consciousness of this real criticism and express it not only theoretically but *politically*. In other words, we must stick closer to the present, which we ourselves have helped create, while conscious of the past and its continuation (and revival). (Gramsci 1992: 234, Q1§156 original emphasis)

Already, then, a more nuanced position is evident, which is borne out by closer scrutiny – or a rereading – of the text. Within the approach of absolute historicism, therefore, Gramsci acknowledged that old and new forms of thought combine within the social relations of a particular epoch so that within every historical period there could be a recurrence of previous questions alongside the need to consider new issues. Putting it a little obliquely, Gramsci (1995: 374, Q10II§41xiv) stated,

> the past is a complex thing, a complex of the living and the dead, in which a choice cannot be made arbitrarily, *a priori*, by an individual or by a political current. . . . What will be conserved of the past in the dialectical process cannot be determined *a priori*, but will be a result of the process itself and will be characterised by historical necessity, and not by arbitrary choice on the part of so-called scientists and philosophers.

To make the point more explicit, a historicist approach to philosophical activity based on critical reflection was conceived by Gramsci which acknowledged the role played by both past forms of thought and previous historical conditions in shaping subsequent ideas and existing social relations. This inherently involved engaging with and criticising previous forms of philosophy and problems proposed by historical development because, 'philosophers cannot ignore the philosophers who went before' (Gramsci 1995: 387, Q10II§31i). 'The working out of the present', Gramsci (1995: 416,

Q10II§59ii) noted elsewhere, 'cannot but continue the past by developing it, cannot but graft itself onto "tradition"'. Past ideas and social practices will inform contemporary understandings. The error is to fail to recognise or acknowledge that there may be 'residues' or survivals of a philosophy that may have 'moments of renewal' and 'fresh intellectual splendour' linked to 'a dead past that is, at the same time, a long time dying' (Gramsci 1995: 331, Q10I§ Summary; 348, Q10I§8; 406, Q10II§41i). Therefore, 'individual critics [*pace* Bellamy, Laclau and Mouffe, or Germain and Kenny] may err by claiming that what is dead or what is not a germ of new life to be developed is actually alive' (Gramsci 1995: 416, Q10II§59ii). As a result, the appropriateness of the position that past ideas, questions, and philosophies still have a bearing on the present, and may thus transcend social context and 'speak' to us, *may* be established. This is the view of Joseph Femia (1981a: 122–3) who maintains that, although a theory is certainly linked to the social relations of a particular epoch, *some* problems are perennial because underlying thoughts about a range of concrete particulars *do* recur. This historicist emphasis on analysing social relations arises as much from the work of Gramsci as it does from the philosophy of Giambattista Vico, although there are clear differences in their theories of history (see Jacobitti 1983).

It was affirmed within Vico's *New Science* that similarities existed between peoples separate from each other in space, time, or customs (Vico 1984: 9–10, 12–13, 67, 135–6, 296). Through common institutions, it was argued, diverse groupings of different people express themselves in a similar manner, which provides scope for limited historical generalities within which historically specific continuities and changes in modes of development may be discerned (Vico 1984: 104, 414–15). By thus situating the particular within the universal, Vico attempted to avoid a totalising interpretation of history whilst comprehending the rise, development, maturity and decline of cultures according to general principles of 'ideal eternal history' (Vico 1984: 79, 104–5, 335). Accordingly, although past ideas have to be firmly located within their socio-historical contexts, and not uncritically applied to divergent circumstances, such ideas, due to the possibility of corresponding social phenomena, could not be dissolved into the historical past (Femia 1981a: 123–4). Ideas may thus transcend their origins although this can only be established by empirical investigation (Femia 1981b: 17).

Following Gramsci, it becomes necessary to analyse the past in an attempt to understand present political realities since both past and present shape each other and condition the future.

> Every historical phase leaves traces of itself in succeeding phases, which then become in a sense the best document of its existence. The process of historical development is a unity in time through which the present contains the whole of the past and in the present is realised that part of the past which is 'essential' – with no residue of any 'unknowable' representing the true 'essence'. (Gramsci 1971: 409, Q7§24)

In similar fashion, Femia (1981a: 124) argues that the 'social' element of a work of philosophy may be rooted in the past but there may remain a 'residue' that cannot be explained by the historical context. Therefore, whilst there is a need for historicity, this does not necessarily entail confining our outlook within a historical straightjacket, as certain ideas and social conditions may transcend historical context (Femia 1981a: 127; Femia 1998: 4–5). By thus rejecting the austere historicism outlined earlier and following the absolute historicism just discussed it is possible to develop a position that articulates the 'contemporary resonance' of Gramsci's thought because, after all, 'an insistence on historicity is one thing; an *a priori* determination to fossilise all past quite another' (Femia 1981b: 17). It is this position, relating Gramsci to his historical context whilst avoiding historical reductionism, that is also shared by other scholars such as Anne Showstack Sassoon (1987, 2000), Christine Buci-Glucksmann (1980: 3–16), Joseph Buttigieg (1986, 1990, 1994, 1995), and Wolfgang Fritz Haug (1999). The overall point is to remain aware of specific contextual issues as part of the general historical process because, after all, Gramsci developed a theory that transcended the 'here and now' of contemporary events (Lawner 1979: 6). It is in this sense that, through the method of absolute historicism, one has to bear an attentiveness to the peculiarities of history, to pay consistent attention to the specificities of historical and cultural conditions, whilst also adopting and adapting Gramsci's insights and concepts, as he indeed adapted and enriched his own concepts, to changing circumstances and to new conditions (Forgacs 1989).

This, at least, seems to be the message of the opening epigraph to this chapter, which cites the Italian poet, film-maker, critic and novelist Pier Paolo Pasolini (1922–75). The poem *Le ceneri di*

Gramsci (*The Ashes of Gramsci*, 1957) avoids becoming anything like a panegyric, instead evoking a critical attitude which at the same time is sympathetic to the 'ashes', or legacy, of Antonio Gramsci, who played a 'fundamental role' in Pasolini's intellectual formation (Stack 1969: 23). Hence, 'Pasolini's Gramsci lives only insofar as he is "ashes"; insofar as his presence is experienced emblematically and at a defining distance' (Sillanpoa 1981: 126). Whilst it is possible to be sceptical of Pasolini's theoretical recourse to Gramsci (see Baránski 1990; Francese 1999), he nevertheless sketches in *Le ceneri di Gramsci* a constantly shifting critical attitude admitting 'the scandal of contradicting myself, of being with you and against you; with you in my heart, in light, but against you in the dark viscera' (Pasolini 1996: 11). Hence the importance of unravelling Gramsci with both 'distrust' and 'hope' in order to appreciate both the limits and the possibilities of his thinking and practice in relation to issues past and present.

Yet, what principal measures are there for establishing the possibility of theoretical generalities within historically specific circumstances? Clearly the possibility of speaking about universally valid 'laws' based on natural science criteria of 'objectivity' or some fixed standard of 'truth' is rejected. The criteria of universal validity and objectivity are legacies of positivist social science, a form of 'cut-price popular science' (Gramsci 1994c: 76). As Robert Cox (1985/1996: 53) has put it, 'the historicist approach to social science does not envisage any general or universally valid laws which can be explained by the development of appropriate generally applicable theories.' Instead, a historicist approach is conscious of its own relativity but through this consciousness aims to achieve a broader time perspective in order to become less relative (Cox 1981: 135). Yet, if the overall plausibility of the above argument does not rely on an extra-historical foundation, what criteria are central to the efficacy of past ideas having a bearing on present political realities? Two criteria will be outlined that provide a general statement on the history of ideas as well as a concrete guideline for establishing the contemporary relevance of past forms of thought. It is no coincidence that these two evaluative principles, related to the unity of theory and practice, are directly drawn from Gramsci's own 'philosophy of praxis' (see also Femia 1981a).

First, theory has to be guided by an interest in understanding practical politics rather than located merely within the realm of ideas. It is crucial to note at this stage that much of Gramsci's arguments on historicism were directed against the speculative and idealist philosophy of Benedetto Croce (1866–1952), who spearheaded liberalism in Italy along with Giovanni Gentile (1874–1944), an official 'philosopher' of Fascism. It was through the diligent use of scholarly journals and the press that Croce set out to saturate the intellectual life of Italy with a liberal point of view (Jacobitti 1980). Yet, for Gramsci, Croce developed a subjective account of history based on the progression of philosophical thought rather than historically specific conditions of class struggle (Gramsci 1995: 343–8, Q10I§7; 369–70, Q10II§1). The dialectical view of historicism developed by Gramsci was therefore part of a practical struggle against the philosophy of Croce which he explicitly cast as *'Anti-Croce'* in contesting liberal reformism in Italy (Gramsci 1995: 354–6, Q10I§11; 379–80, Q6§107; Mansfield 1993; Watkins 1986).[9] Hence the first criterion that stands as a contribution to the history of ideas as well as a concrete guideline in establishing the contemporary relevance of past forms of thought is whether theory can advance a practical understanding of a concrete reality or situation that is *different* from that in which it originated (Gramsci 1971: 201, Q9§63). This is the principal measure upon which one can establish whether a theory has at least some level of generality. After all, 'the philosophy of praxis is precisely the concrete historicisation of philosophy and its iden-tification with history' (Gramsci 1971: 436, Q11§22). Therefore, it is necessary to ask whether the theoretical issues raised in this chapter – involving 'the concrete historicisation of philosophy' – advance knowledge – through an 'identification with history' – related to alternative conditions different in time and space. Put simply, can theory travel? If the argument highlights how Gramsci's ideas may contribute to an understanding of alternative social conditions and concrete realities of hegemony and passive revolution (the task for Part II of this book) then a valid case may be made for limited theoretical generalities. This is the central claim that will come to underpin the unfolding of contemporary conditions of hegemony, passive revolution, and uneven development in the global political economy, especially in Chapters 6 and 7.

Once a theory has advanced an understanding of concrete reality, it is then necessary to determine to what extent such theory actually becomes incorporated within reality *as if it were originally an expression of it* (Gramsci 1971: 201, Q9§63). This second criterion contributing to general debates on the history of ideas as well as providing a guideline to demonstrating the contemporary relevance of past ideas is the hardest but ultimate evaluative principle to fulfil. In this instance theory is assessed in terms of its social embodiment. Under discussion is to what extent theoretical issues actually find expression in people's everyday lives. If history is conceptualised along these lines, as an active theoretical and practical unity (as a 'philosophy of praxis'), then no fixed standard of 'truth' can be assumed outside human construction (Gramsci 1971: 364–5, Q15§22; 440–6, Q11§17). What is more important than any 'absolute truth', to follow Gramsci, is, rather, 'a given, particular truth', because 'for the purpose of human history, the only "truth" is the truth embodied in human action, that becomes a passionate driving force in people's minds' (Gramsci 1977: 185). The tying here of 'truth' to praxis furthers the view that the 'philosophy of praxis' was a return to and advance on Marx (see Sassoon 1987; Haug 2001), in this case echoing Marx's (1843/1975a: 182) sentiment that 'theory . . . becomes a material force as soon as it has gripped the masses'. Or, as it is stated in the *Theses on Feuerbach*: 'The question of whether objective truth can be attributed to human thinking is not a question of theory but is a *practical question*. Man [*sic*] must prove the truth, i.e. the reality and power, the this-sidedness of his thinking in practice' (Marx 1970: 121, original emphasis). This requires an indication of how, through empirical analysis, theoretical issues have practical efficacy (or some form of 'truth' in human action) and how they find expression in the concrete reality of social relations.[10] This task will be taken up later in the book when analysing contemporary conditions of hegemony and passive revolution within world order, the global political economy of uneven development, and conditions of resistance (see Part II: 'Gramsci, World Order, and Resistance'). Yet, it should be recalled that, rather than attempting to apply Gramsci literally, a premium is placed on thinking in a Gramscian way – or internalising Gramsci's method of thinking – about different historical and contemporary social conditions.

Rather than simplistically believing that Gramsci has the answers or holds the key to different historical and contemporary problems, the stress, then, is placed on the importance of thinking in a Gramscian way (or internalising his method). According to Stuart Hall (1988: 161–2), a critical appreciation has to be developed that embraces Gramsci as an intellectual and practical inspiration rather than a prophet. Due to Gramsci's insertion within the specificity of a particular historical moment one cannot literally transpose him to every context. Therefore one has to do one's own work in order to make Gramsci work in alternative social conditions (Hall 1997: 27). Similarly, Anne Showstack Sassoon has noted that it is possible to learn from Gramsci's way of working even if his ideas can only partially fulfil our own analytical requirements. When making use of thinkers from the past, one needs to historicise – by locating the discussion within practical historical and intellectual specificities – whilst deciding what is relevant and what might be historically *limited* about their concepts (Sassoon 1995: 69–70, 77; Sassoon 2000: 66–76). It then becomes possible to argue that Gramsci's writings can be taken as a point of departure to deal with similar problematics in our own time whilst also critically appreciating the need to move *beyond* Gramsci as a necessary reflection on present political conditions (Holub 1992; Landy 1994). This is precisely the political project of various diverse but related neo-Gramscian perspectives within IPE that will be discussed in more detail later in the book (see Chapter 5). For the moment, it is important to stress that any analysis of present social conditions, based on a Gramscian way of thinking, should retain an active engagement both *with* and *against* Gramsci (Nield and Seed 1981: 226): a point that will be affirmed more resolutely in the conclusion to the book, which will fulfil the task of unravelling Gramsci's approach to hegemony and passive revolution by raising some of the anachronisms in his thought and action relative to present day conditions of uneven development within capitalist modernity (see Chapter 8).

Conclusion: Past and Present

This chapter set out to tackle the task of unravelling Gramsci by paying greater attention to issues related to the history of ideas. By outlining a series of interpretative controversies and examining in detail the question of historicising Gramsci, the chapter has addressed one of the principal demands made within the literature across debates in political theory and IPE. This is the demand to return Gramsci to his historical context – to historicise Gramsci – before discerning any contemporary relevance. As a result the chapter has shown that by following a series of 'autobiographical' issues evident in Gramsci's own writings it is possible to develop a reading of his work that can situate ideas both in and beyond their context. This initially involved drawing from a variety of Gramsci's own writings – pre-prison political and journalistic writings, the *Prison Notebooks* and cultural writings, and prison letters – as well as diverse commentaries to capture the leitmotiv or rhythm of thought in his work. This excursus of texts and interpretative controversies is the necessary first step in engaging with and unravelling Gramsci. Different positions were outlined on the issue of historicising Gramsci, with a preference indicated for the absolute historicism evident in Gramsci's own writings, which will further facilitate an appreciation of ideas and conditions linked to hegemony and passive revolution in and beyond their context, related to the enquiry of this book. In contrast, the restrictions of an austere historicism were rejected because of the strictures imposed on trying to appreciate the contemporary relevance of past thinkers. A set of criteria was then outlined which established how theoretical issues, linked to historically specific practices, may be generalised in alternative contexts but without assuming the status of universal laws associated with positivist social science. These criteria provide both a general statement on the history of ideas and a concrete guideline for establishing the contemporary relevance of past forms of thought, and will be revisited in the conclusion to this book (see Chapter 8). The final emphasis was then placed on thinking in a Gramscian way – or internalising Gramsci's method of thinking – about alternative social conditions of hegemony and passive revolution rather than embarking on an ahistorical or mechanical application of his theory.

Consequently, some of the central positions of arguments demanding greater attention to historicising the thought and practice of Gramsci have been undermined according to their own demands and in their own terms. This method of immanent critique could be expanded – for example, by debating the extent to which Gramsci's theory and practice can be inserted within a stream of classic social analysis grappling with forms of modernity and the specific forms of social power deriving from historical processes of capitalist development (see Rosenberg 1994). Questions could then be raised about whether the reductionist stress on principles of historical specificity, articulated by the austere historicists criticised above, acts as an additional 'theoretical veto' that annuls the construction of classic social theory and its relevance to understanding the contemporary world (Rosenberg 2000: 14–15).

To conclude, Pierro Gobetti (1901–26), radical liberal opponent of Italian Fascism, once stated that, 'more than a tactician or a combatant, Gramsci is a prophet' (Gobetti 1924/2000: 22). In contrast, this chapter has implicitly followed a definition that Gramsci provided of himself: as simply neither devil nor saint, neither martyr nor hero

(Gramsci 1994a: 140). By thinking in a Gramscian way about the history of ideas, or focusing on the rhythm of thought in his work, it was possible to establish not only a case for considering ideas in and beyond their context. It was also possible to avoid seeing Gramsci as some sort of prophet and to open up, instead, an invitation to critically question his work. It is by ultimately remaining engaged with strategic sites of political struggle, however, that analysis must also proceed. The fabric of hegemony cannot be analysed at the level of theory but only by a concrete analysis of different forms of state and specific changes in the social relations of production. The invitation to think critically about Gramsci's work and what might be historically *limited* about his theory and practice, as well as to think critically about alternative historical and contemporary circumstances of hegemony and passive revolution in the global political economy, will be taken up in subsequent chapters. The unravelling of Gramsci's approach to hegemony and passive revolution in the global political economy might then lead to the unravelling of his efficacy as an explainer of contemporary conditions of uneven development. Here the immediate task becomes one of moving from abstraction to display how concepts can have explanatory value – or a concrete 'earthliness of thought' (Gramsci 1971: 465, Q11§27) – through the confrontation of theory and practice. Chapter 3 will begin this task by tracing Gramsci's thoughts on the series of class struggles constitutive of European state formation and capitalist production shaping the modern international states-system. Of relevance here are his writings on the concrete historical specificities that fashioned the terms of Italian state formation and uneven development within the European states-system, which acted as a prelude to his more developed theorising on hegemony that will be addressed subsequently in Chapter 4.

3 State Formation, Passive Revolution and the International System

> Public opinion as it is today understood was born on the eve of the fall of the absolutist states, that is, in the period of struggle of the new bourgeois classes for political hegemony and the conquest of state power.
>
> – Antonio Gramsci, *Quaderni del Carcere*, Q7§83

Having established in the last chapter an approach to the history of ideas – consisting of identifying and internalising Gramsci's method of thinking, the leitmotiv, or rhythm of his thought – the task now becomes one of considering his historical and contemporary relevance to understanding the international history of state formation and the rise of the modern capitalist states-system in their linkage to conditions of hegemony and passive revolution. Such a task is undertaken across this and the next chapter in order to demonstrate Gramsci's historical sociological approach to the analysis of the division of labour between city and countryside, between centre and periphery, between north and south, between national and international relations as inscribed within the fragmented process of Italian state formation and the wider dynamics of European history.

In this chapter the aim is to reveal the account Gramsci developed of Italian state formation and how this represents a much overlooked backdrop to the history of the modern capitalist international states-system. For, as Dante Germino (1990: 221) has recognised, 'Gramsci's conviction that one cannot understand the Italian present in isolation from the European past is evident from his fascination with late medieval, renaissance, and early modern European history.' An essential task therefore is to recover Gramsci's historical account of the emergence and development of Italian state formation to demonstrate how this is rooted in wider aspects of transformation shaped by the emerging international states-system and subsequent capitalist transition. As Perry Anderson (2002: 21) noted about Gramsci, 'the logic of his theory, of which he was aware, extended to the international system as well', despite the fact that direct attention towards the explanation of historical state formation in Gramsci's writings has commonly been neglected at the expense of tracing his more developed theorising on hegemony. As will be demonstrated, there is a great deal of significance in the historical account of the series of class struggles that Gramsci traced within the constitution of Italian state formation, which prefigured that state's emergence within an international system of states. Focusing on the situated specificities that fashioned the terms of medieval Italian and European state formation is a necessary prelude to considering Gramsci's more extensive theorisation of the politics of hegemony within capitalist modernity. It is the latter theorising of hegemony that Chapter 4 will tackle in more detail.

This chapter will follow three main lines of enquiry to assist the aim of unravelling Gramsci and his relevance to understanding processes of state formation within medieval and early modern Europe. The first section will trace recent debates in historical sociology on the relationship between sovereign territoriality and capitalism. Of significance here is an important area of scholarship focusing on social property relations that locates trajectories of state formation within the world history of socially uneven and geopolitically combined development. A historical sociological theory of the international causal dynamics of uneven and combined development has thus been developed, which grounds the historical emergence of state societies within the tracks of capitalist modernity (Rosenberg 1994, 1996; Teschke 2003, 2005). These developments build on Leon Trotsky's reflections on the world-historical process of uneven and combined development, indicating the insertion and adaptation of states to different stages of development (Trotsky 1936: 25–32, 72, 334–5; see also Löwy 1981). Yet, as Ralph Miliband (1977: 3) indicates, with no small relevance to debates on uneven and combined development, 'there is a limit to what can properly be squeezed out of a paragraph, a phrase, an allusion or a metaphor'. This necessitates engaging with wider reflections within the canon of historical materialism that also grant due weight to international causal dynamics but have been hitherto neglected within the scramble for theoretical exclusivity.

Out of this dialogue with historical sociological accounts of uneven and combined development comes a focus on processes of Italian state formation, through a two-pronged examination linking the reflections of Niccolò Machiavelli and Antonio Gramsci. These respectively constitute the second and third main sections of the chapter. Machiavelli can be regarded as an interpreter of the rapidly changing social and political conditions of Italy and Europe in his time, marked by the collapse of feudalism, the rise of absolutist states, the dilemmas facing Christianity, the altering power relationships within Italian principalities, and republican attempts to overcome the division of Italy by the foreign occupation of France, Spain, and Austria.[1] He thus developed a 'historicist–sociological approach' to understanding mechanisms of power, antagonisms between social forces, and the structure of situations leading to the social origins of new states (Berlin 1979: 33n.6; Fontana 1993: 49–50). At the same time, 'commentaries on this figure . . . are moments in the intellectual history of the emergence of a politico-philosophical consciousness of modernity' (Balakrishnan 2005: 14–15). This also means that Gramsci's own historical reflections on Machiavelli and the inherent structural weaknesses of Italian state formation, the parochialism of both Papal and mercantile interests, and the insertion of such developments within a European system of states demand attention within any serious explanation of the historical sociology of the modern states-system. The third section therefore outlines the principles of historical research Gramsci provided within his analysis of (1) Renaissance Italy and the role of mercantile capital in shaping the absolutist state; (2) the 'Southern Question' concerning the terms of uneven development of the Mezzogiorno in Italy and beyond; and (3) the Italian Risorgimento, which was represented as a 'passive revolution', a theory of the survival and reorganisation of state identity through which social relations are reproduced in new forms consonant with capitalist property relations. A theory of passive revolution is pivotal in demonstrating how Italian and wider European state formation was shaped by the causal conditioning of 'the international', whether through developments linked to the French Revolution; social forces associated with Fascism; or the growing dominance of Anglo-Saxon capitalism.

Overall, what is significant here is the explicative power of the *method of historical interpretation* offered by Gramsci, which can throw into relief certain factors of state formation and passive revolution. Whilst historians may demur as to the accuracy of his generalisations, there is nevertheless great importance in Gramsci's opinions about the relationship between concepts and circumstances in understanding state formation, passive revolution, and 'the international'. Whilst it might be possible to hold his generalisations against him, Gramsci developed a reasonably clear theory that established a procedure of enquiry into historical conditions. A criterion of interpretation is therefore established that arises out of the way Gramsci sets about writing history. Rather than debating the validity of Gramsci's conclusions, then, it is the relevance of the examples he used that throw light on his theorising of state transition, capitalist modernity, and passive revolution. A genuinely historical sociology is therefore offered, with the caveat that others may want to concentrate on the more fanciful dimensions of the historical analogies he deployed. Where historical inaccuracies might arise, for instance in the positive appreciative character of his writings on Machiavelli, these do not affect the essential argument or the critical hermeneutical judgement (Finocchiaro 1988: 141, 143). The task of establishing scientific truth through historical accuracy can therefore be left to the certitude of others. In short, what matters here, to borrow a phrase from Louis Althusser (1999: 42), is the *dispositif*, 'a series of general theses on history which are literally contradictory, yet organised in such a way as to generate concepts not deducible from them, for the purpose of theorising an "object" which is in fact a determinative object.' For the purposes of this chapter this means that the *dispositif* refers to how, in Gramsci's writings, *theoretical* fragments focus on the formulation of a concrete *political* problem of Italian state formation situated within the world-historical process of uneven and combined development.

State Formation, Sovereign Territoriality and Capitalism

In advancing a frame of reference linking processes of state formation, sovereign territoriality and capitalist modernity, recent scholarship focusing on transformations in social property relations has argued that there was no straight transition from feudalism to the modern capitalist states-system. Instead, the origins of the interstate system lie in a period of absolutist sovereignty – the age of absolutism – that was crucial in determining the constitutive structure of capitalist social relations through which the states-system is mediated and reinforced (Teschke 2003: 7–9). Whilst no precise chronological limit can be applied to the age of absolutism, the period 1660–1815 can be seen as capturing the central social forces that contributed to the development of distinctive institutions (Beloff 1954: 17). Various maps of Europe can be traced at this time. 'In Europe west of the Elbe', in the latter half of the seventeenth century, 'the economic trends of the age worked in favour of the growth of a cash nexus between landlord and tenant, between owner of the soil and tiller, and against the continued exaction of personal services.' In eastern Europe there was a contradictory tendency. 'The cultivator was attached', Max Beloff continues, 'ever more rigorously to the soil; peasantry became almost synonymous with serfdom, social and political power was the monopoly of those who could command the services of this depressed majority.' As he concludes, 'unless this dramatic contrast between East and West is appreciated, there is no beginning of understanding either this period or its successors' (Beloff 1954: 26–7).

The first feature of a social property relations perspective is thus to differentiate pre-capitalist and capitalist property relations in order to comprehend the above contrast. Under feudalism, agrarian property was privately controlled by a class of feudal lords who extracted a surplus from the peasants by politico-legal relations of compulsion: 'extra-economic' coercion was articulated through means of labour services, rents in kind, or customary dues owed to the individual lord by the peasant. Feudalism therefore involved a fusion of the juridical serfdom and military protection of the peasantry by a social class of nobles exercising a monopoly of law and private rights of justice within a framework of fragmented sovereignty (Anderson 1974a: 150–1; Anderson 1974b: 404–7). Accordingly, what distinguished the feudal mode of production in Europe was the specific organisation of seigneurial and serf classes in a vertically articulated system of parcellised sovereignty and scalar property. 'It was this concrete nexus', Anderson (1974b: 408) notes, 'which spelt out the precise type of extra-economic coercion exercised over the direct producer.'

Under capitalist social property relations the direct extraction of surplus is accomplished through 'non-political' relations associated with different forms of social power (see Marx 1887/1996: 577). In capitalist social forms, surplus extraction is indirectly conducted through a contractual relation between those who maintain the power of appropriation, as owners of the means of production, and those who only have their labour to sell, as expropriated producers. The direct producers are thus no longer in possession of their own means of subsistence but are compelled to sell their labour power for a wage in order to gain access to the means of production (Wood 1995: 31–6). Said otherwise, direct producers only have access to the means of production through the sale of their labour power in exchange for a wage, which is mediated by the purely 'economic' mechanisms of the market. The market, in this focus on social property relations, does not therefore represent an opportunity but a compulsion to which both appropriators and expropriators (capital and labour) are subjected, through the imperatives of competition, profit maximisation, and survival (Wood 2002a: 96–8, 102).

The second feature of a social property relations approach is that the origin of capitalism – the displacement of 'politically' constituted property by 'economic' power – is linked to the historical process of *primitive accumulation*, signifying the reconstitution of peasants in possession of the means of subsistence into propertyless individuals compelled to sell their labour. This was 'the historical process of divorcing the producer from the means of production' leading to a situation in which 'capitalist production is once on its own legs' (Marx 1887/1996: 705–6). According to Marx (1850/1978: 122) 'the peasant's title to property is the talisman by which capital held him [*sic*] hitherto under its spell, the pretext under which it set him against the industrial proletariat'. Leading to this situation, the historical rupture of primitive accumulation means

> the transformation of the individualised and scattered means of production into socially concentrated ones, of the pigmy property of the many into the huge property of the few, the expropriation of the great mass of the people from the soil, from the means of subsistence, and from the means of labour, this fearful and painful expropriation of the mass of the people forms the prelude to the history of capital. (Marx 1887/1996: 749)

It is in the outcome of this historical process of class struggle that Benno Teschke (2003: 57–73) has framed the question of modern sovereignty, turning to the consequences of developments in late medieval and early modern Europe and the 'transition' from feudalism to capitalism. Following Robert Brenner's analysis, the 'transition' historically involved a comparative decline in serfdom in western Europe and its intensification in eastern Europe. Alongside this, Brenner has examined the divergent effects of the emergence of secure small peasant property versus the rise of landlord/large tenant farmer relations on the land, linked to the rise of agrarian capitalism and the growth of agricultural productivity in England, in contrast to the role played by an absolutist state in France based on centralised tax/office surplus extraction (Brenner 1985a: 10–63; 1985b: 213–327).

The third major contribution of a social property relations approach is therefore the capacity to distinguish between the differential outcomes to the 'general crisis' that faced the European economy in the seventeenth century and the ensuing class confrontations, which resulted in totally divergent paths of subsequent social and economic development (see also Hobsbawm 1960: 97–112; Hobsbawm 1965: 5–58). To summarise, in central and eastern Europe, faced with a relatively weak and disorganised peasantry, lords politically reconstituted themselves through a greater concentration of power within large serf-estates (magnates) alongside the growing centralised states. Such 'servile agriculture' covered parts of Germany, a region to the east of a line running roughly along the Elbe, the western frontiers of what are today the Czech and Slovak Republics, and then south to Trieste, cutting off eastern and western Austria. This eastern area was 'servile' because it was largely a food and raw-material producing dependent economy of western Europe that encompassed the Mediterranean plains and Baltic areas which, as early as the fifteenth century, was required to export, among other products, cereals and wood to countries such as Holland, England, and the Iberian peninsula. Eastern Europe therefore played the role of raw-materials producer for the industrialising west in exchange for manufactured goods, notably textiles, and other luxuries (Hobsbawm 1962/1976: 162). This led to a *re*-feudalisation that stifled the productivity of the direct peasant producers, precluding the emergence of an 'internal' dynamic of development and the expansion of social productive powers (Brenner 1977: 73). As a result, 'the lords of eastern Europe constructed a form of state peculiarly appropriate to their rather simple needs. It was a form in which they could represent themselves in the most immediate and direct way' (Brenner 1985b: 282–3).

In areas of western Europe, the transformation of the feudal order and serfdom was determined by further differences in class structure. In England, the agrarian situation would be uniquely transformed through the monopolisation of land by commercially minded landlords, cultivated by tenant farmers employing the landless as smallholders. As Brenner (1985b: 298) details, a 'tripartite capitalist hierarchy' would therefore become established, consisting of commercial landlords, capitalist tenants, and wage labourers, as a result of which the landed classes had no need to revert to direct 'extra-economic' compulsion to extract a surplus. What is significant here was the increasing reliance on purely 'economic' modes of appropriation – the productive and competitive utilisation of land rather than direct coercive surplus extraction, which was central to creating conditions under which the primitive accumulation of capital could proceed.[2] This meant that the nascent ruling class of landlords could largely depend on the 'impersonal' logic of 'economic' processes of exploitation by capitalist tenants of relatively free wage labourers leading to greater intra-capitalist competition throughout the economy as a whole (Katz 1993/1999: 71–2). Hence, 'by the end of the seventeenth century the English evolution towards agrarian capitalism had brought about the end of the age-old "fusion" of the "economic" and the "political", and the emergence of an institutional separation between state and civil society' (Brenner 1985b: 299).

With regard to the connection between the emergence of capitalism and the rise of the state, it is argued that in the historically peculiar and specific case of England the processes developed in tandem. State formation and capitalist development went hand in hand as the social transformations that brought about capitalism were the same that characterised the separation of state and civil society, leading to the constitution of the capitalist state (Wood 1991: 26–8, 91). According to Marx (1843/1975a: 32, 77–8, 81), this induces a mystification of the powers of the state to the extent that public and private spheres are split and individual freedom forms the foundation of civil society, giving decisive status to the abstraction of citizenship above class exploitation. Civil society therefore becomes equated with individual rights and private interests and 'appears as a framework external to the individuals, as a restriction of their original independence' (Marx 1843/1975b: 164). State formation and the transition from feudal to capitalist social property relations, in the example of England, thus proceeded in a manner that was 'both more tardy and more direct' with only 'precarious existence to the absolutist state' (Poulantzas 1973: 161–2). Therefore, the 'specificity of state sovereignty lies in its "abstraction" from civil society – an abstraction which is constitutive of the private sphere of the market, and hence inseparable from capitalist relations of production' (Rosenberg 1994: 123–4). Whilst additional features distinguishing state formation in western Europe, from a social property relations point of view, have been detailed elsewhere (Morton 2005b), it is important to highlight that absolutist sovereignty in France is clearly distinguished from modern sovereignty due to its proprietary and dynastic character, which imposed a different logic of political accumulation on the emerging states-system (Teschke 2003: 167–88, 233–45). The absolutist state was rooted in pre-capitalist property relations and 'should be understood as a social formation *sui generis*, a fundamentally non-capitalist form of social organisation characterised by a form of state that was precisely non-modern' (Lacher 2003: 539, Lacher 2005: 30–4; Teschke 2003: 152).

By extension, the end of the absolutist age from a social property relations approach has been cast as a set of specific processes linked to a crisis in class power, the advent of 'bourgeois revolutions' across Europe, and the emergence of uneven and combined development.[3] In France, 'the state structure and concordant ruling culture perfected in the reign of Louis XIV was to become the model for much of the rest of the nobility in Europe', directly extending to Spain, Portugal, Piedmont, and Russia (Anderson 1974b: 42, 102). This means that earlier trajectories of state formation became influenced by the *uneven* social development and worldwide spread of capitalism that was *combined* with the geopolitical emergence of the modern state (Rosenberg 1996: 3–15; Rosenberg 2005: 68–9).[4] As capitalism chronologically expanded in an *uneven* fashion, due to the precocity of development such as that in England, states configured by pre-capitalist relations were required to adapt by *combining* different forms of development. This was because 'once breakthroughs to ongoing capitalist economic development took place in various regions, these irrevocably transformed the conditions and character of the analogous processes which were to subsequently occur elsewhere' (Brenner 1985b: 322). Absolutist sovereignty in certain cases would therefore be forcibly abbreviated by conditions of underdevelopment as the state came to give an external impulse to the progress of capitalism through primitive accumulation, as earlier defined. Through mechanisms of centralised political power, primitive accumulation would then be impelled by employing 'the power of the state, the concentrated and organised force of society, to hasten, hothouse fashion, the process of transformation' (Marx 1887/1996: 739). As Trostky (1936: 26) explains, 'a backward country assimilates the material and intellectual conquests of the advanced countries. But this does not mean that it follows them slavishly, reproduces all the stages of their past.' What this means is that, within the history of capitalism, conditions of unevenness have engendered mimetic processes of state-led combined development as the primary channel of primitive accumulation (Rosenberg 2005: 31, 43). Additionally, the internal relation of sovereignty and capitalism is understood in such a way that uneven international dynamics are worked into the conception of combined developmental tendencies within different state forms (Rosenberg 2005: 10). The result is a method of analysis that is cognisant of international causal dynamics in shaping the development trajectories of state formation. Hence integrating 'the international' as constitutive of the peculiarities of development within state forms to realise the 'internationally-mediated causation' of specific socio-political state transformations (Teschke 2005: 9–10).

Nevertheless, social property relations approaches can be held to account for their analysis of state formation processes within the 'transition' to capitalist modernity in three main ways. First, the missing link in this account of state formation is that between the rise of specific social property relations and the making of new social identities and subjectivities, so that identities become simply read off from transformations in social property relations. What needs to be demonstrated more clearly is how, through the series of class struggles constitutive of absolutist and, later, capitalist state formation, customary practices of folklore and modes of social organisation were equally transformed into 'modern' moral classifications and social definitions of property, value, customs, and rights. Illustrative of this is Comninel's acknowledgement that the abolition of normative rules of social regulation linked to 'traditional' peasant communities within English feudalism was intrinsic to constituting capitalist society. Yet equally revealing is his confession that no 'adequate attention to the character and social relationships of the "traditional" peasant community', is given in his analysis, nor to 'the dissolution of this characteristic peasant community . . . through the intrusion of radically different social relationships rooted in the common law, based on fundamentally individualistic property rights' (Comninel 2000: 32). As Perry Anderson (2005: 249) also notes, the understatement in the contrast between extra-economic coercion and politically constituted property, so central to social property relations analysis, 'is the extent to which landed property was still "ideologically constituted"'.

Second, there is a related focus that privileges *intra*-ruling class conflict rather than the self-organisation of producer classes (Teschke 2003). The theory of state formation that ensues is a prioritisation of changes in noble proprietary consciousness, in the form of property titles and the social identity of the noble family through primogeniture, which then provides the basis for a system of feudal polities headed by dynasties. 'The self-organisation of the ruling, arms-bearing class – the form of the "state" – should thus be understood in the light of definite property regimes governing inter-lordly redistributional struggles' (Teschke 2003: 88). The result is a framework that views changes in property relations as responsible for changes in the noble family, or the struggle among lords through intra-class conflict, resulting in a 'political economy of lordships' at the expense of an appreciation of the struggles of direct producers (Teschke 2003: 87, 90–1, 93, 107). The background presence of the peasantry become cyphers subject to the power dynamics of political institutions central to absolutist state formation. By granting priority to inter-noble arrangements, or the 'reproductive imperatives of the ruling elite' (Teschke 2003: 191), the structural conditions of absolutist state formation are given priority over the agency of peasant production through which the absolutist state ruled and was reinforced. This leads to the reduction of the history of state formation to the history of state classes, missing state forms in terms of what they have made of producing classes through whom they rule and function. As Brenner reminds us (1977: 59–60):

> The historical evolution or emergence of any given class structure is not comprehensible as the mere product of a ruling-class choice and imposition, but . . . represents the outcome of class conflicts through which the direct producers, have, to a greater or lesser extent, succeeded in restricting the form and extent of ruling-class access to surplus labour.[5]

Yet, whilst class conflict between direct producers and non-producers is invoked, it is intra-ruling-class conflict that retains analysis in terms of proprietary kingship, office venality, and the social relations of warfare in relaying the logic of absolutist state formation and the rules and norms of international relations (Teschke 2005: 22). Beyond the polarising forces dividing the gentry within the London merchant community of Robert Brenner's analysis of the roots of revolution in early modern England, 'the trajectory of popular politics in the capital becomes yet more of an enigma' (Anderson 2005: 244; Brenner 1993). Anyone anticipating a detailed account of class struggles between direct producers and lordly appropriators from a social property relations line of argument would therefore be disappointed, as these receive scant attention (Davidson 2005a: 16).

Third, there is a problem of 'Eurocentric diffusionism' within social property relations analysis meaning that capitalism is examined through the notion of uneven and combined development as a wave of diffusion unfolding outward from western Europe to the non-European periphery (Blaut 1993). The privileged focus therefore becomes the spatial system of Europe without making connections between intertwined histories that lie both within and beyond the European context. As a result, the periphery of non-Europe is portrayed as a passive recipient of diffusions from the European core, so that the modern expansion of capitalism is presented largely in terms of internal, immanent forces (Blaut 1999: 130–2). This is evident in Robert Brenner's dispensation to acclaim 'the dynamic of capitalist development in a *self-expanding* process of capital accumulation by way of innovation in the *core*' (Brenner 1977: 29, emphases added). As James Blaut (1993: 206) counters:

> Capitalism became centrated in Europe because colonialism gave Europeans the power both to develop their own society and to prevent development from occurring elsewhere. It is this dynamic of development and underdevelopment which mainly explains the modern world.

By contrast, as Blaut (1999: 136) notes, such work on development and underdevelopment is simply dismissed as 'Third-Worldist ideology' (Brenner 1977: 92).

Yet the historical narrative of the emergence and development of the international system can be developed in a way that directly contributes to overcoming these areas of oversight. The following will highlight how Gramsci has precise relevance to debates in historical sociology on the uneven and combined development of the international states-system shaped by the mediation of international pressures. Revealing this detailed appreciation of the causal significance of 'the international', shaping the peculiarities of national developments, will also vitiate the hasty claims that 'Gramsci's praxis of hegemony broke on the rocks of the national border', or that he failed to consider the international dimension of social transformations in capitalist world history (Shilliam 2004: 73). Furthermore, within Gramsci's recourse to understanding modern state formation there is discernible emphasis on the socio-cultural aspects of class rule that encompassed peasant producers. The making and unmaking of social identities and subjectivities within the series of class struggles constitutive of modern European state formation and capitalist production will therefore be shown to be of primary focus. Likewise it will be demonstrated how Gramsci challenges Eurocentrism, when he speaks of 'international and cosmopolitan outward radiation and of imperialistic and hegemonic expansion'

(Gramsci 1971: 18, Q12§1), but in a way that linked relations between different territorial and social dimensions. Before revealing these aspects of the theory of passive revolution that shaped the uneven and combined development of capitalism across the eighteenth and nineteenth centuries, the prior context of Italian state formation – linked to altering power relationships within principalities and republican attempts to overcome the division of Italy by foreign intervention – demands discussion. Hence a focus that shifts from, first, discussing the concrete historical situation shaping the ideas of Machiavelli on the exigencies of Renaissance Italy to, second, analysing Gramsci's principles of historical research on coeval and subsequent developments. 'The Prince', after all, was meant 'to put an end to feudal anarchy' (Gramsci 1971: 141, Q13§13).

Machiavelli in Perspective: Renaissance Italy

As noted above, the structural identity of the feudal mode of production in western Europe was marked by the parcellisation of sovereignty involving overlapping claims to authority and a scalar organisation of property. As Anderson (1974a: 150–1) has detailed, the medieval towns of Italy that practised trade and manufacture, were self-governing communes identified by commodity exchange controlled by merchants and organised in guilds and corporations, which were in dynamic opposition to the rural economy that was controlled by nobles over peasant producers. Whilst there were diverse social formations in the medieval epoch, the evolution of feudalism in Italy reflected this town–country opposition: urban communes were based on merchant communities regulating production through guilds and striving to assert autonomy from the ecclesiastical power of the Papacy, whilst rural society in different regions combined fiefs, freehold peasants, latifundia, and urban landowners. Pivotal to this process in the thirteenth century was the constitution of the *contado* across northern and central Italy, a territorial expansion of the town over a rural hinterland to extract taxes, grain, and military service. 'The most advanced regions of Italy thus became a chequerboard of competing city-states, in which the intervening countryside, unlike any other part of Europe, was annexed to the towns' (Anderson 1974a: 167). This led to the distinctive institutional form of corporate urban communes in Italy, so that merchants in the medieval towns of the feudal order exercised autonomy from Papal authority as well as direct seigneurial or monarchical control (Anderson 1974a:

192–4; Rosenberg 1994: 73). This pattern differed from the characteristic configuration of surplus extraction of European feudalism, discussed in the preceding section of this chapter, based on the fusion of political and economic power through serfdom, with lords acting as both exploiters and rulers over appropriated producers (Wood 2002b: 49).

Similarly, within the framework of absolutism, the emergence of the centralised monarchies of Renaissance Europe, and the recharged state apparatus of noble domination, were experienced differently in Italy. A national absolutism was not apparent on the basis of 'the premature development of mercantile capital in the North Italian cities [the communes of Lombardy, Liguria and Tuscany], which prevented the emergence of a powerful reorganised feudal state at the national level' (Anderson 1974b: 143). Whilst the communes were capable of resisting territorial regroupment under feudal domination, the predominance of merchant capital within the communes meant that peninsular unification was unachievable in the face of royal and seigneurial threats. Italian political development was deadlocked between, on one hand, the organisation of guilds and corporate traditions of mercantile capital in the towns, that acted as a fetter on the development of capitalist wage labour, and on the other hand the assertiveness of seigneurial nobles in the countryside. As Anderson (1974b: 169) details, 'unable to produce a national absolutism from within, Italy was condemned to suffer an alien one from without', through Spanish interventions in Sicily, Naples, and Milan. The *national absence* of a dominant feudal nobility capable of organising a unitary state coeval with Spain or France was eventually succeeded by the *regional presence* of such a nobility in Piedmont. It was this royal dynasty that would later facilitate the creation of a state 'that would provide the trampoline for a belated unification in the era of industrial capitalism' (Anderson 1974b: 169n.52).

It is in the writings of Machiavelli that one can witness the dissolution of the structure of medieval state societies through the prism of the Italian Renaissance. Machiavelli distils various factors confronting Italian social and political development in the cradle of the Renaissance. In the *Discourses* he links chiefly the presence of the Church to the domination of competing interests, from the many princes of the communes and the *signori* of the countryside (both creating disunion and weakness), to the influence of 'barbarian potentates', to foreign subvention. The result was the constant occurrence of civil wars and foreign wars, with Italy easy prey, as it was 'downtrodden by all the ultramontanes' (Machiavelli 2003: 330, Book II.18). According to Machiavelli, the church kept Italy divided, 'for, though the Church has its headquarters in Italy and has temporal power, neither its power nor its virtue has been sufficiently great for it to be able to usurp power in Italy and become its leader'. At the same time, the commentary continues, Papal authority could call upon the absolute princes and rulers of republics contesting Italian state formation as well as the foreign interests of outside monarchies in the shape of French and Spanish principalities (Machiavelli 2003: 145, Book I.12; 244, Book I.55). The Church encouraged factional revolts against nobles, as Machiavelli also details in *The Prince*, to increase its temporal power; 'because Italy had largely come under the control of the Church and of some republics, and because these priests and citizen-rulers had little experience of military matters, they all began to use outsiders to fight their battles'. The 'arbiters of Italy', as he goes on to indicate, were therefore mercenary leaders who contributed to Italian disorder, such as Andrea Fortebraccio, employed by the Papal armies, and Francesco Sforza, of the 'Sforza mercenary troops' (Machiavelli 1993: 47, XII). This was contrasted with 'stability' in France and Spain where monarchies ensured unity through constitutional methods and, 'in the province of Germany', where observance of order had ensured that, 'neither outsiders nor their own inhabitants dare to usurp power' (Machiavelli 2003: 244, Book I.55). The type of polity specifically emergent in Germany was seen to offer opposition to the yoke of foreign intervention whilst drawing other states into forms of competitive expansion (Machiavelli 2003: 336–7, Book II.19).

Meanwhile, in the Italian communes of Venice and Florence, territorial expansion was attempted through the acquisition of dominion and military strength. Whilst these aims were sometimes contradictorily articulated – with both cities weakened by their expansion as a result of their respective holds over Lombardy and Tuscany (Machiavelli 2003: 337–8, Book II.19, see also 441, Book III.12) – Machiavelli nevertheless became a witness through these examples to political accumulation in the form of the violent dispossession thrown up by the beginnings of state formation (Althusser 1999: 124–5). More broadly, in the provinces dominated by the gentry (Naples, the Papal states, Romagna) attempts to establish republican government proved difficult, whilst 'faction-ridden cities' marked the rest of Italy (Machiavelli 1993: 73, XX). The gentry thus became upbraided as 'those who live in idleness on the abundant revenue derived from their estates, without having anything to do with their cultivation or with other forms of labour essential to life. Such men are a pest in any republic and in any province.' The best way to reconstitute power, Machiavelli advocated, was through absolute monarchy: 'it is necessary to have, besides laws, a superior force, such as appertains to a monarch, who has such absolute and overwhelming power that he can restrain excesses due to ambition and the corrupt practices of the powerful' (Machiavelli 2003: 246, Book I.55). This counsel reflected Machiavelli's analysis of the reassertion of rural lordship, of the seigneurialised countryside, that was at loggerheads with mercantile capital in republican towns. Hence his important twofold advice to establish a principality where notable inequality prevails and a republic where notable equality abounds (Machiavelli 2003: 247–8, Book I.55). In the case of Florence, this is where the crucial requisite of *prestige* is elaborated, with reference to Cesare Borgia and his campaign in the Romagna 'to inspire both devotion and respectful fear in the people' as long as it is 'solidly established in power' (Machiavelli 1993: 28–9, VII). The successful foundation of a state is therefore ensured as along as 'the ruler has the prestige attaching to his office', which arises within internal institutions rather than external force (Machiavelli 1993: 65, XIX; Machiavelli 2003: 385–90, Book III.1). Where such prestige cannot be maintained, the less desirable means of *fraud and force* become amenable, albeit with the attendant risks associated with failing to imitate both the fox and the lion (or laws and force) (Machiavelli 1993: 61–2, XVIII; Machiavelli 2003: 310–12, Book II.13).

On the basis of this historical account, Gramsci came to recognise Machiavelli as 'the theoretician of national states ruled by absolute monarchies' (Gramsci 1994a: 153). The priorities that shaped Machiavelli's ideas can therefore be summarised as: (1) the internal struggles of the Florentine republic and the particular structure of the state that was unable to free itself of the residues of commune and municipality; (2) the regional struggles between the Italian states for a balance of power throughout the peninsula, which was obstructed by the existence of the Papacy and other feudal residues of forms of state based on city rather than territory; and (3) the struggles of the Italian states within a European balance of power or 'the contradictions between the requirements of an internal balance of power in Italy and the exigencies of the European states struggling for hegemony' (Gramsci 1971: 140, Q13§13). As a result, the Italian state was subjected to foreign dominance that was a consequence of a condition of backwardness and of stagnation of Italian political and social history from 1500 until 1700 – *a condition which was to a great extent due to the preponderance of international relations over internal ones, which were paralysed and congealed.* (Gramsci 1971: 143, Q13§13, emphasis added)

Italy was therefore posed the problem of uneven development by international factors that would shape subsequent state identity. At the same time, the communes existed as 'the urban forms of feudalism' that were incapable of economic transformation and expansion and thus political conversion towards unifying the national state (Althusser 1999: 71; *vide* Althusser 1993: 220, 242). Machiavelli therefore theorised the constituent power of state-forming processes in terms of the problem of how a state begins to produce and reproduce itself within a conjuncture of events. Whilst the historical account provided by Machiavelli has been criticised for its inattention to dynastic authority, which was central to emergent absolutist states, and his approach has been dismissed as suffering from an 'unseeing empiricism', which overlooked the structural causes of the events he recorded (Anderson 1974b: 168), he nevertheless does reflect upon traits that would become associated with the modern territorial state – notably, transitions in terms of relations between city and countryside, the role of urban classes in not forgoing feudal privileges, and thus the integration of rural classes into the state (Gramsci 1995: 163–4, Q8§162). However, Machiavelli *is* missing a full exploration of the economic and social causes of Italy's enfeeblement (Finocchiaro 1988: 131). 'Nowhere does he discuss the decline of economic dynamism brought about by guild restrictions and established privileges, and exacerbated by parochial attachments to small administrative units' (Femia 2004: 87). It was this task, that of delineating the inherent weakness in Italian state formation, the corporative basis of guild formation, and the parochialism of both Papal and mercantile interests, that was bequeathed to Gramsci. Since 'Gramsci discovers the means of understanding the political project to which Machiavelli devoted all his efforts . . . we may suppose that Machiavelli "speaks" to Gramsci if in large part historically and retrospectively' (Althusser 1999: 10). Although Gramsci declared with exaggeration that 'Machiavelli represents in Italy the realisation that there can be no real Renaissance without the foundation of a national state' (Gramsci 1985: 222, Q17§8), it was left to the diminutive Sardinian himself to contribute towards unravelling the concrete historical relations of which Machiavelli's ideas are the product and consciousness.

Gramsci in Perspective: towards the Italian Risorgimento

According to Hoare and Nowell-Smith (1971: 44–5), within the *Prison Notebooks* the term 'Renaissance' encapsulates a number of key developments linked to the historical experience of Italian state formation. Chiefly, these can be summarised as (1) the failure of the Italian communes to create a national state due to the role of mercantile capital in acting as a fetter on the transition of the absolutist state; (2) the specific historical 'backwardness' of Italy and the problems posed by the 'southern question' of uneven development in Italy; and (3) the regressive 'cosmopolitan' character of Italian intellectual classes that carried forward a passive revolution in the shape of the Italian Risorgimento. As outlined in the introduction to this chapter, these features will be examined in detail in order to highlight the much neglected priority given by Gramsci to the conditions of uneven development in shaping the Italian state and thus the due regard he gave to the causal dynamics of 'the international' as a constitutive moment in the dynamics of state formation. At the same time this will include tracing the dispensation he exhibited when analysing the subaltern class struggles of peasant producers in his account of state formation processes. First, the legacy of pre-capitalist territorial and spatial relations – that preceded and prefigured the expansion of capitalism – will be traced during the age of absolutism in relation to the medieval communes of the Italian Renaissance.

Renaissance Italy

After the year 1000 and the disintegration of the Carolingian Empire, Gramsci indicates a gradual break developed that would culminate in the Renaissance and humanism and lead to the presence of 'regressive' classes, from the point of view of Italian history, which contrasted with developments throughout the rest of Europe. In Italy, specific class interests linked to the Papacy became reactionary in character whilst the new intellectual classes across Europe became absorbed in developments that would eventually lead to the organisation of modern states (Gramsci 1985: 220, Q17§3). Hence the 'double face of Humanism and the Renaissance' in the history of European state formation (Gramsci 1985: 188, Q29§7; Gramsci 1994a: 360). The communes were pivotal in this account in that they were unable to transcend feudal property relations, or 'unable to develop beyond middle feudalism, i.e. that which succeeded the absolute feudalism . . . which had existed before the year AD 1000, and which was itself succeeded by the absolute monarchy in the fifteenth century, up to the French Revolution' (Gramsci 1971: 54n.4, Q25§2). What is central here is the focus on the medieval communes – autonomous city-states like Florence, Genoa, and Venice – that represented a phase of Italian history that was incapable of creating a unified state. Linking with the earlier reflections of Machiavelli, the problem facing Gramsci was 'the real constitution of the communes' that was to be studied in terms of 'the concrete stances that the representatives adopted towards the government of the commune' (Gramsci 1995: 20, Q5§85).

Fundamental to Gramsci's analysis of the specificity of Italian development is therefore the medieval commune. The communes were understood as laden with an inability to transcend a syndicalist phase of development, so that they represented 'the economic–corporate phase' in the history of Italian state formation. 'In Italy, the communes were unable to go beyond the corporative phase, feudal anarchy triumphed in a form appropriate to the new situation and then came the period of foreign domination' (Gramsci 1971: 54n.4, Q25§2). The unfolding of Italian history would thus have to be understood from a viewpoint that grants importance to the development of the communes in order to recognise the Renaissance as a reactionary movement due to the inability to establish an integral relationship of the city over the countryside (Gramsci 1994b: 67–8). 'In the rest of Europe . . . ', Gramsci elaborates, 'the general movement culminated in the formation of national states and then in the world expansion of Spain, France, England and Portugal. What corresponded in Italy to the national states of these countries was the organisation – begun by Pope Alexander VI – of the papacy as an absolute state, an organisation which broke up the rest of Italy' (Gramsci 1985: 222, Q17§8). As alluded to earlier, alongside the rise of humanism the possibility of establishing united sovereign territorial relations became diluted. Humanism assumed an aspect of restitution, 'politically, an aristocracy made up mostly of *parvenus* dominated, gathered as it was round the courts of the lords and protected by mercenary troops: it produced the culture of the sixteenth century and helped the various arts, but it was politically limited and ended up under foreign domination' (Gramsci 1985: Q5§123). The Italian state came to rely on 'specific auxilaries' of foreign domination in the organisation of its specific form of state due to the failure of the mercantile classes within the medieval communes – the autonomous city-states – to unite nationally. This inability of the communal classes to unite the people around itself 'was the cause of its defeats and the interruptions in its development' (Gramsci 1971: 53, Q25§5). The ensuing results of humanism included 'retractions before the stake', with the most notable example, of course, being that of Girolamo Savonarola (1452–1498), the Dominican friar who was leader of Florence between 1495 and 1498 before excommunication by the Papacy and rejection by the Florentine *signoria* leading to his burning at the stake (Gramsci 1985: 234, Q5§123).

Gramsci thus points to differences in development during the Renaissance between Italy and Europe, notably France where 'the protective shell of monarchy' permitted the struggle within and between feudal classes, whereas in Italy the interests of mercantile capital were 'incapable of going beyond a narrow-minded corporatism or of creating their own integral state civilisation' (Gramsci 1985: 227–8, Q5§123). 'In France . . . the origin of absolutism lay in the struggle between bourgeoisie and feudal classes', with the former drawing in 'the common people and peasants' (Gramsci 1985: 229, Q5§123; 1992: 22–4, Q3§16). Elsewhere he notes that 'only in the Netherlands was there an organic passage from the commune or city-state to a regime that was no longer feudal' (Gramsci 1985: 223, Q5§123). Meanwhile, in France, reaction against Papal authority spread in the form of the Protestant Reformation whilst, in Italy, it took the form of support for Savonarola. Returning to our earlier theme, 'Machiavelli's political thought', therefore, 'was also a reaction to the Renaissance, a reminder of the political and national need to return to the people as the absolute monarchies of France and Spain had done' (Gramsci 1985: Q5§123).

Emergent here is what Gramsci designated 'the method of historical analogy as an interpretative criterion' (Gramsci 1971: 54n.4, Q25§2). This can be defined as a mode of analysis from which a certain explicative power can be derived on the basis of comparing different historical processes and, therein, the particular configuration of social, cultural, and political state forms. On the basis of this method he derives certain principles of historical research linked to the conditioning circumstances of Italian state formation in relation to the wider emerging European states-system. As will become clear, the explanatory value of this method of historical analogy, as an interpretative criterion, revolves around the causal sequence of events he deems important in shaping Italian and European state formation. The importance of this method for historical sociology is in the sense of historical process that is brought to bear on the conditions and structural developments of state formation. At times, as noted earlier in this chapter and elaborated further below, such analysis may serve only by negative example, due to the simplified reading of the historical conditions in question. Nevertheless this does not detract from the relevance Gramsci has for understanding the causal sequencing of Italian state development within the wider history of the European states-system. At the very least, it throws into relief specific elements that can be proposed as paramount for future discussion. This method will be further discussed when delineating the contours of the Italian Risorgimento and the conditions of passive revolution.

The 'Southern Question' and Uneven Development

Within the national structure of Italian state formation Gramsci also traced the relationship between city and countryside that was intrinsic to the conditions of uneven development within the country and the broader division of Europe. The relationship between cities and countryside was seen as a microcosm of the historical relationship between north and south in Italy, which would shape the series of political crises surrounding the Risorgimento. The spatial distinction of north and south reflected a 'relatively homogenous politico-economic structure' that configured the uneven development of Italian state formation from approximately 1815 onwards (Gramsci 1971: 93, Q19§26). 'The relation between city and countryside', argued Gramsci, 'is the necessary starting-point for the study of the fundamental motor forces of Italian history' (Gramsci 1971: 98, Q19§26). Hence an equation between the leadership or *prestige* (echoing Machiavelli) of the north over the south, city over countryside, within which questions of agrarian reform were posed, albeit in an unresolved way that would have favoured the peasantry (Gramsci 1971: 99, Q19§26; 101, Q19§26). Within the national structure, the prevalence of so-called 'cities of silence'[6] was spotlighted as a residue of the feudal past, 'a legacy of parasitism bequeathed to modern times by the disintegration as a class of the communal bourgeoisie' (Gramsci 1971: 131, Q13§1). These numerous cities (including Assisi, Brescia, Pisa, Volterra, and Vicenza) came to have an aversion to the countryside, holding the 'backwardness' of the peasantry in contempt (Gramsci

1971: 91, Q19§26). From the point of view of these non-rural centres, poverty in the Mezzogiorno was explained in terms of the presumed incapacity or 'backwardness' of the southerners rather than as being linked to the fetters on development grounded in structural political and economic conditions (Gramsci 1971: Q10§24). As a result, 'the Mezzogiorno was reduced to the status of a semi-colonial market', controlled through direct police measures and more general political measures of coercion and co-option (Gramsci 1971: 94, Q19§27).

These issues are perhaps spelt out most clearly in Gramsci's essay 'Some Aspects of the Southern Question' (1926) which also traces the question of intellectuals and the function they perform in the class struggle as mediators between the *latifondisti* (or great landowners), the rural bourgeoisie, and the peasantry (Gramsci 1994c: 313–37). Here one can witness a consideration of the city–countryside relationship through a focus on 'differing cultural conceptions and mental attitudes' (Gramsci 1971: 93, Q19§26). Within the countryside of the south of Italy Gramsci maintained a focus on the *morti di fame*, or 'starvelings', constituted by the peasantry and agricultural day-labourers, who often embarked on confused expressions of class struggle. Their 'intellectual and moral condition' would be '"semi-feudal" rather than modern in character', manifested in 'a negative rather than a positive class position' expressed through the identification of the *signori* of officialdom, on the basis of dress codes, their role as civil servants, and their dislike of country in favour of town. Hence the peasantry could 'only achieve self-awareness via a series of negations, via their consciousness of the identity and class limits of their enemies' as representatives of the state (Gramsci 1971: 272–3, Q3§46). This could be discernible in terms of the 'anarchic turbulence' of brigandage, blackmail, burning down woods, the maiming of livestock, or attacks on municipal buildings that all constituted 'a form of elementary terrorism, without long term or effective consequences' (Gramsci 1971: 94, Q19§26; Gramsci 1978: 84). Through these forms of organising, the peasantry were 'in perpetual ferment, but as a mass . . . incapable of giving a centralised expression to their aspiration and needs' (Gramsci 1994c: 327). Such action was 'characteristic of the "history of the subaltern classes", and indeed of their most marginal and peripheral elements' for they 'have not achieved any consciousness of the class "for itself"' (Gramsci 1971: 196, Q3§48). At the same time, linked to their class background, southern intellectuals came to 'derive a fierce antipathy to the working peasant, considered as a work machine that can be bled dry and then replaced, given the excess working population' (Gramsci 1994c: 329). However, through 'capillary processes' linked to the composition of local parties or communal and provincial councils, various strata of intellectuals would seek 'the realignment of political currents and mental attitudes' linked to the peasantry to forge an agrarian bloc that could act as an overseer for the industrial bourgeoisie in the north (Gramsci 1994c: 324–5).

What is granted priority here is a focus on the struggles between appropriators and producers, landlords and peasants. According to Gramsci, 'capitalism begins the dissolution of traditional relations inherent in the institution of the family and religious myth' (Gramsci 1975: 113), dimensions commonly overlooked from a social property relations approach. Gramsci thus draws direct attention to the means by which the personalised political and military power of appropriating groups was reconstituted in the impersonal form of the Italian state. The peasant therefore comes to feel the state through the economy or the direct struggle over property rights represented by the 'war' between the feudal right of acquisition, based on extra-economic surplus extraction, and the emergence of surplus extraction conducted through the purely 'economic' mechanisms of the market (Gramsci 1975: 75–9). The way in which the state begins to assert itself through political consciousness in shaping the class feeling and mentality of producers is thus traced, whilst peasant producers, at the same time, become transformed into propertyless individuals compelled to sell their labour. As a result, 'reality is the deep and bottomless abyss that capitalism has dug between proletariat and bourgeoisie and the ever growing antagonism between the two classes' (Gramsci 1975: 134). In contrast to social property relations approaches, the 'epistemological significance' of class struggle is thus granted priority, revolving around shaping state and subaltern class intersubjectivities internally related to the emergence of capitalism (Gramsci 1971: 365, Q10II§12). This is furthered by tracing the residues of 'common sense' – taken-for-granted 'beliefs, superstitions, opinions, ways of seeing and of acting' – whether in popular folklore or customs, religious beliefs, or practices that are transformed in the attempt to engender a 'modern outlook' (Gramsci 1971: 34, Q12§2; 323, Q11§12).

The principal world-view of peasant producers' 'common sense' is splintered in the first instance in terms of religion, with differences existing amongst the peasantry, the petits bourgeois, town workers, women, and intellectuals (Gramsci 1971: 420). Subsequently, the constitution of the human subject is composed of very contradictory ideological formations with 'common sense' standing between elements of folklore and modern philosophy, science, and economics. Identity here is protean; 'it contains Stone Age elements and principles of a more advanced science, prejudices from all past phases of history at the local level and intuitions of a future philosophy', often based on educational practices intended to call modernity into existence through the rudiments of natural science, a belief in objective laws, civic rights and duties, and the disciplining of work (Gramsci 1971: 33–5, Q12§2; 324, Q11§12; cf. Thompson 1968: 67–73). The criteria that Gramsci developed to understand the history of subaltern classes are therefore pivotal in understanding how subaltern classes are intertwined with processes of state formation (Gramsci 1971: 52–5, Q25§2 and §5). These involved, first, identifying the 'objective' formation of subaltern social classes by analysing developments and transformations within social property relations (Gramsci 1971: 52, Q25§2 and §5). For example, by incorporating as much as possible a consideration of the mentalities and ideologies of subaltern classes, their active as well as passive affiliation to dominant social forms of political association, and thus their involvement in formations that might conserve dissent or maintain control (Gramsci 1971: 52, Q25§2 and §5). Second, it entailed focusing on the formations which subaltern classes themselves produce (e.g. trade unions, workers' co-operatives, peasant associations) in order to press claims or assert their autonomy within the existing conditions of state formation. What we are left with is a historical materialist methodology for subaltern historical analysis of the role of producer classes in constituting the history of states and groups of states (Green 2002: 19–20). This 'moral economy' of the poor is thus important in indicating the 'fragmented débris' of older patterns of class formation and consciousness that originated over hundreds of years as well as emergent patterns operative in the transition to a modern state (Thompson 1971/1993: 12, 293–4). Overall, the experiential historical process of class formation is therefore recognised, situated within the lives and cognitive systems of ruler and ruled within specific contexts of antagonism and exploitation (cf. Thompson 1978: 148). These insights thus provide a pathway to addressing the structuring of identities and subjectivities embedded in transformations to modernity but often missed in social property relations accounts. The underlying basis of this cultural assimilation, however, was the emergence of capitalism through processes of primitive accumulation;

'we shall thus see the "colonial" economic exploitation and impoverishment of the south increased', anticipated Gramsci, 'and the slow detachment of the southern petty bourgeoisie from the state accelerated' (Gramsci 1978: 352; cf. Gramsci 1977: 179–81). Hence the tracing of the nexus of ideological and class relations between class fractions of the north and south in the organisation of the national economy and the Italian state so intrinsic to the history of the Risorgimento.

The Italian Risorgimento, Passive Revolution and the Presence of 'the International'

Gramsci also understood issues of uneven and combined development across eighteenth- and nineteenth-century European history as a series of passive revolutions. This is evident within his analysis of the dissemination of the French Revolution through 'class "meatuses"' that influenced the creation of modern European states. Such events unfolded through modernising strategies and 'successive waves' of class struggle and national wars known as passive revolution. (Gramsci 1992: 230–1, Q1§151)

> In France . . . there was a split between the nobles and the monarchy, as well as an alliance among the monarchy, the nobles and the upper bourgeoisie. In France, however, the Revolution was also propelled by the popular classes, who prevented it from stalling in its early stages; this did not happen in southern Italy or, subsequently, during the entire Risorgimento. (Gramsci 1996: 97, Q3§103)

Initially developed to explain the Risorgimento, the movement for Italian national liberation that culminated in the political unification of the country in 1860–61, the notion of passive revolution was expanded to encompass a whole series of other historical phenomena.[7] In the case of Italy, the 'passive' aspect refers to the restrictive form of hegemony that emerged out of the Risorgimento because of the failure of potential 'Jacobins' in the *Partito d'Azione* led by Giuseppe Mazzini and Giuseppe Garibaldi, among others, to establish a programme reflecting the demands of the popular masses and, significantly, the peasantry. Instead, challenges were thwarted and changes in property relations accommodated due to the 'Moderates', led by (Count) Camillo Benso Cavour, establishing alliances between big landowners in the Mezzogiorno and the northern bourgeoisie, whilst absorbing opposition in parliament through continually assimilated change (or *trasformismo*) within the current social formation. 'Indeed one might say', Gramsci noted, 'that the entire state of Italy from 1848 onwards has been characterised by *trasformismo*' (Gramsci 1971: 58, Q19§24). The *Partito d'Azione* did not succeed in emulating a Jacobin force, reflecting the relative weakness of the Italian bourgeoisie within the international states-system of uneven development after 1815, so that

> in Italy the struggle manifested itself as a struggle against old treaties and the existing international order, and against a foreign power – Austria – which represented these and upheld them in Italy, occupying a part of the peninsula and controlling the rest. (Gramsci 1971: 80–2, Q19§24)

The process is not therefore literally 'passive' but refers to the attempt at 'revolution' through state intervention, or the inclusion of new social groups within the hegemony of a political order without an expansion of mass-producer control over politics (Sassoon 1987: 210). Significant here is the way the Moderates thought 'the national question required a bloc of all the right-wing forces – including the classes of the great landowners – around Piedmont as a state and as an army' (Gramsci 1971: 100, Q19§26). This left intact the sedimentations of pre-capitalist social relations bequeathed, as noted earlier, by the parasitism of the rural southern bourgeoisie – those 'pensioners of economic history' – residing in the quiescent 'cities of silence' (Gramsci 1971: 281, Q22§2). In the words of Giuseppe Garibaldi (2004: 15):

> the whole country, so full of enthusiasm and energy, capable not only of resisting but of overcoming the enemy occupying its territory, was reduced to a state of prostration and inertia through the folly and the treachery of the men who ruled it: its monarchy, its intelligentsia, its clergy.

The result was a process of fundamental social change but without an attempt to embrace the interests of subordinate classes, and crucially the peasantry, within a national state. That is why 'the concept of "passive revolution"', as Neil Davidson (2005b: 19) has stated, 'is perhaps the most evocative one to describe the process of "revolution from above"', developed within the classical tradition of historical materialism. In Italy, what was lacking was a Jacobin force, 'which in other nations awakened and organised the national–popular collective will, and founded the modern states' (Gramsci 1971: 131, Q13§1). Or, as Fred Halliday (1999: 246) notes, 'in the case of the uncompleted bourgeois revolution in Italy itself . . . [Gramsci] had a powerful example of the impact of combined and uneven development'.

Whilst the notion of passive revolution was rooted in his writings on the crisis of the liberal state in Italy, Gramsci also linked it to transformations across Europe cast in the shadow of revolutionary French Jacobinism (Gramsci 1995: 330, Q10I§0; 348–50, Q10I§9). Specifically, this was the case in terms of a transformation of society in a 'bourgeois' direction but without the active participation of the peasant producing masses, unlike the upheaval of the French Revolution where the Jacobins 'made the bourgeoisie into the leading, hegemonic class of the nation, in other words gave the new state a permanent basis and created the compact modern French nation' (Gramsci 1971: 79, Q19§28). According to Gramsci, the French Revolution established a 'bourgeois' state on the basis of popular support and the elimination of old feudal classes yet, across Europe, the institution of political forms suitable to the expansion of capitalism occurred differently – hence highlighting 'differences between France, Germany and Italy in the process by which the bourgeoisie took power (and England)', for 'it was in France that the process was richest in development, and in active and positive political elements' (Gramsci 1971: 82–3, Q19§24). Following the post-Napoleonic restoration (1815–1848), the tendency to establish 'bourgeois' social and political order was regarded as something of a universal principle, but not in an absolute or fixed sense (Gramsci 1994c: 230–3). 'All history from 1815 onwards', wrote Gramsci, 'shows the efforts of the traditional classes to prevent the formation of a collective will . . . and to maintain "economic–corporate" power in an international system of passive equilibrium' (Gramsci 1971: 132, Q13§1). Moreover 'the "successive waves" [of class struggle] were made up of a combination of social struggles, interventions from above of the enlightened monarchy type, and national wars – with the latter two predominating' (Gramsci 1971: 115, Q10II§61). This was indicative of mid-nineteenth-century European national unifications during which people became (albeit active) ancillaries of change organised from above; a process that in other parts of the world would be mimetic. For, as Hobsbawm (1975: 73, 166) puts it, in a statement that resonates with the force of Trotsky's arguments on uneven and combined development, 'countries seeking to break through modernity are normally derivative and unoriginal in their ideas, though necessarily not so in their practices'. A passive revolution, therefore, *was* a revolution, marked by violent social upheaval, but it involved a relatively small elite leading to the creation of state power and an institutional framework consonant with capitalist property relations.[8] Analysing the 1848 revolutions, Gramsci thus argued that the 'precise *coups d'état*' of the 'Eighteenth Brumaire type' had been changed to such an extent that 'the Forty-Eightist formula of the "Permanent Revolution"' became 'expanded and transcended in political science by the formula of "civil hegemony"' (Gramsci 1971: 220, Q13§27; 243, Q13§7). Hence the resultant dialectical combination of progressive and reactionary elements within conditions of passive revolution, described as 'revolution–restoration' or 'revolution without revolution' (Gramsci 1992: 137, Q1§44).

These trajectories of state formation manifested within the uneven and combined development of various passive revolutions were, once again, the precise legacy of absolutism. Recall from the first section of this chapter that the absolutist state in eastern Europe was highly centralised, with serfdom consolidated and seigneurial power concentrated over the peasantry as 'territorial, personal and economic lordship were generally fused in a single manorial authority, which exercised cumulative rights over its subject serfs' (Anderson 1974b: 223–4). Here, the legacy of absolutism was a heavily concentrated, hierarchical and centralised state structure that unequivocally displayed its class composition and function alongside its oppression and exploitation of the peasantry through blunt coercion (Anderson 1974b: 430). It is this bequest that led Gramsci famously to formulate that,

> In Russia [i.e. the East] the state was everything, civil society was primordial and gelatinous; in the West, there was a proper relation between state and civil society, and when the state trembled a sturdy structure of civil society was at once revealed. (Gramsci 1971: 238, Q7§16)

As also outlined earlier, the rich background of the age of absolutism in Europe provides an insight into the posterior processes of state formation, divergent trajectories of development, and the relationship between state and civil society shaping different regions. But what Gramsci offers, perhaps uniquely, is recognition of *both* the internal fragmentation of Europe in terms of an east–west division *and* a realisation of the north–south structuring of geography, territory, place, and space. The latter, as noted earlier in relation to the 'southern question' of Italian development, was just as significant in shaping transitions to modernity and associated forms of cultural representation (Moe 2002: 297). Linked to the concept of passive revolution, this realisation of different regional axes of development makes it possible to appreciate similar but discrete questions of 'north–south uneven development' characterised by the expansion of capital and the emergence of the modern state (see Chapter 1). 'The concept of passive revolution, it seems to me', declared Gramsci (1996: 232, Q4§57), 'applies not only to Italy but also to those countries that modernise the state through a series of reforms or national wars without undergoing a political revolution of a radical Jacobin-type.'

At issue here is not the question of the historical validity of the examples deployed. After all, as Gramsci himself noted, 'historians are by no means of one mind (and it is impossible that they should be) in fixing the limits of the group of events which constitutes the French Revolution' (Gramsci 1971: 179–80, Q13§17).[9] As Gramsci himself was also more than aware, the theory he developed is merely a 'criterion of interpretation' that 'cannot be applied mechanically to . . . Italian and European history from the French Revolution throughout the nineteenth century'. Danger exists 'in making what is a principle of research and interpretation into a "historical cause"' (Gramsci 1971: 114, Q15§62; 116, Q10II§61; 180, Q13§17). Highly specific regional diversities in the pattern of capitalist development, the relationship between city and countryside, and the forms of political representation and tensions between social classes within Italy have been raised elsewhere (see Davis 1979; Davis 1994; Morris 1997; Schneider 1998). But it is all too easy to question the historical account of modern revolution that Gramsci provides without considering the wider import this might have in throwing into relief certain questions of comparative method in historical sociology (Ghosh 2001: 16–19). On this basis it would be too precocious to dismiss Gramsci on the basis of his conflating the historical problems of absolutism and the 'bourgeois' character of monarchies unifying France, England, or Spain or for carrying categories from one historical epoch and reading them back into history (Anderson 1974b: 169n.52). The error of telescoping the transformations of feudalism and the medieval church with the historical conditions and developments of the modern world are evident more in subsequent commentaries (e.g. Fontana 1993).

By contrast, one can observe in Gramsci a periodisation that distinguishes aspects of absolutist state forms in the case of medieval communes from the early modern epoch of capitalism and the Risorgimento marking Italian historical development. To reiterate, this mode of interpreting the historical sociology of late medieval and early modern state formation is not presented as a mechanical schema. The method of historical analogy as a criterion of interpretation merely attempts to elucidate some comparative principles of political science, in which the history of modern states can be situated in terms both of general trajectories and historical specificities (Gramsci 1971: 107, Q15§17; 108–9, Q15§11; 114, Q15§62). The point made here is the need to appreciate specific outcomes within the formative conditions of the creation of modern states, or 'the significance of a "Piedmont"-type function in passive revolutions – i.e. the fact that a state replaces the local social groups in leading a struggle of renewal' (Gramsci 1971: 105–6, Q15§59). This refers to the manner in which the Piedmontese monarchy provided a regional base for the nobility onto which the political forms of absolutism could be grafted, resulting in the creation of a distorted unitary state. The theory exposes a situation in Italy whereby the 'bourgeoisie obtained economic–industrial power, but the old feudal classes remained as the government stratum of the political class' (Gramsci 1971: 83, Q19§24; 104–6, Q15§59; 115–20, Q10II§61 and Q10I§9). It is this weakness in the 'function' of Piedmont that then became the analogue to state-building attempts elsewhere marking the history of Europe across the nineteenth century, most significantly between 1848 and 1871 (Gramsci 1971: 110, Q15§11).

Passive revolution is therefore a portmanteau concept that reveals continuities and changes within the order of capital. Processes, in the example of the Risorgimento, that exemplified the inability of the ruling class to fully integrate the producer classes through conditions of hegemony, when the leaders 'were aiming at the creation of a modern state in Italy [but] in fact produced a bastard' (Gramsci 1971: 90, Q19§28). Hence a situation when 'more or less far-reaching modifications . . . into the economic structure of the country' are made in a situation of 'domination without that of "leadership": dictatorship without hegemony' (Gramsci 1995: 350, Q10I§9; Gramsci 1971: 105–6, Q15§59). This might be because 'the impetus of progress is not tightly linked to a vast local economic development . . . but is instead the reflection of *international developments* which transmit their ideological currents to the periphery – currents born of the productive development of the more advanced countries' (Gramsci 1971: 116–17, Q10II§61, emphasis added).

Lest the international dimensions of this analysis are neglected, Gramsci linked the above conditions of passive revolution and the method of historical analogy to processes of social transformation and capitalist expansion. The Risorgimento was an attempt 'to "patch up" structural weaknesses' engendered by the position of the Italian state within an international system of uneven development (Gramsci 1985: 245, Q19§5). For 'international relations were certainly very important in determining the line of development of the Italian Risorgimento' (Gramsci 1971: 84, Q19§24). As a result, 'variations in the actual process whereby the same historical development [i.e. passive revolution] manifests itself in different countries have to be related not only to the differing combinations of internal relations within the different nations, but also to the differing international relations' (Gramsci 1971: 84, Q19§24). Alluding to the very causal presence of 'the international', within an historical methodology, therefore entailed tracing how 'the complex problem arises of the relation of internal forces in the country in question, of the relation of international forces, [and] of the country's geo-political position' (Gramsci 1971: 116, Q10II§61). This entailed analysing organic and conjunctural historical movements that were dealt with by the same concepts, so that *'relations within society'* (involving the development of productive forces, the level of coercion, or relations between political parties) that constitute *'hegemonic systems within the state'*, were inextricably linked to *'relations between international forces'* (involving the requisites of great powers, sovereignty and independence) that constitute *'the combinations of states in hegemonic systems'* (Gramsci 1971: 176, Q13§2). The 'close play of the class struggle' was analysed, then, by linking both the 'development of international relations between states' and the 'relations between various groups that form a class within a nation' (Gramsci 1975: 62). Therefore 'in the international sphere, competition, the struggle to acquire private and national property, creates the same hierarchies and system of slavery as in the national sphere' (Gramsci 1977: 69). Three examples of the causal presence of 'the international' in Gramsci's method of historical analogy can be briefly detailed.

First, the uneven and combined development of capitalism was represented through a distinction between (1) the group of capitalist states which formed the keystone of the international states-system (Britain, France, Germany, the United States); and (2) those states which represented, at the time, the immediate periphery of the capitalist world (Italy, Poland, Russia, Spain, Portugal) (Gramsci 1978: 408–10). Within the former, 'the global politico-economic system' was being more and more marked by 'Anglo-Saxon world hegemony' accompanied by the 'colonial subjection of the whole world to Anglo-Saxon capitalism' (Gramsci 1977: 81, 89). In Gramsci's view that is why the 'uneven development' of capitalism is a 'world historical phenomenon' within which 'the colonial populations become the foundation on which the whole edifice of capitalist exploitation is erected' (Gramsci 1977: 69–72, 302). Hence, as a counter to the problem of Eurocentric diffusionism outlined earlier, there was the need to grant due regard to 'the class struggle of the coloured peoples against their white exploiters and murderers' producing 'cheap raw materials for industry . . . for the benefit of European civilisation' (Gramsci 1977: 60, 302).[10] At the same time, the late entrance of peripheral European societies into capitalist activity meant that state forces were 'less efficient' in creating ideological mechanisms to defer the immediate consequences of economic crisis, so that the form of state transformation was circumscribed by 'the prevailing conditions within the international capitalist system' (Gramsci 1975: 95; Gramsci 1977: 128; Gramsci 1978: 408–10). Within his historical sociological method, Gramsci therefore traced specific contexts of uneven development as constitutive features of the international states-system.

The potential break from Eurocentrism is offered by Gramsci's prompt to think through and collectively interpret discrepant experiences in order to appreciate the coexistence and interaction of interconnected and overlapping histories or the 'connective tissues' binding together Europe and its colonies (Gramsci 1977: 60). Theorising 'the international' in this way speaks to what Philip McMichael has established as the method of *incorporated comparison*. This is an interpretative approach to historical sociology focusing on interrelated instances of state transition within world-historical processes, where the *particulars* of state formation are realised within the *general* features of capitalist modernity. To put it in McMichael's words (1990: 392, original emphasis), this method 'views comparable social phenomena as differentiated *outcomes* or *moments* of an historically integrated process, whereas conventional comparison treats such social phenomena as parallel *cases'*. Instances of different passive revolutions can thus be understood as part of a cumulative process of historically linked state formation moments within the world market order of capitalism and the international states-system. Incorporated comparison encapsulates the method of viewing processes of passive revolution as *specific* instances of state transition that are internally related through the *general* world-historical conditions of uneven and combined development. Different historically peculiar *national* processes of passive revolution across the postcolonial world can therefore be traced as connected variants within the *international* conditions of world capitalism.

Such factors were, second, similarly evident in Gramsci's questioning of Fascism as the most recent attempt in Italian history to further the expansion of capital: 'Is not "fascism" precisely a new "liberalism"? Is not fascism precisely the form of "passive revolution" proper to the twentieth century as liberalism was to the nineteenth?' (Gramsci 1988: 264–5; 1971: 119, Q10I§9). Within the uneven development of the world economy, the ideology of Fascism was recognised as an attempt by the ruling classes in Italy – allied with a social base in the urban and rural petty bourgeoisie that was created as a result of trans-formations in rural property – to develop the productive forces 'in competition with the more advanced industrial formations' (Gramsci 1971: 120, Q10I§9; 1978: 350). The political economy of Fascism was therefore a response to 'the intervention of Anglo-American capital in Italy' that signified the growing predominance of finance capital over the state (Gramsci 1978: 352, 403). 'What is fascism, observed on an international scale?', asks Gramsci. 'It is the attempt to resolve the problems of production and exchange with machine-guns and pistol-shots' (Gramsci 1978: 23). Quite clearly that is why the representative of passive revolution 'both practical (for Italy) and ideological (for Europe)' was Fascism (Gramsci 1971: 120, Q10I§9; 1995: 350, Q10I§9). In the former, Fascism was held to be a modification of conservative reaction that had always dominated Italian politics within the conditions of passive revolution. This resulted in both colonial exploitation at home (in the form of exploiting the southern masses of the Mezzogiorno with the support of Catholic Action and the monarchy as the 'state form' of the Fascist regime) and colonial exploitation abroad (in the form of expansion in Ethiopia) (Gramsci 1978: 352, 371). These should be regarded as conjoined forms of colonial exploitation, with leaders such as Francesco Crispi

(1818–1901), Italian prime minister on various occasions between 1876 and 1896, responding to exigencies of internal politics by conjuring up 'the mirage of colonial lands to be exploited' in an attempt to displace exploitation from the Mezzogiorno onto colonial expansion (Gramsci 1971: 68, Q19§24). Italian responses to uneven and combined development were therefore reflections of wider tendencies of colonialism in that

> capitalist Europe, rich in resources and arrived at the point at which the rate of profit was beginning to reveal its tendency to fall, had a need to widen the area of expansion of its income-bearing investments; thus after 1890, the great colonial empires were created. (Gramsci 1971: 68, Q19§24)

Therefore:

> All the ideological propaganda and the political and economic activity of fascism is crowned by its tendency to 'imperialism' . . . It contains the germs of a war, but in which fascist Italy will in reality be an instrument in the hands of one of the imperialist groups which are striving for world domination. (Gramsci 1978: 352)

Once more we witness here Gramsci's understanding of history and his potential break with Eurocentrism.

Third, chief amongst the conditions of uneven and combined development in the international states-system of the early twentieth century was the specific context of the Russian Revolution and (as a response) the liberal internationalism of Woodrow Wilson. With reference to the latter, issues of liberal reformism were generally noted, with Gramsci stating that 'on the economic level, the bourgeois class is international: it must necessarily wield across national differences', to result in a class doctrine that is 'liberalism in politics and free trade in economics' (Gramsci 1975: 105). More specifically, the dissemination of Wilsonian cosmopolitanism and the League of Nations was regarded as 'the proper ideology of modern capitalism':

> It seeks to liberate the individual from all collective authoritarian shackles dependent on pre-capitalist economic structures, in order to establish the bourgeois cosmopolis and allow a more unrestrained race for individual enrichment, possible only with

the fall of national monopolies in the world's markets. The Wilsonian ideology is anti-Catholic, anti-hierarchical: it is the demonic capitalist revolution that the Pope has always exorcised without being able to defend the traditional economic and political patrimony of feudal Catholicism against it. (Gramsci 1975: 114, cf. 129–31)

The Russian Revolution was also sketched in a manner that accorded due regard to particular national characteristics of historical development whilst noting that these differed in their 'normal development' from the Western world. As Gramsci stated, 'the unfolding causation is coupled and entangled', but penetrating research must not view history as 'a mathematical calculation: it does not have a metric decimal system, a progressive numbering of equal quantities'. Therefore, he continued, 'the process of causation must be studied within Russian events and not from an abstract and general viewpoint'. This entailed rejecting a conception of history based on the progression of 'fixed stages of predictable development' to focus instead on the specific manner in which relations of capitalist necessity shaped both the international circumstances of the states-system as well as the particular conditions of state formation in Russia (Gramsci 1975: 149–55; cf. Gramsci 1994c: 39–42). This approach was posed in the following oft-cited question: 'Do international relations precede or follow (logically) fundamental social relations? There can be no doubt that they follow . . . However, international relations react both passively and actively on political relations' (Gramsci 1971: 176, Q13§2). It is in this manner that Gramsci linked issues of class struggle to elements of world history and national history, 'which forms a part of the world system and obeys the pressures of international events'. Therefore such conditions within the national sphere 'can only be understood and resolved within a world context' (Gramsci 1977: 69, 128, 357).

Conclusion: 'the Riddle of History'

This chapter has endeavoured to further the aim of this book by unravelling Gramsci with reference to his historical sociological approach to understanding the relation of capitalism to the sovereign states-system. It has done so by taking its point of departure from social property relations accounts of state formation, sovereign territoriality and capitalism to highlight the contribution Gramsci can make to understanding the uneven development of the states-system and the international causal dimension of transitions to capitalist modernity through the notion of passive revolution. Principally, this has involved demonstrating how Gramsci's own reflections on the beginnings of state formation in Italy were attuned to the social realities facing Machiavelli in the form of the absolutist state and Renaissance Italy. Linking with contentions outlined in Chapter 1, the argument then moved to discuss the terms of uneven development and the 'southern question' of the Mezzogiorno in Italy, whilst privileging the secular struggle of subaltern classes within an overall account of class struggle. This promotes enquiry into the processes through which new social identities and subjectivities are made through the series of class struggles constitutive of state formation and capitalist production; elements that are left unspoken within a social property relations approach. Ignoring such dimensions risks reducing the history of state formation to the history of state classes, missing state forms in terms of what they have made of subaltern classes through whom they rule and function. As Marx and Engels (1848/1998: 48) sketched in the *Communist Manifesto*, it is imperative to trace how the social definitions of property, the family, law, customs, and rights materialised within and through the actions of producer classes in their 'modern subjection to capital'. For this is the 'riddle of history': that 'strife between existence and essence, objectification and self-confirmation, between freedom and necessity, between the individual and the species' (Marx 1844/1975: 296–7).

The focus on subjectivities embedded in Gramsci's historical sociological approach to the transition to modernity assists in addressing this riddle in terms of the making and unmaking of identities embedded within historically specific state formation processes. Recourse to the notion of passive revolution also reveals how the furtherance of state power and the reorganisation of state and subaltern producer class identities have been forged within a causally constitutive realm of 'the international', whether in relation to the emerging dominance of Anglo-Saxon capitalism and colonial exploitation; the European response of Fascism to the growing intervention and predominance of Anglo-American capital; or the specific manner in which the late entrance of states' development trajectories within an international system of states hastened conditions of catch-up, e.g. in the case of Piedmont or Russia. Such processes are not that far removed from the practices of passive revolutions of the twentieth century in postcolonial countries, which were tied to state mechanisms that assisted in the emergence of capitalism and became the primary organs of primitive accumulation through elaborate institutions of public power, administration, planning, and national development (Hobsbawm 1986: 29–31; cf. Morton 2003b, 2003c). These processes of imitation have been referred to as the 'pathos of semi-peripheral escape' exhibited in those states that were not at the forefront of capitalism but nevertheless embarked on development routes through *étatist* state-building strategies of passive revolution (Halliday 1992: 458–9; Badie and Birnbaum 1983: 97–9).

What Gramsci's method of historical analogy as an interpretative criterion offers almost uniquely to debates on the historical sociology of uneven and combined development is a realisation of the complex issues of interscalar articulation affecting state formation processes. Unravelling Gramsci in this instance entails recognising the reciprocal influence he accorded to the 'national' and 'the international', but in a scalar manner within which the national was *nodal* rather than *dominant* in relation to the international sphere (Jessop 2006a: 37–40). Put differently, Gramsci's spatial awareness of the uneven development of social power provided a stimulus to taking a 'national' point of departure that was intertwined with the mediations and active (as well as passive) reactions of 'the international' dimension (Gramsci 1971: 176, Q13§2; Sassoon 2001: 11–13). The next chapter furthers the unravelling of Gramsci and this nodal 'national' point of departure by focusing on those world-historical developments linked to the specific institutional forms he deemed fundamental to the structuring of capital and the organisation of consent. In short, it is now time to examine the notion of hegemony, which can be considered to be the gravamen of the philosophy of praxis.

4   A Return to Gramsci: 'The Moment of Hegemony'

> The greatest modern theoretician of the philosophy of praxis [i.e. Lenin] has – on the terrain of political organisation and struggle and with political terminology – in opposition to the various tendencies of 'economism', reappraised the front of cultural struggle and constructed the doctrine of hegemony as a complement to the theory of the state-as-force.
>
> — Antonio Gramsci, *Quaderni del carcere*, Q10I§12

It should be clear from the previous chapters that any active development of a focus on questions of hegemony and passive revolution requires direct engagement with Gramsci's own writings and the contextual issues that embroiled the Italian thinker. To do otherwise would be to commit the error of developing an interpretation by proxy. Hence, the preceding chapters have tackled the tasks of historicising and engaging with Gramsci's thought and practice by displaying a greater sensitivity to the problems of meaning and understanding in the history of ideas. At the same time, there was a consideration of Gramsci's historical writings on processes of state formation within the emerging international states-system, which in many ways act as a prelude to his subsequent consideration of the politics of hegemony in modern capitalism. As a result, it has been possible in the first part of this book to situate ideas in and beyond their context. Without forcing the text, this has been accomplished by developing a dialectical understanding of historicism, consistent with Gramsci's own 'absolute historicism' (Chapter 2). It is this 'strangely composite' approach that was then deployed to reveal Gramsci's historical account of the emergence and development of Italian state formation (Chapter 3). Central here was a method of historical interpretation that analysed the role of the Renaissance in shaping the absolutist state in Italy; the problem of the 'Southern Question' concerning the terms of uneven and combined development in Italy and beyond; and the centrality of the Italian Risorgimento to understanding the condition of passive revolution shaping Italian and European state formation. The approach of granting attention to both text and context, or focusing on the leitmotiv or rhythm of thought in Gramsci's work, will be extended in the present chapter to outline in more detail the features shaping capitalist modernity. This chapter will therefore extend the 'strangely composite' approach outlined earlier to focus on and remain engaged with Gramsci's wider concepts and theoretical and practical labours. As a result the chapter develops a (re)reading of Gramsci, with particular emphasis placed on 'the moment of hegemony', which draws attention to the full weight of cultural–political–economic class struggle within capitalist development and the social function of intellectuals in state–civil society relations (Gramsci 1995: 343–6, Q10I§7). As will be discussed, an understanding of the moment of hegemony is essential to developing a conception of social relations that goes beyond a 'theory of the state-as-force' (Gramsci 1995: 357–8, Q10I§12). By developing a (re)reading of the moment of hegemony it will be possible to remain engaged with Gramsci's wider thought and practice, a central aim of Part I of the book. This will then assist the objective of thinking in a Gramscian way about the construction and contestation of hegemony in the global political economy, a feature of Part II of the book, which is directed towards concrete issues of world order and resistance. For the present focus on unravelling Gramsci's theory of hegemony, five main sections shape the argument in this chapter.

Following the stress in the previous chapters on social context, the first section will outline some of the crucial formative influences on Gramsci's thought and action. As a result there will be a discussion of the social and institutional context of Italian politics within which Gramsci's thinking developed. Whilst space restrictions are imposed on such a discussion, an overview will be provided of Gramsci's political apprenticeship as a journalist and his involvement in forming the Turin weekly journal *L'Ordine Nuovo*. This journal fused theory and practice and became a basis of support for the Factory Councils movement in Turin during the *biennio rosso* (two red years) period across much of Italy (1919–20). Experiences at this time and the ideas that emerged during the occupation of the FIAT factories influenced subsequent political reorganisation and would lead to the founding of the *Partito Communista d'Italia* (PCd'I: Communist Party of Italy) in January 1921. Similarly, the experiences of factionalism and sectarianism within the PCd'I, whilst under threat from the rise of Fascism, and a lack of unity between Italy's regions, held sway over Gramsci's thought and action. This period included his involvement in the PCd'I between 1921 and 1926, as well as his direct leadership after 1924, and his writings in the paper *L'Unità* on the organic crisis of capitalism in Italy (1924–26). By tracing this unfolding social context of political thought and action, the historical experiences through which Gramsci's concepts developed will be emphasised. Once these 'biographical' and historical issues have been traced, subsequent sections will then take an excursus through Gramsci's writings to indicate how certain terms and concepts emerged. Rather than literally or mechanically applying a series of reified concepts, it should be recalled that the emphasis is on thinking in a Gramscian way about hegemony and passive revolution (see Chapter 2). Yet, clearly, one has to have some knowledge of and about a political theorist before attempting to think in a similar way about alternative social conditions.

The second section will therefore elaborate on 'the moment of hegemony', which, to be clear, is a dynamic process constantly constructed as well as contested through different forms of class struggle or 'counter'hegemonic initiatives. The section will indicate how hegemony is conceived in relation to an expanded notion of the state, and the key role intellectual activity plays in constructing and contesting hegemony. The emphasis is thus on the *social basis* of hegemony. Following the unravelling of Gramsci in Chapter 2, it will also be shown how hegemony is conceived as a transcendence of idealist philosophy, particularly represented by the figure of Benedetto Croce (1866–1952). Also, this section will highlight how hegemony is understood as a contested, fragile, and tenuous process, rather than simply a structure or edifice, involving active struggle between a variety of 'relations of force'.

One of the major theoretical and practical innovations developed by Gramsci to appreciate the dialectical relationship between economic and socio-cultural factors in the struggle over hegemony was the notion of historical bloc. This concept is discussed in the third section of the chapter to indicate how the formation of hegemony is essential to the development of a historical bloc within a social formation. At the 'national' level the hegemony of a social group over subordinate groups is indicated by the notion of historical bloc. Once again, though, hegemony is always a contested process. The section therefore also details aspects of Gramsci's strategic theory concerning the practical feasibility of counterhegemonic struggle. Whilst the formation of a historical bloc is discussed as a 'national' phenomenon, it will become apparent that hegemony is understood as part of a dialectical complex of 'national' and 'international' elements represented by the expansion of a particular mode of production on a world scale. Linking back to Chapter 3, the fourth section of this chapter will further advance not only what the 'national' point of departure means, but also how Gramsci directly understood the 'international' expressions of hegemony. The way Gramsci juxtaposed 'national' developments within 'international' trends is often overlooked and has fundamental importance for the development of the argument in Part II of the book, specifically in relation to explaining the constitution of neoliberalism in Mexico as an expression of the passive revolution of capital (see Chapter 6).

Intrinsically linked to Gramsci's preoccupation with 'national' and 'international' elements was his concern with the geopolitical and sociological aspects of 'Americanism and Fordism' in the struggle over hegemony. Therefore, a fifth section examines how Gramsci related these aspects to the hegemony of production *and* social reproduction. In particular, Gramsci drew attention to 'psychoanalysis . . . as the expression of the increased moral coercion exercised by the apparatus of state and society on single individuals, and of the pathological crisis determined by coercion' (Gramsci 1971: 280, Q22§1). The features of this geopolitical and sociological view of hegemony retain relevance beyond the specific historical frame of reference he outlined. Pulling all the above strands together, it will be noted in conclusion how the 'moment of hegemony' is both related to, but also differs from, the condition of passive revolution. Crucial to the unravelling of Gramsci is the presentation of his understanding of 'the moment of hegemony' and how the expansion of capital may be maintained when hegemony is weakened or a crisis of authority prevails. The conclusion will therefore round up this issue of contrasts and connections between conditions of hegemony and passive revolution to indicate how such notions may be useful in generating additional insights relative to alternative historical and contemporary contexts, which is of the utmost importance to the second part of the book in its focus on the class strategies of neoliberalism and resistance within the global political economy of uneven development.

From *L'Ordine Nuovo* and the *Biennio Rosso* to the *Quaderni del Carcere*

Ever since Gramsci's death in 1937, diverse currents of political thought and practice have embarked on a variety of appropriations. Indeed, the historians Paolo Spriano and Gwyn A. Williams have both documented how the making of Gramsci into a myth had already begun even before he had died. In particular, the role of Palmiro Togliatti (1893–1964) was crucial, as leader of the PCd'I in 1927 – renamed the *Partito Communista Italiano* (PCI: Italian Communist Party) after 1943 – and as a member of the Executive of the Communist International (Comintern) from 1927 until its dissolution in 1943 (Spriano 1979). It was Togliatti who initially administered 'a masterly handling of truths, half-truths and the minimum of untruth' to create a 'Gramscian tradition' (Williams 1974: 7–15). 'When Italian Communists invoke the authority of Gramsci', states Leszek Kołakowski (2005: 963), 'to justify their deviations from the Soviet ideological model, it is convenient to emphasise that they are basically of one mind with the tutelary genius of the Communist movement.' As a result, Gramsci's posthumous support was claimed for the 'Italian Road to Socialism' after the 1950s, his image as an 'Italian Leninist' was deployed up to the 1970s, a post-Leninist Gramsci was formulated to underpin the Eurocommunist movements in the 1970s and 1980s, and a post-Communist image of Gramsci emerged in the 1990s as the PCI evolved into the *Partito Democratico della Sinistra* (PDS: Party of the Democratic Left) (see Gundle 1995; or Togliatti 1979). The image of Gramsci as a congenial figure for liberal democratic audiences has also diffused throughout the academy and is often evident in arguments that have initiated an incipient slide away from historical materialism, most notably within the debates on post-Marxism (see Harris 1992: 190–1; Ives 2004b: 153–60; Lester 2000: 134–42 for critiques). It should therefore be remembered that any interpretation always succumbs to some kind of appropriation, although this does not license reading Gramsci in any which way that suits us, because to do so would risk annulling the very principles he adhered to (see Morton 2005a). By returning to a discussion of social context, it is possible to appreciate (as noted in Chapter 1) that, despite various potential appropriations, Gramsci still remained within a Marxist orientation that was preoccupied with issues of cultural–political–economic class struggle and a refusal to accept the capitalist order.

Gramsci frequently crossed boundaries between language and identity, not least in terms of his own background as a young Sardinian studying philology at Turin University (see Ives 2004a). In many ways Gramsci's Sardinian background was a paramount influence on his thinking and practice, and yet, in other ways, he was acutely aware of the need to avoid the parochialism and romanticism sometimes associated with nationalist folklore. Thus, at times, he would assert the importance of the Sardinian language and regional forms of identity (Gramsci 1994a: 88–91). Yet, at others, he would emphasise that his family was only 'half Sardinian', due to his father's Albanian origin, whilst announcing that 'my culture is fundamentally Italian and this is my world' (Gramsci 1994a: 267; 1994b: 87, 173–4). It is significant in this sense that, whilst in prison, Gramsci approvingly cited Julien Benda (1867–1956), French philosopher and novelist, to note how it is one thing to *be* particular, or 'national', and another to *preach* particularism, or 'nationalism'. After all, 'those who lack personality find it useful to decree that the essential thing is to be national' (Gramsci 1996: 6–8, Q3§2). Hence, as Giuseppe Fiori has argued, Gramsci refused the alternatives of either remaining cocooned within Sardinian national experiences or becoming totally assimilated within Italian culture. 'Gramsci refused either to shelter within the Sardinian nationalism of his youth, or to let himself be converted passively to the ideology and political outlook of the northern working class' (Fiori 1970: 94).

It is my view that resorting to simple divisions should also be resisted when attempting to describe the different phases or periods in Gramsci's life. For instance, on the one hand, commentators have warned against drawing too close a connection between Gramsci's role as a political activist prior to his imprisonment and the notes penned thereafter (Bellamy 1987: 119). However, on the other hand, it has been advised that one should avoid creating divisions or imposing artificial barriers between Gramsci's pre-prison activity and the *Prison Notebooks*, including his involvement in Third International Marxism (Buci-Glucksmann 1980: 7). In this regard Gwyn A. Williams (1975: 91) has referred to Gramsci's involvement and experience in launching *L'Ordine Nuovo* as 'central to the achievement of that problematic which was to govern his leadership of the Communist Party and, in some senses, his lonely and desperate work in prison'. Hence the following discussion begins with a brief summary of the historical context of Gramsci's political activity, to indicate how similar themes were subsequently to preoccupy him whilst he was engaged in work on the *Prison Notebooks* related to the theory of hegemony.

In May 1919 four activists – all involved in the youth section of the *Partito Socialista Italiano* (PSI: Italian Socialist Party) – formed the Turin weekly journal *L'Ordine Nuovo* (the *New Order*) to promote questions of socialism and workers' democracy in Italy. The initial group of *ordinovisti* included Angelo Tasca (1895–1960) and Umberto Terracini (1895–1983) alongside Togliatti and Gramsci (Cammet 1967: 71–7). Even in early journal issues, efforts were made to harness the workers' movement unleashed by economic and political crisis following the First World War and to raise critical and active consciousness amongst the exploited working classes (Gramsci 1977: 65–8). Notably, the journal was distributed by 'communist' methods, outside the normal commercial outlets, directly to the workers (via factory distribution) and intellectuals (via subscription), and became a fulcrum in promoting the rise of new workers' organisations known as Factory Councils (Clark 1977: 72). Alongside other socialist newspapers, the focus was on economic and political crisis within Italian society that, nevertheless, was situated within a world context of uneven development. After all, as detailed in the previous chapter, 'capitalism is a world historical phenomenon' to the extent that 'in the international sphere, competition, the struggle to acquire private and national property, creates the same hierarchies and system of slavery as in the national sphere' (Gramsci 1977: 69–72). Therefore,

the elaboration of the 'conciliar theory' of the *ordinovisti* . . . was directly, and dialectically, integrated into the movement of the factory workers. It was [also] inserted, however, into a global perspective whose master-themes had already been established, largely by Gramsci, even in the earliest numbers of the journal. (Williams 1975: 99)

These themes involved criticism of established labour institutions such as the reformist–socialist *Confederazione Generale del Lavoro* (CGL: General Confederation of Labour) and the approach to trade unionism espoused by key labour figures – such as Bruno Buozzi (1881–1944) or Mario Guarneri (1886–1974) – affiliated to the *Federazione Italiana Operai Metallurgici* (FIOM: Italian Federation of Metal–Mechanical Workers). The latter developed a very rigid and bureaucratic conception of trade unionism based on centralised authority, discipline and the legality of contractual power (Spriano 1975: 28). As a result, the leaders of the Italian workers' movement, as well as 'bureaucratic industrialists', were heavily criticised by Gramsci as being shortsighted and, therefore, as superstitious as 'protestant ministers' or 'conceited ministerial flunkies' (Gramsci 1970: 17–25). In contrast, an alternative conception of popular participation was developed through *L'Ordine Nuovo* in co-operation with worker agitation. At the time, the trade unions were seen in a rather negative light. Although, they might have been important phenomena, as tools or organisms of revolution rather than simply as 'slaves' to capital, they had taken on a rather determinate character (Gramsci 1977: 103–8, 265). Hence they were ultimately seen as organisations that regulated the relations between capital and labour *within* capitalist society, and their function only made sense within capitalist institutions. As integral parts of capitalist society they might therefore just as easily become instruments of control achieving only limited reforms (Gramsci 1977: 65–8, 98–102).

> *Objectively*, the trade union is nothing other than a commercial company, of a purely capitalistic type, which aims to secure, in the interests of the proletariat, the maximum price for the commodity labour, and to establish a monopoly over this commodity in the national and international fields. The trade union is distinguished from capitalist mercantilism only *subjectively*, insofar as, being formed necessarily of workers, it tends to create among the workers an awareness that it is impossible to achieve industrial autonomy of the producers within the bounds of trade-unionism. (Gramsci 1978: 76, original emphasis)

Hence, it was more likely that trade unions would tend to represent reformist opportunism, incapable of overthrowing capitalist society, due to their incorporation within the machinery of the bourgeois state (Gramsci 1977: 103–8, 190–6). As such, trade unions were determined rather than determining (Gramsci 1977: 332).[1]

In contrast, the Factory Councils were conceived as a dynamic and democratic movement 'from below', based on worker participation. They constituted an alternative set of legitimacy-creating institutions and an embryonic form of political organisation. Workers were *automatic* members of the Councils, in contrast to the voluntary bodies existing within bourgeois society, such as the trade unions and the PSI, which were created 'from above' (Clark 1977: 61–2). The task was therefore to transform the essential legality of the trade unions and the PSI by infusing them with revolutionary structures. The councils were envisaged as the social institutions that would replace those of capitalist society in the endeavour to emancipate labour and create a new form of 'anti-state' organised on a national and ultimately an international basis (Gramsci 1977: 58, 80).

These ideas were developed within the context of the ongoing conflict between capital and labour after the First World War, represented respectively by the employers' organisation Confindustria (General Confederation of Italian Industry) and the CGL, along with the PSI and the metal workers led by FIOM. By 1920 the situation reached a 'frontier crisis', in the form of a head-on clash between the main protagonists over normal wage agitation within a global context of challenges to established state, political, and social structures (Spriano 1975: 39). Following the failure of the Piedmontese general strike in April 1920, the occupation of factories proceeded in September as employers attempted to lock out workers in Rome, Turin, and Genoa. Hence a normal wage dispute was forced into 'revolutionary' channels by the refusal of employers to grant concessions; by the failure of the reformist labour movement to develop adequate support; and by the strength of anarcho-syndicalist ideas alongside those of the council movement (Spriano 1975: 156; Williams 1975: 193, 199). The recurrent pattern throughout much of Italy was occupation – as a substitute for the weapon of the general strike – in response to potential lockout. Between 1 and 4 September 1920 the occupation of factories reached its peak involving workers at Giovanni Agnelli's FIAT assembly plants as well as engineering factories, steelworks, foundries, shipbuilding plants, and small workshops linked to the metallurgical industry. The occupation was total, affecting nearly all parts of Italy, involving over 400,000 workers; the figure would reach over half a million when the labour force of non-metallurgical industries moved into occupation (Spriano 1975: 157). In Turin, the Factory Council movement was hailed as a success for the *ordinovisti* group, with Gramsci addressing workers in the Garrone-FIAT assembly plant during 'Red Sunday' on 5 September 1920.

Yet the movement as a whole lacked co-ordination and there was no common revolutionary programme around which to organise. By 10 September the industrialists and the government were waiting for divisions between the revolutionary and reformist factions of the workers to develop. The CGL favoured the pursuit of compromise, the militants in Turin could not undertake offensive action on their own due to limited military preparation, and the PSI was unable to galvanise leadership of the situation. The government, led by Giovanni Giolitti (1842–1928), aligned itself with 'moderates' on all sides and those committed to the political system and existing ideas of social change. Within the framework of bourgeois liberal democracy the workers put the future of the occupations to a vote, in a way renouncing revolutionary aspirations in favour of legal forms of participation. With an awareness that no revolution could take place through the ballot box, one activist, Gaetano Bensi, declared,

> We felt the revolution could not be made. Because a revolution is not made by first calling a convention to decide whether there is going to be a revolution or not. This was Mexican stuff [i.e. labour reformism] they were trying to import. (Cited by Spriano 1975: 92)

The Factory Council movement, whilst still embedded within the existing state apparatus, therefore suffered from the vacillations of the PSI and Giolitti's policies of compromise. Also, the workers of the industrial factories were isolated from the occupation of agrarian estates and uncultivated land by rural masses in the south, which further thwarted any unified socialist movement. Isolation therefore provided the opportunity for assimilation. As Giolitti himself stated, on 11 September 1920, to Camillo Corradini, then under-secretary at the Ministry of the Interior,

> A final solution of the industrial question lies in the integration of workers, if necessary as shareholders, into the structure of industry, in full practical participation. Above all, workers' representatives must participate in administrative councils, so that they learn the real conditions of industry and the state of profits. (Cited by Spriano 1975: 99)

The absence of a well-organised and disciplined party, capable of unifying the dispersed elements and factions of agitation, fatally isolated the Factory Council movement. A realisation therefore arose that the formation of mass organisations based on the workplace, in the form of Factory Councils, had to emerge at the same time as a political party was organising and forming support. Each form of political practice had to proceed simultaneously rather than in the chronological sequence in which events actually progressed (Davidson 1977: 155–7). Eventually, after the Livorno Congress, on 15 January 1921, a communist fraction split from the PSI to form the PCd'I (Cammet 1967: 156–86). Notably, emphasis was initially placed on the territoriality of the Party, as a section of the Comintern based in Italy, rather than on an 'Italian' Communist Party solely preoccupied with national policies (Williams 1975: 298–9). Yet, whilst the idea of the Factory Councils was not abandoned, the Party was too small, with little mass support, to establish any immediate impact or unifying force.

The first leader of the PCd'I, between 1921 and 1923, was Amadeo Bordiga (1889–1970), who developed a somewhat rigid and purist conception of the party, based on a narrowly defined proletariat that avoided alliances with other parties and groups. This tendency was particularly evident in the document presented at the Second Congress of the PCd'I at Rome in the form of the 'Rome Theses' (see Gramsci 1978: 93–125). Although Gramsci's thinking should not be severed from Bordiga's own approach, it is acknowledged that Gramsci propagated a more organic conception of the party aimed at establishing a dialectical relationship with the masses (Williams 1975: 175–84). This stress was evident in his writings for *L'Ordine Nuovo*.

It would be disastrous if a sectarian conception of the Party's role in the revolution were to prompt the claim that this apparatus had actually assumed a concrete form, that the system for controlling the masses in movement had been frozen in mechanical forms of immediate power, forcing the revolutionary process into the forms of the Party. The result would be to successfully divert a number of men [*sic*], to 'master' history: but the real revolutionary process would slip from the control and influence of the party, which would unconsciously become an organ of conservatism. (Gramsci 1977: 144)

Between 1921 and 1926 Gramsci therefore devoted his energy to creating a party that could raise class consciousness and unite the disparate forces and regions across Italy into a cohesive political movement. Yet the effort to engender a greater degree of homogeneity and self-awareness amongst certain social-class forces was confronted by serious obstacles.

Although it seemed that Giolitti's government had maintained equilibrium by marginalising and dividing elements within the Italian socialist movement, vital groups among the ruling classes were also isolated. As Gramsci (1978: 160) would state, the schism in the left 'was without a doubt the greatest triumph of reaction', creating the conditions for a convulsion from the right in the form of Fascism. In March 1922 this reaction was represented by Benito Mussolini's (1883–1945) seizure of power and the 'March on Rome'. At this time Gramsci had suffered a nervous breakdown and spent a spell recuperating in Moscow and Vienna (1922–24) (see Fiori 1970: 155–63). Meanwhile, a new Communist Party daily newspaper was formed, in 1924, called *L'Unità*, that was designed to appeal both to Italy's industrial workers and to the southern peasant masses. By this time Gramsci's own thinking on the contemporary situation in Italy had begun to evolve into a mature interpretation of Fascism. This included situating Fascism within a historical perspective related to the successive attempts throughout Italian history since the Risorgimento to unify the country as well as reflecting on Italy's 'Southern Question', or the role of the south in the development of the Italian state. These issues were combined in the drafting of a document for the Third Congress of the PCd'I, held at Lyons in January 1926, that became known as the 'Lyons Theses', which linked Fascism in Italy to the intervention of Anglo-American capital (see Chapter 3). As also outlined in the preceding chapter, these points were extended in the essay 'Some Aspects of the Southern Question' (1926), in which the institutional structures linking relations between agrarian landowners in vast landed estates and the southern peasantry to the activities of the bourgeoisie in the north of the country were analysed. As Bellamy and Schecter (1993: 79) argue, Gramsci thus sketched out of this context a theory of uneven development on a world scale, within which ideological struggle for the support of certain classes in peripheral states took great significance.

Therefore, prior to his arrest by the Fascist authorities in 1926, during a period of intense intellectual and political struggle, Gramsci had begun to outline many of the themes that would preoccupy his thoughts in the *Prison Notebooks*. Indeed, in prison Gramsci was constantly to refer back to his *Ordine Nuovo* experiences, the failure of the revolutionary Factory Council movement in 1919–20, and the ability of the capitalist state in Italy to survive through periods of crisis with Fascism representing the latest disintegration of Italian society. As Clark (1977: 225) states, 'his analysis of why revolutions fail is a major theme of the *Prison Notebooks*, and provided the stimulus for his views on the nature of "hegemony", of political organisations and parties, and of intellectuals'. The next sections turn to these issues in more detail.

The 'Moment of Hegemony' and Ethico-political History

Questions of hegemony, the relationship of civil society to the state, and the role of ideology in developing and maintaining the dominant position of the ruling classes and the expansion of capital came to preoccupy Gramsci in greater detail within the period during which he wrote the *Prison Notebooks*, between 1929 and 1935. However, it is rather unproductive to try and locate Gramsci's concepts within a neat series of models and assess their internal coherence as part of a unified discourse and then find them wanting due to a series of slippages (*pace* Anderson 1976/1977). The attempt to calibrate with precision the 'hidden' meaning of hegemony – or fix exactly the order of concepts such as state and civil society – runs the risk of abstracting ideas from the context of the argument in order to provide a set of prescriptions (Femia 1979: 472–83; Forgacs 1989: 70–88).[2] By contrast, an immanent (re)reading, as discussed in Chapter 2, may promote a guideline for thinking about the relationship of state–civil society and an analysis of hegemony in alternative historical and contemporary contexts. Therefore, whilst Gramsci's prison writings did not develop in a linear fashion or pursue a single line of enquiry, it is possible to trace themes and subjects indicative of a prolonged intellectual project. Moreover it is possible to argue that these themes were consistent with Gramsci's analysis prior to imprisonment concerning the crisis of bourgeois rule in Italy and the attempt to engender feasible revolutionary transformation (Martin 1998: 42).

Clearly there is no single point of authorial reference on the term hegemony. The lineage of such a term can be traced through the writings of the nineteenth-century Italian philosopher Vincenzo Gioberti as much as through the Russian labour movement and the writings of Georgi V. Plekhanov or Vladimir I. Lenin (Anderson 1976/1977: 15). As evidenced in the epigraph, Gramsci partially acknowledged such precursors, drawing attention to Lenin (with a little over-exaggeration) as the theorist who developed the notion of hegemony as a complement to the theory of the state-as-force (Gramsci 1995: 357, Q10I§12). Gramsci probably had in mind Lenin's *Two Tactics of Social Democracy* (1905), which stressed how the proletariat should aim to exercise 'hegemony', implying leadership with the consent of allied classes such as the peasantry. Yet, as Lenin's propositions do not really support Gramsci's interpretation (Williams 1960: 588), it is possible to highlight Gramsci's theory of hegemony as that which is 'a complement to the theory of the state-as-force'. The reworking of historical materialism that was undertaken by Gramsci in the *Prison Notebooks* involved affirming an alternative conception of the state that was identified with the struggle over hegemony in civil society. He regarded the most common error in politics to be that of overlooking an extended notion of the state that he referred to as the 'integral state', meaning a combination of dictatorship and hegemony (Gramsci 1971: 239, Q6§155; also see Buttigieg 1995). As outlined in one of his prison letters to Tatiana Schucht:

> My study . . . leads to certain definitions of the concept of the state that is usually understood as a political society (or dictatorship, or coercive apparatus meant to mould the popular mass in accordance with the type of production and economy at a given moment) and not as a balance between the political society and the civil society (or the hegemony of a social group over the entire national society, exercised through the so-called private organisations, such as the church, the unions, the schools, etc.). (Gramsci 1994b: 67)

The state was not conceived as a thing in itself, or as a rational absolute, that was extraneous to individuals in a reified or fetishistic sense (Gramsci 1992: 229, Q1§150). The latter refers to when individuals consider the state as a thing, expecting it to act, leading them to believe that:

> in actual fact there exists above them a phantom entity, the abstraction of the collective organism, a species of autonomous divinity that thinks, not with the head of a specific being, yet nevertheless thinks, that moves, not with the real legs of a person, yet still moves. (Gramsci 1995: 15, Q15§13)

In contrast, the state is but a form of social relations within which methodological distinctions can be made between the ensemble of 'private' organisms in civil society and that of the state or 'political' society (Gramsci 1971: 158–67, Q13§18). In turn, these two spheres respectively correspond to the function of 'hegemony' and 'direct domination'. The tendency to view the state as both a perpetual entity and to concentrate solely on direct governmental responsibilities within political society was also criticised as 'statolatry': viewing the state as a perpetual entity limited to actions within political society (Gramsci 1971: 268–9, Q8§130).

Extending this discussion, it is important to note that the notion of the 'integral state' was developed in order to counter the separation of powers embedded in liberal conceptions of politics. A critique was particularly developed of the notion that the state simply referred to the representative apparatus of government, which did not intervene in the economy except as a 'nightwatchman' safeguarding public order (Gramsci 1971: 245–6, Q6§81; 262–3, Q6§88). By equating power simply with the state apparatus, the significance of organised opposition outside the parameters of the state, in the narrow sense, was diminished, leading to the formula: '"Everything within the state, nothing outside the state, nothing against the state"' (Gramsci 1971: 261, Q8§190). Notably, Gramsci furthered his criticisms of Croce on this issue, in terms of the latter's history of nineteenth-century liberalism, which provided the conditions for the emergence and prevalence of a liberal view of history propagated as a universal principle (Gramsci 1995: 351–4, Q10I§10). In contrast, the construction of abstract hypotheses, based on generalised, historically indeterminate conditions and a universal 'homo oeconomicus', were rejected by Gramsci's critical conception of the state and political economy (Gramsci 1995: 165–6, Q10II§37i; see Bieler and Morton 2003: 481–5). Within a historicist conception of 'critical economy', any 'individualised' representation of states was merely metaphorical. States were distinguished as historically determined combinations of 'vertical' groups and 'horizontal' stratifications, involving a coexistence of different cultures bound together by coercion and moral consciousness or consent (Gramsci 1995: 176–9, Q10II§37ii; 344, Q10I§7). It was therefore acknowledged that the state plays a role in the economy as a substitute for so-called private enterprise by 'manufacturing the manufacturers' through protectionism and privileges (Gramsci 1995: 243–4, Q15§1; 248–53, Q19§7). Hence the state was not agnostic and the ensemble of classes that constituted it had a formative activity in the economy and society to the extent that 'one cannot speak of the power of the state but only of the camouflaging of power', through hegemony in civil society (Gramsci 1985: 191, Q27§1; Gramsci 1995: 217–18, Q6§75; 237–9, Q19§6). Therefore 'laissez-faire too is a form of state "regulation", introduced and maintained by legislative and coercive means' (Gramsci 1971: 160, Q13§18).

An 'integral' concept of the state is central to understanding the moment of hegemony involving leadership and the development of active consent through the social relations of state–civil society. Like many other themes, Gramsci's theory of hegemony developed by shadow-boxing with the philosophy of Croce and, in this case, his ethico-political conception of history.[3] For Gramsci, Croce promoted an abstract idealist philosophy that separated theory from practice and ignored concrete struggles between social-class forces (Gramsci 1995: 348–50, Q10I§9). Hence Croce's view of ethico-political history was abstract and speculative and separated ideas from concrete circumstances. As a result, Croce's ideas were considered to be supportive of liberal reformist conceptions of history and provided the intellectual legitimacy for specific political groups in everyday politics, particularly due to his links with the Giolittian government (Gramsci 1995: 376–7, Q10II§41vxi; 379–80, Q6§107; 444–5, Q6§112; 473–5, Q10II§41v). 'It might be one of the numerous paradoxical manifestations of history', wrote Gramsci, '. . . that Croce, stimulated by his particular preoccupations, should have contributed to strengthening fascism by indirectly providing it with an intellectual justification' (Gramsci 1995: 349, Q10I§9). Affirming his earlier analysis of Croce in 'Some Aspects of the Southern Question', the philosopher was thus regarded as a 'priest of the religion Liberty': the ideologue of political and economic liberalism (Gramsci 1995: 396, Q10II§41xii). Hence the importance, to Gramsci, of producing an *Anti-Croce* comparable to the *Anti-Dühring* (see Chapter 2 and also Watkins 1986).

However, it was possible within a philosophy of praxis not only to incorporate ethico-political history, by attaching full weight to cultural factors, but also to focus on the significance of political and economic class conflict; thus avoiding an account that would rely on developing an 'extrinsic history' of objective economic forces. This was possible, argued Gramsci, because the moment of hegemony included the function of intellectuals within civil society and the role played by ideologies as consensual instruments of intellectual and moral leadership in relation to material conditions. In broad terms, a range of intellectuals may be distinguished within society. This may include 'traditional' intellectuals, such as ecclesiastics or idealist philosophers, who consider themselves to be autonomous of social-class forces. Yet, despite their claims to independence, traditional intellectuals would often play a conservative role by supporting preceding socio-economic and political forms. The links Croce had with senators Giovanni Agnelli, head of FIAT, and Antonio Stefano Benni, head of Montecatini chemicals, were regarded as paradigmatic of this category (Gramsci 1971: 7–8, Q12§1). Beyond this, it is significant that all people were actually recognised by Gramsci as intellectuals but only some were noted to have an immediate social function as professional intellectuals. This latter function would involve active participation in everyday life as an agent within the economic, political, social, and cultural fields acting as a constructor, organiser, and 'permanent persuader' in forming or contesting hegemony (Gramsci 1971: 9–10, Q12§3). Hence, a further category was distinguished by acknowledging the social function of what Gramsci termed 'organic intellectuals'. This function was crucial in two senses. First, in terms of a connection with the active formation of hegemony by particular social-class forces that constantly construct and maintain a social order; and second, in terms of a connection to alternative initiatives attempting to forge a 'counter'hegemony by connecting many different forms of struggle. By propagating certain ideas, intellectuals therefore play an essential mediating function in the struggle over hegemony between social-class forces, by acting as 'deputies' or instruments of hegemony, or by performing a valuable supporting role for subaltern classes engaged in promoting social change (Gramsci 1971: 5–23, Q12§1; 52–5, Q25§5). Thereby we are able to appreciate the links intellectuals may have, or the wider social function they perform, in relation to the world of production within capitalist society, leading to a materialist and social-class analysis of intellectuals (Morton 2003b). Ideas in this sense are not mere epiphenomena. They 'are anything but arbitrary; they are real historical facts which must be combated and their nature as instruments of domination exposed . . . precisely for reasons of political struggle' (Gramsci 1995: 395, Q10II§41xii). This amounted to a 'state–hegemony–moral consciousness conception' of ethico-political history, with *ethical* referring to the activity of civil society, to hegemony, and *political* referring to coercive initiatives conducted by the state (Gramsci 1995: 343–6, Q10I§7; 357–8, Q10I§12; 372–3, Q10II§41iii).

Attention could therefore be directed to the 'material structure of ideology' in civil society, consisting of publishing houses, newspapers, journals, literature, libraries, museums, theatres, art galleries, schools, architecture, or street names which all operate as factors or elements in the struggle over hegemony (Gramsci 1996: 52–3, Q3§49; Gramsci 1995: 153–4, Q14§56).[4] Various social condensations of hegemony are highlighted here as the means by which a '"diffused" and capillary form of indirect pressure' becomes mediated through various organisations – or 'capillary intellectual meatuses' – to exercise hegemonic class relations (Gramsci 1971: 110, Q15§11; Gramsci 1985: 194, Q27§2). Gramsci can thus be described as a paramount theorist of capillary power, due to his attentiveness to the social class meatuses of 'capillary sources of capitalist profit' (Gramsci 1977: 82; Gramsci 1992: 230–1, Q1§151).[5] Hegemony within the realm of civil society is then grasped when the citizenry come to believe that authority over their lives emanates from the self. Hegemony is therefore articulated through capillary power – akin to 'an incorporeal government' – when it is transmitted organically through various 'social infusoria', such as schools, street layout and names, architecture, the family, workplace, or church (Gramsci 1977: 143–4; Bieler and Morton forthcoming). Hence, 'within the husk of political society a complex and well-articulated civil society', is evident, '*in which the individual can govern himself* without his self-government thereby entering into conflict with political society but rather becoming its normal continuation, its organic complement' (Gramsci 1971: 268 emphasis added).

The scope of intellectual activity is thus amplified within the notion of the 'integral state' and the wider ensemble of social relations. An understanding of the *social basis* of hegemony is also therefore developed. How hegemony is exercised throughout state–civil society relations by the mediating function of intellectuals organically tied to particular social classes, not only in the economic but also the social and political fields, is then realised.

> The intellectuals have the function of organising the social hegemony of a group and that group's domination of the state . . . they have the function of organising the consent that comes from the prestige attached to the function in the world of production and the apparatus of coercion for those who do not 'consent' either actively or passively or for those moments of crisis of command and leadership when spontaneous consent undergoes a crisis. (Gramsci 1996: 200–1, Q4§49)

Hegemony is therefore in part associated with conflicts over 'class "prestige"' (Gramsci 1971: 184, Q13§17). As a result, by going beyond a theory of the state-as-force and expanding on conventional notions of the intellectual, the struggle over hegemony revolves around shaping intersubjective forms of consciousness in civil society – which 'are like the trench-systems of modern warfare' – rather than simply focusing on gaining control of the coercive state apparatus (Gramsci 1971: 235, Q13§24; 365, Q10II§12).

This focus on aspects of intersubjectivity in the struggle over hegemony was particularly drawn out in Gramsci's elaboration of the various 'relations of force' that impact on historically concrete situations (Gramsci 1971: 175–85, Q13 §2, §17). He highlighted three 'moments' within the 'relations of force' (see Figure 4.1). First,

Gramsci accorded primacy to the relations of production that provide a basis for the emergence of the 'relation of social forces'. Within a second 'moment', referred to as the 'relation of political forces', various social forces may subsequently vie for influence in a bid to propagate a hegemonic position throughout society. However, a third 'moment', the 'relation of military forces', could prove decisive in any struggle over hegemony, understood in a strict technical sense as a politico-military function.

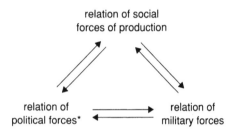

Figure 4.1   The relations of force

Within the relation of political forces in the struggle over hegemony the articulation of ideas and subjective elements beyond narrow 'economic–corporate' interests involves three additional relations (see Figure 4.2). This entails raising intersubjective consciousness among a variety of social forces, to move from a solidarity of interests, to transcended interests (beyond the economic sphere) through an appeal to wider social groups.[6] The struggle between social forces supportive of contesting and conflicting ideologies was thus described as 'the most purely political phase' and involved propagating an ideology throughout society. Hence the goal of establishing

> not only a unison of economic and political aims, but also intellectual and moral unity, posing all the questions around which the struggle rages not on a corporate but on a 'universal' plane, and thus creating a hegemony of a fundamental social group over subordinate groups. (Gramsci 1971: 181–2, Q13§17)

Hegemonic social forces have to make sacrifices of an 'economic–corporate' kind by appealing to general interests to ensure the expansion of their activity.

Overall, though, the role of force within a hegemonic order should not be discounted. 'The "normal" exercise of hegemony . . . is

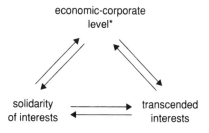

Figure 4.2 The political relation of hegemony

characterised by the combination of force and consent, which balance each other reciprocally, without force predominating excessively over consent' (Gramsci 1971: 80n.4, Q19§24). The creation of hegemony through capillary power crucially encapsulates processes on the terrain of ideology involved in forming consciousness but without losing an appreciation of the material basis that is at stake in the struggle between social-class forces; thereby analysing discourse with reference to the relations of force that structure the field of knowledge (Bieler and Morton forthcoming).[7] Moreover, 'between consent and force stands corruption/fraud (which is characteristic of certain situations when it is hard to exercise the hegemonic function, and when the use of force is too risky)' (Gramsci 1971: 80n.4, Q19§24). To sum up, hegemony is marked by, 'the decisive passage from the structure to the sphere of the complex superstructures' (Gramsci 1971: 181, Q13§17). The theoretical and practical innovation introduced by Gramsci to capture this dialectical relationship between economic 'structure' and ideological 'superstructures' was the notion of historical bloc. As outlined in the next section, the very nature of a historical bloc is linked to the successful formation of hegemony by certain social-class forces or, alternatively, via the 'counter'hegemonic challenges of subaltern social classes.

Historical Bloc and 'Counter'hegemony: Theoretical and Practical Aspects

It has been established that 'the moment of hegemony' involves *both* the consensual diffusion of a particular cultural and moral view throughout society *and* its interconnection with coercive functions of power; or when there is a corresponding equilibrium between ethico-political ideas and prevailing socio-economic conditions fortified by coercion (Gramsci 1995: 360, Q10I§13). The traditional

Marxist division between 'economic structure' and 'ideological superstructure' is thus fundamentally reworked. Hence, an internal relationship is acknowledged that includes, for example, the way private property is legally ensured by the state, so that forms of power such as 'the law' may be seen as *both* an instrument through which definitions of property are imposed or maintained *and* an ideology in active relationship to social norms through which class relations are mediated. Productive relations are therefore in part meaningful in terms of their very definition in law in civil society, although 'the anatomy of this civil society . . . has to be sought in political economy' (Marx 1859/1987: 262; Thompson 1975: 261; Wood 1995: 22).

For Gramsci, the interrelated and reciprocal development of structure and superstructure was encapsulated within the concept of *historical bloc*.[8] 'Structures and superstructures form an "historical bloc". That is to say the complex, contradictory and discordant *ensemble* of the superstructures is the reflection of the social relations of production' (Gramsci 1971: 366, Q8§182). The theoretical innovation Gramsci introduced was that whilst the economic 'structure' may set certain limits, it was also acknowledged that so-called 'superstructural' factors have a degree of independent autonomy. Thus it was possible to theoretically understand how regressive or exploitative social relations of production may still persist because of supportive ideologies (Femia 1975: 36–7). There was a 'necessary reciprocity' between the social relations of production and ideas within the realm of state–civil society relations, which was represented by the concept of historical bloc. As Martin (1998: 82) has clarified, production relations could not therefore secure the power of a social group or even be conceived without articulating supportive ideas that gave form to the economic structure. Hence Gramsci, following Marx in the 'Preface' to *A Contribution to the Critique of Political Economy*, declares, 'it is on the level of ideologies that men [*sic*] become conscious of conflicts in the world of the economy' (Gramsci 1971: 162, Q13§18; Marx 1959/1987: 263).

Yet the notion of historical bloc was also used in a second way to refer to concrete or practical relationships between social-class forces (Sassoon 1987: 121). This emphasis bore the weight of Gramsci's experiences in the socialist movement, outlined in the first section of this chapter, and the failure to unite industrial workers in the north and the rural masses in the south of Italy. Hence, in terms both of constructing and of contesting hegemony, various social-class forces with competing and heterogeneous interests had to be fused to bring about at least some kind of unity in aims and beliefs (see Figure 4.2). A historical bloc therefore indicates the integration of a variety of different class interests and forms of identity within a 'national–popular' alliance (Forgacs 1984). Following Gramsci, it was within the moment of hegemony that a fundamental social group created this kind of universal expansion and established the *necessary form* of a concrete historical bloc (Gramsci 1995: 357–8, Q10I§12). This means that the very existence of hegemony is therefore necessary for the emergence of a historical bloc. Only when hegemony has been established by a social group across the domain of state–civil society relations, in the integral sense, 'can it represent a fully developed and maximally extended historical bloc' (Sassoon 1987: 123). Moreover, although formed within an 'international' conjuncture, the historical bloc is specific to the 'national' context (Sassoon 1987: 121). Following Marcia Landy (1994: 49), '[t]he concept of hegemony is inextricably tied to Gramsci's notion of the "historical bloc", which offers a theoretical analysis of the relationship between base and superstructure and a particular and specific analysis of a given historical and national moment'. This does not imply, however, that there is a neat one-to-one correspondence between hegemony and historical bloc, as some may presume (Adamson 1980: 178). Instead, the relationship is constantly constructed and contested and is never a static reflection of an alliance of social class forces.

This emphasis on the continual construction, maintenance, and defence of hegemony in the face of constant resistance and pressures is reflected in Gramsci's strategic theory and the potential for 'counter'hegemony. Once again, the failure of the Factory Council movement – or the Italian 'soviets' – during 1919–20 pushed Gramsci to consider different revolutionary tactics. He therefore continued his pre-prison writings on the differences between frontal struggle in Russia and the need for more complex and long-term tactics in central and western Europe (see Chapter 3). Hence the strategic phase of a frontal attack, or war of manoeuvre, targeted directly at attaining state power might prove ineffective and transitory in certain countries. Therefore, amongst a range of strategies that should not be regarded as separate options, a more protracted form of 'trench warfare' could be conducted, known as the war of position. This involved a struggle on the cultural front in civil society – to overcome the 'powerful system of fortresses and earthworks' – in an attempt to penetrate and subvert the mechanisms of ideological diffusion (Gramsci 1971: 238, Q7§16). Additionally, a 'counter'hegemony could entail an 'underground war' involving the clandestine gathering of arms and assault troops (Gramsci 1992: 219, Q1§134). However, in terms of the war-of-position strategy, one has to bear in mind that a 'counter'hegemonic movement may lack an internal logic or social basis. This means that the formation of a 'collective will' might be thwarted and resistance dispersed into 'an infinity of individual wills' scattered into separate and conflicting paths (Gramsci 1971: 128–9, Q13§1).

The struggle to establish a 'counter'hegemony could therefore be particularly weakened by absorbing or co-opting the active elements of opposition involved in projecting a war of position. Such attempts to remove substantive differences and establish a convergence between contending social-class forces was encapsulated within the process of *trasformismo*. In the context of Italian parliamentary politics, these were the tactics used by Agostino Depretis (1813–87), Franceso Crispi (1818–1901), and notably Giovanni Giolitti against the Factory Councils movement, by isolating and then assimilating formerly recalcitrant fractions (Gramsci 1992: 125–36, Q1§43; Gramsci 1996: 105–6, Q3§119). In pedagogical terms Croce's role was again pivotal in acting as a mediator between dominant and subaltern classes and adjusting the interests of 'counter'hegemonic forces (Gramsci 1994b: 166–7, 170–3, 179–82). The notion of *trasformismo* was also importantly related to processes that were not exclusively Italian; it thereby applied to other countries with analogous conditions (Gramsci 1996: 114–15, Q3§137).

To summarise this section, it is important to remember that the political process remains open because of the various strategies and courses of action available to social-class forces struggling for hegemony. Hence the importance of recognising the constant attempts by social-class forces to actively construct and contest hegemonic initiatives within or against a specific historical bloc at the 'national' level. Through 'counter'hegemonic struggle it is thus possible to envisage how diverse aims and interests could be welded together to 'change the political direction of certain forces which have to be absorbed if a new, homogenous politico-economic historical bloc . . . is to be successfully formed' (Gramsci 1971: 168, Q13§23). However, whilst the formation of a historical bloc was situated at the 'national' level, hegemony could manifest itself as an 'international' phenomenon through the outward expansion on a world scale of a particular mode of production. 'Every relationship of "hegemony" is necessarily an educational relationship and occurs not only within a nation, between the various forces that comprise it, but in the entire international and world field, between complexes of national and continental civilisations' (Gramsci 1995: 156–7, Q10II§44).

Juxtaposing the 'National' Point of Departure and 'the International'

Whilst Gramsci was obsessively concerned with Italian 'national' experience, his role as a revolutionary internationalist thinker and practitioner should not be diminished. After all, he was not only a participant in the Comintern but also a fastidious student of the international circumstances of hegemony. The propensity to insert 'national' problems within the wider context of 'the international' was particularly evident in his pre-prison journalistic writings as well as the *Prison Notebooks*. As early as 1919 he argued that, although the national sphere remained the starting point for eliminating class exploitation and private property, capitalism was a world-historical phenomenon with uneven development.

> The economic and political crisis into which Italian society is plunging can only be understood and resolved within a world context. The essential conditions for its resolution lie beyond the reach and power of the Italian state, and hence all the ministries that may succeed each other in government. (Gramsci 1977: 69–72)

This social context was outlined earlier in the chapter. In his early writings stemming from this period, Gramsci embarked on frequent analysis of world capitalist production, which he referred to as 'the global politico-economic system' of Anglo-Saxon capitalism or 'Anglo-Saxon world hegemony' (Gramsci 1977: 79–82, 89–93). Capitalism in Italy had to be situated within the wider context of the international states-system and the relative decline of 'English' hegemony that had led to 'a gigantic struggle to divide the world between hegemonic forces' (Gramsci 1977: 127–9, 356–9). These writings can be regarded as entirely consonant with his prison writings and the focus on issues of 'Americanism and Fordism', to be discussed shortly, concerning the introduction of mass-production techniques and scientific management processes on a world scale (Gramsci 1971: 279–318, Q22 §1-§15). Therefore, linking in with the discussion in Chapter 3, we can see that Gramsci sustained a focus on relationships between the advanced capitalist world and developing countries, highlighting forms of 'American global hegemony' (Gramsci 1996: 275, Q5§8).

The United States was described as 'the supreme arbiter of world finance', which was trying to 'impose a network of organisations and movements under its leadership' (Gramsci 1992: 259–65, Q2§16; Gramsci 1996: 11–13, Q3§5). In terms of the latter, Gramsci analysed the roles of international voluntary associations as well as those of international public and private organisations promoting American liberalism and supporting the universal projection of mass production. This included the Young Men's Christian Association (YMCA), international groups like the Rotary Club, or Pan-Christian movements (Gramsci 1992: 167–70, Q1§61; 291, Q2§46: 354–5, Q2§135; Gramsci 1996: 269–71, Q5§2; 282, Q5§17; 318–20, Q5§61). Forms of regional and international economic integration, within which 'hegemonic states' might organise national and 'international (interstate) markets', were also discussed (Gramsci 1992: 285–7, Q2§40; 318–20, Q2§125). As, indeed, was the role of the Catholic Church, which was described as a 'worldwide hegemonic institution' that promoted an imperialistic (religious) spirit of 'international hegemony' (Gramsci 1985: 220–2, Q17§8). As a result it is fair to say, consistently with the argument in Chapter 3, that Gramsci dealt with 'relations within society' and 'hegemonic systems within the state' with the same concepts as he did 'relations between international forces' that constitute 'the combinations of states in hegemonic systems' (Gramsci 1971: 176, Q13§2). Nowhere is this more evident than in the following representative passage:

> Just as, in a certain sense, in a given state history is the history of the ruling classes, so, on a world scale, history is the history of the hegemonic states. The history of the subaltern states is explained by the history of hegemonic states. (Gramsci 1995: 222–3, Q15§5)

This, however, was not a recommendation to focus simply on hegemonic forces either in terms of social classes within a country or of states at the international level. Such a stance would merely produce 'negative history'. Instead, the making of history should be sought on the margins, because 'the decisive forces of world history' are those involving struggles *between* social classes, including subaltern class elements (Gramsci 1995: 222–3, Q15§5). The history of subaltern social classes is intertwined with that of the history of states and groups of states (Gramsci 1971: 52, Q25§5).

The implication of all of this is that, once more, claims that Gramsci's concepts 'were used exclusively' in the grounding of national societies (Germain and Kenny 1998: 20), or that Gramsci 'rejected the international dimension' as a causal factor of social transformation (Shilliam 2004: 73), fail to stand up to critical scrutiny. Indeed, it is entirely possible to argue that the concept of hegemony can sustain explanatory power beyond the 'national' context in relation to 'the international' because this was already how Gramsci developed the concept. As Bob Jessop (2006a: 32) has argued, by taking the 'national' point of departure as nodal, or focusing on the form of state, it is possible to analyse the concrete development of the social relations of production and the relationship between politics and economics which is inscribed in the struggle for hegemony within a state, whilst also acknowledging that 'the perspective is international and cannot be otherwise' (Gramsci 1971: 240, Q14§68). Hence the need to appreciate the meaning conveyed by taking the 'national' point of departure. One must begin with analysing the originality and uniqueness of 'national' specificities and historical differences, whilst displaying an awareness of 'the international' as a constitutive moment in the dynamics of state formation. Relations within a society may then react both passively and actively to the mediations of international trends and local differences or global and regional forces (Gramsci 1971: 176, Q13§2; Sassoon 1990: 14–25; Sassoon 2001: 11–13). One of the ways in which these relations became intertwined during Gramsci's time was through the rise of Americanism and Fordism and the outward expansion on a world scale of a particular mode of production supported by mechanisms of international organisation. It was also expressed through aspects of modern culture, or the variety of 'artistic flowerings' related to the American capitalist industrial system (Gramsci 1992: 357–8, Q2§138; Gramsci 1995: 256–7, Q15§30). A particularly personal cultural expression of such Americanism pondered by Gramsci was the fondness of his son, Delio, for the toy Meccano, and whether such toys would deprive children of an inventive spirit of their own (Gramsci 1994a: 242, 276–7). An alternative expression was through literature and how American 'civilisation' was able at the time to remain self-critical and understand its strengths and weaknesses through novels such as Sinclair Lewis' *Babbit* (Gramsci 1985: 278–9, Q5§105; 279–80, Q6§49).[9] Indeed, nowhere was the admixture of the 'national' point of departure and 'the international' more evident than in Gramsci's wider engagement with aspects of 'Americanism and Fordism' that is considered in more detail in the next section.

'Americanism and Fordism'

Within the remarks on 'Americanism and Fordism' in the *Prison Notebooks*, Gramsci draws a distinct contrast between the socio-economic structure of feudalism in Europe and the social formation of the United States. Whilst America had never experienced a feudal phase as such, Europe was characterised precisely by the 'absolute parasitism' of the sedimentations of past history embodied by the existence of the old feudal classes. These 'pensioners of economic history' (Gramsci 1971: 281, Q22§2) prevailed in two senses. First, there was the existence in a number of cities – 'the famous hundred cities' of silence, referred to in the previous chapter – of a class who maintained property in rural areas, the property being divided amongst a small-town bourgeoisie that gave the land over to peasant cultivators for share cropping rented in exchange for natural goods and services or leased against rent. Hence the existence of an 'enormous bulk of petty and middle bourgeoisie living on "pensions" and "rents"' (Gramsci 1971: 283, Q22§2). These classes were a 'semi-feudal type of *rentier*' existing as 'predators of surplus value' produced by the primitive labour of the peasantry (Gramsci, 1971: 291–3, Q22§6). 'This is the most hideous and unhealthy means of capital accumulation', states Gramsci, 'because it is founded on the iniquitous usurial exploitation of a peasantry kept on the verge of malnutrition' (Gramsci 1971: 283, Q22§2). Second, a similar function of 'absolute parasitism' was carried out through the state administration that was itself embedded in various aspects of 'backward' economic development in Italy, as detailed in Chapter 3. Hence 'the state is creating new *rentiers*, that is to say it is promoting the old forms of parasitic accumulation of savings and tending to create closed social formations' (Gramsci 1971: 293–4, Q22§3, Q22§6). As examined in this and earlier chapters, this is the measure of control that is exercised in conditions of passive revolution where 'bourgeois' hegemony does not prevail and the state becomes pivotal in furthering the establishment of capitalism. These features contrasted with the situation in the United States which had not experienced the European historical phase of feudalism and absolutism. That was why in Italy socio-economic modernisation had to proceed through the renovation of passive revolution, 'while remaining within the framework of the old industrialism' (Gramsci 1971: 293, Q22§6).

With reference to Americanism and Fordism, cultural and sociological features, conjoined with emergent patterns of production, are what differentiate the character and predominance of this form of hegemony. As John Agnew (2005: 9, emphases added) has put it, 'the *place* that comes to exercise hegemony [*Americanism*] matters, therefore, in the *content* and *form* that hegemony takes [*Fordism*]'. Gramsci's formulation at the time therefore recognised the 'transformation of the material bases of European civilisation' induced by the 'repercussion of American super-power' that resulted in 'the superficial apish initiative' of emulative economic policies (Gramsci 1971: 317, Q22§15). Simultaneously, however, the role of high wages within the 'Fordian ideology' of mass production affects a 'tempering of compulsion (self-discipline) with persuasion' (Gramsci 1971: 310–12, Q22§13). The phenomenon of hegemony springing forth from the conditions of Fordism involves 'coercion [that] has therefore to be ingeniously combined with persuasion and consent' (Gramsci 1971: 310, Q22§13). Americanism is an ideology manifested in 'café life' that 'can appear like a form of make-up, a superficial foreign fashion' whilst capitalism itself (expressed by the character and relationships between fundamental class relations) is not transformed, it simply acquires 'a new coating' in the climate of Americanism (Gramsci 1971: 317–18, Q22§15).

At the geopolitical level, Gramsci drew attention – through the focus on 'Americanism and Fordism' – to the changing geography and spatiality of power emerging in the twentieth century. That is why there was inquiry into 'Fordism as the ultimate stage in the process of progressive attempts by industry to overcome the law of the tendency of the rate of profit to fall' (Gramsci 1971: 279, Q22§1). At a sociological level, this equally led Gramsci directly to issues of capillary power, which were raised earlier in this chapter. These two dimensions were woven together through a number of features involving the ways in which the new methods of disciplining labour were linked to wider aspects of familial relations; to the sexual division of labour; and to changing norms of identity. Taking the first of these, the dangers inherent within the mechanisation of labour were spotlighted, whether in terms of contrasting tasks in the modern epoch, such as that of a compositor seen as increasingly alienated from the art of writing,[10] or of the worker in general, viewed as an automaton or some '"trained gorilla"' of Fordist mass production

(Gramsci 1971: 308–10, Q22§12). Instead, it was argued that the opportunity for critical reflection and independence of thought will always arise: 'not only does the worker think, but the fact that he [sic] gets no immediate satisfaction from his work and realises that they are trying to reduce him to a trained gorilla, can lead him into a train of thought that is far from conformist' (Gramsci 1971: 310, Q22§12). Second, the rationalisation of production methods was regarded as 'inescapable from a specific mode of living and of thinking and feeling' that became internalised by the worker rather than 'imposed from the outside' (Gramsci 1971: 302–3, Q22§11). This included new methods that demanded 'a rigorous discipline of the sexual instincts . . . and with it a strengthening of the "Family" in the wide sense . . and of the regulation and stability of sexual relations' (Gramsci 1971: 300, Q22§10). Alongside the preference for monogamy within industrial society, the threat of alcoholism to the 'destruction of labour power' was also noted as central to 'state ideology' (Gramsci 1971: 304, Q22§11). Third, there was a specific focus on the 'economic function of reproduction' that was described as a molecular process operating through the family and institutionalised medical practices of population control, hospitalisation, and psychoanalysis. Within Gramsci's stray remarks on gender (clumsily phrased as the 'sexual question') he notes that in society 'the "aesthetic" ideal of woman oscillates between the conceptions of "brood mare" and of "dolly"' (Gramsci 1971: 295, Q22§3). The latter was becoming especially significant due to the prevalence of 'beauty competitions, competitions for new film actresses . . . the theatre etc. all of which select the feminine beauty of the world and put it up for auction' (Gramsci 1971: 306, Q22§11). This is not to romanticise the growing preoccupation Gramsci had with the relationship between public and private forms of social experience and the commodification of life in terms of gender and the role of theatre and film in positioning women as sexual objects. After all, despite Gramsci's promotion of plays that addressed standards of 'female liberation' – such as Henrik Ibsen's *A Doll's House* – as well as his involvement with women's study circles, he equally displayed a deeply chauvinistic and sexist attitude toward women.[11] Whilst some aspects of 'Americanism and Fordism' may have taken precedence over others, it was nevertheless stated that

> [t]he formation of a new feminine personality is the most important question of an ethical and civil order connected with the sexual

question. Until women can attain not only a genuine independence in relation to men but also a new way of conceiving themselves and their role in sexual relations, the sexual question will remain full of unhealthy characteristics and caution must be exercised in proposals for new legislation. (Gramsci 1971: 296, Q22§3)

What is central to unravelling Gramsci's take on hegemony, then, is that there is an overall growing analysis of forms of 'United States world expansionism' that he envisaged as causally significant on the world stage in struggles over the 'security of American capital' (Gramsci 1996: 56, Q3§55). At the same time, though, this was categorically linked to the changing articulation of capillary power within state forms characteristic of modern capitalism, tingeing all aspects of social production and reproduction. That is why Gramsci presciently questioned 'whether Americanism can constitute an historical "epoch", that is whether it can determine a gradual evolution of the same type as the "passive revolution"' (Gramsci 1971: 279, Q22§1).

Conclusion: 'Resisting "Encrocement"'

This chapter has unravelled Gramsci on the basis of an interpretative (re)reading of the question of hegemony by carrying through the 'strangely composite' approach introduced in Chapter 2. This involved analysing the unfolding historical context and the social and political experiences through which Gramsci's concepts were developed. Hence a focus on unravelling 'biographical' and historical issues that included discussion of Gramsci's involvement in the journal *L'Ordine Nuovo*, his commitment to the Factory Councils movement, and his participation and leadership of the PCd'I. Rather than separating such practical activity from the work undertaken in prison, a focus on this period assisted in emphasising the reciprocal relationship between Gramsci's theory and practice. The 'strangely composite' approach was then extended across the unravelling of pre-prison writings, the *Prison Notebooks* themselves, and various commentaries. As a result, five interrelated elements were elaborated that all aided the unravelling of Gramsci's understanding of 'the moment of hegemony'.

First, it was shown how hegemony is conceived as a dynamic process and how intellectual activity plays a crucial formative role in its construction and contestation in relation to an expanded or 'integral' notion of the state. However, whilst due weight was accorded to ethico-political factors, such an approach to hegemony is not limited to the realm of ideas. Indeed, this notion of hegemony was conceived as a transcendence of the idealist philosophy of Croce, so that, 'though hegemony is ethical-political, it must also be economic' (Gramsci 1971: 161, Q13§18). Moreover, it was clearly emphasised how ideas can 'assume the fanatical granite compactness of . . . "popular beliefs" which assume the same energy as "material forces"' (Gramsci 1971: 404, Q11§62). Hence a need to highlight the role of ideas as a material force, whilst resisting the '"encrocement"' of idealist philosophy, which tends to overemphasise the indeterminate and decentred character of politics (Mansfield 1993: 81–103).

Second, this was fulfilled by focusing on what was referred to as the *social basis* of hegemony – beyond simply understanding the state-as-force – and the phase of struggle between social-class forces within the 'relations of force'. Attention is therefore granted to the articulation of ideas and subjective elements supportive of contesting and conflicting ideologies beyond narrow 'economic–corporate' interests. This is crucial in the bid to raise intersubjective consciousness among a variety of social-class forces and thus transcend particular interests limited to the economic sphere by appealing to wider social groups. The scope of intellectual activity is therefore amplified without arbitrarily presupposing how the struggle over hegemony may be exercised.

Intrinsically linked to the struggle over hegemony is the concept of historical bloc, which was discussed in the third section, and how this relates to the formation of hegemony within a national social formation. Similarly, the task of launching a 'counter'hegemonic movement was highlighted – according to various but not necessarily separate strategies – and how such attempts are also shaped by the material possibilities of the society within which they arise. It would be a mistake to focus solely on the unity of the ruling classes within a state or group of states, because this would result in 'negative history'. Hence the importance of focusing on 'positive forces' represented by subaltern social classes, whose history is intertwined with that of civil society, the history of states, and groups of states.

Fourth, it became essential to indicate how hegemony, whilst understood within a 'national' point of departure, was part of a dialectical complex with 'the international', represented by the expansion of a mode of production on a world scale, i.e. through 'Americanism and Fordism'. It was therefore shown that, by taking the 'national' point of departure as nodal, one can appreciate how relations within a society react both passively and actively to the mediations of 'the international'. It was indicated not only how this nodal approach to the 'national' point of departure was evident in Gramsci's writings but also how he directly focused on forms of 'American global hegemony' and 'American super-power' status – hence rejecting the claim that concepts such as hegemony are exclusively national. Gramsci, instead, brings awareness to both an understanding of specific dynamics of state formation and the rise of the 'international' moment of hegemony within capitalist modernity.

Unravelling Gramsci also yielded more detailed discussion in a fifth section by focusing on aspects of 'Americanism and Fordism', which is linked to the discussion of passive revolution throughout this and the immediately preceding chapter. This revolved around Gramsci's interest in 'whether America, through the implacable weight of its economic production (and therefore indirectly), will compel or is already compelling Europe to overturn its excessively antiquated economic and social basis' (Gramsci 1971: 317, Q22§15). The feature of 'Americanism and Fordism' therefore represented not so much 'the "normal" exercise of hegemony', discussed in detail throughout the chapter, 'characterised by the combination of force and consent, which balance each other reciprocally' (Gramsci 1971: 80n.4, Q19§24). Rather, 'Americanism and Fordism' can be understood as the *passive revolution of capital* emanating through the state as a necessary condition for the stabilisation of capitalism (Chatterjee 1986: 46–7). In modern capitalist society, conditions of passive revolution can therefore be understood not so much as the constitution of 'normal' conditions of hegemony. This situation occurs only at exceptional moments: 'if the relationship between intellectuals and people–nation, between the leaders and led, the rulers and ruled, is provided by organic cohesion . . . then and only then is the relationship one of representation' (Gramsci 1971: 418, Q11§67). The historical path of passive revolution is instead the basis of a minimal hegemony that rests on an unstable equilibrium of narrow consensus among modernising elite classes to maintain the extant order. To put it in Hugues Portelli's (1973: 30) apt words: 'There is no social system where consensus serves as the sole basis of hegemony nor a state where the same [*mismo*] social group can durably maintain its domination on the basis of pure coercion.'[12] Hence the importance of recognising different variations of hegemony that may prevail within a social order, or shifts in the threshold of power between consensual and coercive means indicative of state crisis and rule through *trasformismo* (Femia 1981b: 46–8).

By unravelling Gramsci in this and the preceding chapters, the discussion of Part I of the book is now complete. As a result, these chapters provide suitable preparation for beginning to think in a Gramscian way about hegemony and passive revolution related to alternative historical and contemporary conditions. This endeavour is the task of Part II of the book. Rather than mechanically 'applying' a series of reified concepts, however, the focus on unravelling Gramsci's leitmotiv or rhythm of thought, about questions of hegemony, passive revolution and uneven development, promotes not only concrete analysis of the peculiarity of alternative historical phenomena but also an interest in actual practices related to present political activity. The following chapters therefore aim to reveal what is offered by a Gramscian way of thinking about the construction, renewal and contestation of hegemony and passive revolution within the global political economy of uneven development.

Part II

Gramsci, World Order, and Resistance

5 Hegemony and World Order: Neo-Gramscian Perspectives and the Global Political Economy

Reality produces a wealth of the most bizarre combinations. It is up to the theoretician to unravel these in order to discover fresh proof of his theory, to 'translate' into theoretical language the elements of historical life.
— Antonio Gramsci, *Quaderni del Carcere*, Q3§48

This chapter continues the central focus of the book by analysing how various perspectives in international political economy (IPE) have contributed to thinking in a Gramscian way about the contemporary constitution of hegemony and passive revolution in world order. Located within a historical materialist problematic of social transformation and deploying many insights from Antonio Gramsci, a crucial break with mainstream international relations (IR) approaches had emerged by the 1980s in the work of Robert Cox. In contrast to such mainstream routes to hegemony in IR, which develop a static theory of politics (e.g. Keohane 1984 and 1989; Waltz 1979), debate shifted towards a critical theory of hegemony, world order and historical change (for the classic critique, see Ashley 1984). Rather than a problem-solving preoccupation with the maintenance of social power relationships, a critical theory of hegemony directs attention to questioning the prevailing order of the world.[1] 'Critical theory', adds Herbert Marcuse (1937/1968: 156), '. . . is critical of itself and of the social forces that make up its own basis.' It 'does not take institutions and social and power relations for granted but calls them into question by concerning itself with their origins and whether they might be in the process of changing' (Cox 1981: 129). Thus, it is specifically critical in the sense of asking how existing social or world orders have come into being and what class forces may have the emancipatory potential to change or transform a prevailing order (see Morton 2006a; 2007).

What is crucial to the argument of the chapter is that a critical theory of the practice of hegemony is still relevant to understanding the changing spatial and territorial structure of power in the global political economy. Clearly there has been much recent debate about aspects of 'empire' shaping the terrain of power within global politics (Hardt and Negri 2000). Elsewhere it has been argued that events surrounding the invasion of Iraq in 2003 signal the transformation of US hegemony into sheer domination (Arrighi 2005a, 2005b). Given that the United States has military bases in over 69 countries, a figure that is continually increasing through additional presence in Central Asia and the occupation of Iraq, it would be out of place to deny the role of territorial occupation within projections of global power (Mészáros 2001: 44). At the same time it can be said that imperialism is a labile term both in theoretical and practical dynamics that goes, as Eric Hobsbawm (1987: 60) notes, to the heart of arguments about Marxism. 'Imperialism', then, '. . . is a rather loose concept which in practice has to be newly defined with reference to each historical period' (Cox 1981: 142). Rather than identifying global power according to some unchanging essence of imperialism, the somewhat distinct claim in this chapter is that the articulation of hegemony better explains the construction and altering configuration of global power (see Agnew 2005). As Leo Panitch and Sam Ginden (2005: 121) pointedly argue, 'hegemony is a variable quality of rule; conjunctural shifts in the balance between coercion and consent in the deployment of structural power should not be mistaken for epochal ones', such as the unravelling of hegemony into coercive dominance. What is central to this chapter is therefore the elaboration of a framework that attempts to account for the possibilities of change and transformation within world order through the notions of hegemony and passive revolution. Linking the structural and historical characteristics of imperialism to the contemporary hegemonic phases of world order is outside the scope of the present study. Instead, the task in the first section of this chapter is to outline the conceptual framework developed by Robert Cox, connecting it back to Gramsci's own work, in order to trace features in the articulation of hegemony and passive revolution through world order. This includes situating the world economic crisis of the 1970s within more recent debates about globalisation and how this period of 'structural change' has been conceptualised. Attention will then turn to what has been recognised as similar, but diverse, neo-Gramscian perspectives in IPE (see Morton 2001). These build on Cox's work and constitute a distinct critical theory route to considering structural issues of hegemony and passive revolution, world order and historical change. Finally, various controversies surrounding the neo-Gramscian perspectives will be traced and, in conclusion, the directions along which current debate is proceeding will be elaborated. This undertaking will act as a necessary backdrop to the discussion in Chapter 6 that will address the scale of uneven development within the global political economy by engaging with those endeavours to account for the increasing shift from a 'national' to a 'transnational' pattern of global capitalism.

A Critical Theory Route to Hegemony, World Order and Historical Change

Unlike conventional IR theory, which reduces hegemony to a single dimension of dominance based on the economic and military capabilities of states, the neo-Gramscian perspective developed by Cox broadens the domain of hegemony. Hegemony here is the articulation and justification of a particular set of interests as general interests. It appears as an expression of broadly based consent, manifested in the acceptance of ideas and supported by material resources and institutions, which is initially established by social-class forces occupying a leading role within a state, but is then projected outwards on a world scale. Within a world order, a situation of hegemony may prevail 'based on a coherent conjunction or fit between a configuration of material power, the prevalent collective image of world order (including certain norms) and a set of institutions which administer the order with a certain semblance of universality' (Cox 1981: 139). As Cox (1994: 366) has elaborated elsewhere,

hegemony is a form in which dominance is obscured by achieving an appearance of acquiescence . . . as if it were the natural order of things . . . [it] is an internalised coherence which has most probably arisen from an externally imposed order but has been transformed into an intersubjectively constituted reality.

Hegemony is therefore a form of dominance, but it refers more to a consensual order, so that 'dominance by a powerful state may be a necessary but not a sufficient condition of hegemony' (Cox 1981: 139). If hegemony is understood as an 'opinion-moulding activity', rather than brute force or dominance, then consideration has to turn to how a hegemonic social or world order is based on values and understandings that permeate the nature of that order (Cox 1992/1996: 151). Hence consideration turns to how intersubjective meanings – shared notions about social relations – shape reality. '"Reality" is not only the physical environment of human action but also the institutional, moral and ideological context that shapes thoughts and actions' (Cox 1997: 252). The crucial point to make, then, is that hegemony filters through structures of society, economy, culture, gender, ethnicity, class, and ideology. These are dimensions that escape conventional IR routes to hegemony, which simply equate the notion with state dominance. As a result, they conflate the two forms of power. There is a failure to acknowledge that 'there can be dominance without hegemony; [and that] hegemony is one possible form dominance may take' (Cox 1981: 153n.27).

By including the intersubjective realm within a theory of hegemony it is also possible to begin appreciating alternative conceptions and different understandings of the world. In this sense Cox refers to civilisations as different realms of intersubjectivity, although there might exist common ground or points of contact between the distinct and separate subjectivities of different coexisting civilisations (Cox 2002). Similarly Gramsci appreciated the need to understand cultural overlaps between civilisations rather than worrying about 'the danger to the homogeneity of beliefs and the ways of thinking of Western culture' (Gramsci 1994a: 179). Ridiculing those who envisaged a threat from different religious, ethnic, and cultural backgrounds, Gramsci (1994a: 180) noted the growing importance of musical phenomena such as jazz bands and their ideological influence, because they are 'manifestations that express themselves in the most universal language in existence today, in the language that most rapidly communicates total images and impressions of a civilisation'.[2] At the same time, rival forms of capitalism are tied up with struggles between different civilisations or ways of life, so that the challenge is to articulate shared ideas that can bridge the different realms of inter-subjectivity within a 'critique of capitalist civilisation' (Cox 1995b: 16; Gramsci 1977: 10–13). This applies as much to the maintenance of a hegemonic situation as it does to bids for 'counter'hegemony that aim to challenge and transform a prevailing hegemony.

Hegemony within a historical structure is constituted on three spheres of activity: *the social relations of production*, encompassing the totality of social relations in material, institutional, and discursive forms that engender particular social forces; *forms of state*, consisting of historically contingent state–civil society complexes; and *world orders*, which not only represent phases of stability and conflict but also permit scope for thinking about how alternative forms of world order might emerge (Cox 1981: 135–8). These are represented schematically in Figure 5.1 (Cox 1981: 138).

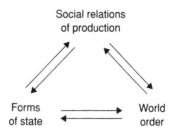

Figure 5.1   The dialectical relation of forces

What is striking here is the manner in which Gramsci's rendering of historical relations of force and his focus on the political relation of hegemony are consistent with this revision of power dynamics (see Chapter 4, Figure 4.1). If considered dialectically, in relation to each other, then it becomes possible to represent the historical process through the particular configuration of historical structures. Social forces, as the main collective actors engendered by the social relations of production, operate within and across all spheres of activity similar to the 'relations of force' as articulated by Gramsci. Through the rise of contending social forces, linked to changes in production, there may occur mutually reinforcing transformations in forms of state and world order. There is no unilinear relationship between the spheres of activity, so that the point of departure to explain the historical process may equally be that of forms of state or world order (Cox 1981: 153n.26). Again this is significant as space is left open to consider the 'national' point of departure as *nodal* rather than *dominant* in relation to 'the international', which is consistent with Gramsci's spatial awareness of the uneven development of social power (see Chapter 3). Within each of the three main spheres, it is argued that three further elements reciprocally combine to constitute a historical structure: *ideas*, understood as intersubjective meanings as well as collective images of world order; *material capabilities*, referring to accumulated resources; and *institutions*, which are amalgams of the previous two elements and are means of stabilising a particular order. These again are represented schematically (see Figure 5.2) (Cox 1981: 136).

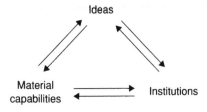

Figure 5.2   The dialectical moment of hegemony

The aim is to break down over time coherent historical structures – consisting of different patterns of social relations of production, forms of state and world order – that have existed within the capitalist mode of production (Cox 1987: 396–8). In the following, the main characteristics of the three spheres of activity are outlined whilst attention is given to how this framework, as discussed in the preceding chapter, develops Gramsci's focus on the political moment of hegemony (see Chapter 4, Figure 4.2), by drawing attention to the full weight of cultural–political–economic class struggle within capitalist development (Gramsci 1995: 343–6, Q10I§7). This framework will then become significant in assisting an explanation of capitalist reproduction and resistance within conditions of uneven development in Chapters 6 and 7 in relation to thinking in a Gramscian way about empirical contexts of hegemony and passive revolution in Mexico.

The Constitution of Hegemony

The Social Relations of Production

According to Cox (1987: 1–9), patterns of production relations are the starting point for analysing the operation and mechanisms of hegemony. Yet, from the start, this should not be taken as a move that reduces everything to production in an economistic sense.

> Production . . . is to be understood in the broadest sense. It is not confined to the production of physical goods used or consumed. It covers the production and reproduction of knowledge and of the social relations, morals and institutions that are prerequisites to the production of physical goods. (Cox 1989: 39)

These patterns are referred to as modes of social relations of production, which encapsulate configurations of social-class forces engaged in the process of production. By discerning different modes of social relations of production, it is possible to consider how changing production relations give rise to particular social-class forces that become the bases of power within and across states and within a specific world order (Cox 1987: 4). The objective of outlining different modes of social relations of production is to question what promotes the emergence of particular modes and what might explain the way in which modes combine or undergo transformation (Cox 1987: 103). It is argued that the reciprocal relationship between production and power is crucial. To examine this relationship, a framework is developed that focuses on how power in *social relations of production* may give rise to certain *social forces*, how these social forces may become the bases of power in *forms of state* and how this might shape *world order*. This framework revolves around the social ontology of historical structures. A social ontology merely refers to the key properties that are thought to constitute the social world, representing claims about the nature and relationship of agents and social structures. It refers to 'persistent social practices, made by collective human activity and transformed through collective human activity' (Cox 1987: 4). An attempt is thus made to capture the reciprocal relationship of agents and structures (see Bieler and Morton 2001b).

Hegemony is therefore understood as a form of class rule, not primarily as a hierarchy of states (Overbeek 1994). For Cox, class is viewed as a historical category and employed in a heuristic way rather than as a static analytical category (Cox 1987: 355–7, 1985/1996: 57). This means that class identity emerges within and through historical processes of economic exploitation. 'Bring back exploitation as the hallmark of class, and at once class struggle is in the forefront, as it should be' (Ste. Croix 1981: 57). As such, class-consciousness emerges out of particular historical contexts of struggle rather than mechanically deriving from objective determinations that have an automatic place in production relations (see Thompson 1978). Yet the focus on exploitation and resistance to it ensures that social forces are not simply reduced to material aspects, but also include other forms of identity involved in struggle, such as ethnic, nationalist, religious, gender or sexual forms. In short, '"non-class" issues – peace, ecology, and feminism – are not to be set aside but given a firm and conscious basis in the social realities shaped through the production process' (Cox 1987: 353). The point then, as E.P. Thompson (1968: 226) explained, is not to constitute the social subject as a set of disaggregated individuals but instead to focus on those class relations that bear on life in a way often mediated 'through the refraction of a particular system of ownership and power'. An understanding of social relations of production thus ensures that due regard is granted to new social relationships, institutions, and cultural codes shaped by the inner compulsions of production. Class struggle is thereby faced rather than effaced in this historical materialist conceptualisation of critical theory – as an enquiry into distinct capitalist relations corresponding to forms of property ownership, state power, and *un*freedom (Morton 2006a; 2007).

Forms of State

The conceptual framework outlined so far considers how new modes of social relations of production become established. Changes in the social relations of production give rise to new configurations of *social forces*. State power rests on these configurations. Therefore, rather than taking the state as a given or pre-constituted institutional category, consideration is given to the historical construction of various forms of state and the social context of political struggle. This is accomplished by drawing upon the concept of historical bloc and by widening a theory of the state to include relations within civil society. A historical bloc refers to the way in which leading social-class forces within a specific 'national' context establish a relationship over contending social forces. It is more than simply a political alliance between social forces represented by classes or fractions of classes. It indicates the integration of a variety of different class interests that are propagated throughout society, 'bringing about not only a unison of economic and political aims, but also intellectual and moral unity . . . on a "universal" plane' (Gramsci 1971: 181–2, Q13§17). The very nature of a historical bloc, as Anne Showstack Sassoon (1987: 123) has explained, necessarily implies the existence of hegemony. Indeed, the 'universal plane' that Gramsci had in mind was the creation of hegemony by a fundamental social group over subordinate groups. Hegemony would therefore be established

> if the relationship between intellectuals and people–nation, between the leaders and the led, the rulers and the ruled, is provided by an organic cohesion . . . Only then can there take

place an exchange of individual elements between the rulers and ruled, leaders . . . and led, and can the shared life be realised which alone is a social force – with the creation of the 'historical bloc'. (Gramsci 1971: 418, Q11§67)

These issues are encompassed within the focus on different forms of state which, as Cox notes, are principally distinguished by

the characteristics of their historic[al] blocs, i.e. the configurations of social forces upon which state power ultimately rests. A particular configuration of social forces defines in practice the limits or parameters of state purposes, and the modus operandi of state action, defines, in other words, the *raison d'état* for a particular state. (Cox 1987: 105)

In short, by considering different forms of state, it becomes possible to analyse the social basis of the state or to conceive of the historical 'content' of different states. The notion of historical bloc aids this endeavour by directing attention to which social-class forces may have been crucial in the formation of a historical bloc or particular state; what contradictions may be contained within a historical bloc upon which a form of state is founded; and what potential might exist for the formation of a rival historical bloc that may transform a particular form of state (Cox 1987: 409 n.10). In contrast, therefore, to conventional state-centric approaches in IR, a wider theory of the state emerges within this framework. Instead of underrating state power and explaining it away, attention is given to social-class forces and processes and how these relate to the development of states (Cox 1981: 128) as well as to states in alternative conditions of development (Bilgin and Morton 2002). Considering different forms of state as the expressions of particular historical blocs, and thus relations across state–civil society, fulfils this objective. Overall, this relationship is referred to as the state–civil society complex and, clearly, it owes an intellectual debt to Gramsci.

For Gramsci, the state was not simply understood as an institution limited to the 'government of the functionaries' or the 'top political leaders and personalities with direct governmental responsibilities'. This tendency to concentrate solely on such features of the state, it will be recalled from the previous chapter, was pejoratively termed 'statolatry': it entailed viewing the state as a perpetual entity limited to actions within political society (Gramsci 1971: 178, Q13§17; 268,

Q8§130). Again, it can be argued that certain neo-Realist approaches in IR succumb to the tendency of 'statolatry'. Yet the state presents itself in a different way beyond the political society of public figures and top leaders so that 'the state is the entire complex of practical and theoretical activities with which the ruling class not only justifies and maintains its dominance, but manages to win the active consent of those over whom it rules' (Gramsci 1971: 178, Q13§17; 244, Q15§10). This alternative conception of the state is inclusive of the realm of civil society.

The state should be understood, then, not just as the apparatus of government operating within the 'public' sphere (government, political parties, military) but also as part of the 'private' sphere of civil society (church, media, education) through which hegemony functions (Gramsci 1971: 261, Q6§137).

> What we can do . . . is to fix two major . . . 'levels': the one that can be called 'civil society', that is the ensemble of organisms commonly called 'private', and that of 'political society' or 'the state'. These two levels correspond on the one hand to the function of 'hegemony' which the dominant group exercises throughout society and on the other hand to that of 'direct domination' or command exercised through the state and 'juridical' government. (Gramsci, 1971: 12, Q12§1)

It can therefore be argued that the state in this conception is understood as a social relation. The state is not unquestioningly taken as a distinct institutional category, or thing in itself, but conceived as a form of social relations through which capitalism and hegemony are expressed (see Bieler and Morton 2003). At an analytical level, then, 'the general notion of the state includes elements which need to be referred back to the notion of civil society (in the sense that one might say that state = political society + civil society, in other words hegemony protected by the armour of coercion)' (Gramsci, 1971: 263, Q6§88). Linking back to Chapter 4, it is this combination of political and civil society that is referred to as the integral state through which ruling classes organise intellectual and moral functions as part of the political and cultural struggle for hegemony in the effort to establish an 'ethical' state (Gramsci 1971: 258, Q8§179; 271, Q6§10). Furthermore, different social relations of production engender different fractions of social-class forces. This means that 'foreign' capital, for example, is not simply represented as an autonomous force beyond the power of the state but instead is represented by certain classes or fractions of classes *within* the constitution of the state apparatus. There are contradictory and heterogeneous relations internal to the state, which are induced by class antagonisms between nationally and transnationally based capital and labour (Bieler 2006: 32). The state, then, is the condensation of a hegemonic relationship between dominant classes and class fractions. This occurs when a leading class develops a 'hegemonic project' or solidarity of interests that transcends particular economic–corporate interests within the political relation of hegemony (see Chapter 4, Figure 4.2). A hegemonic project or 'comprehensive concept of control' becomes capable of binding and making coherent the diverse aspirations and general interests of various social classes and class fractions (van der Pijl 1984, 1998; Overbeek 1990, 1993). It is a process that involves the 'most purely political phase' of class struggle and occurs on a '"universal" plane' to result in the forging of a historical bloc (Gramsci 1971: 181–2, Q13§17).

Hegemony and World Orders

The construction of a historical bloc cannot exist without a hegemonic social class and is therefore a 'national' phenomenon (Cox 1983: 168, 174). This is because the very nature of a historical bloc is bound up with how various classes and fractions of classes construct, or contest, hegemony through 'national' political frameworks taken as nodal points of departure (see above and Chapter 4). Yet the hegemony of a leading class can manifest itself as an 'international' phenomenon insofar as it represents the development of a particular form of the social relations of production. Once hegemony has been consolidated domestically it may expand beyond a particular social order to move outward on a world scale and insert itself through the world order (Cox 1983: 171; Cox 1987: 149–50). By doing so it can connect social class forces across different countries. 'A world hegemony is thus in its beginnings an outward expansion of the internal (national) hegemony established by a . . . social class' (Cox 1983: 171). The outward expansion of particular modes of social relations of production and the interests of a leading class on a world scale can also become supported by institutional mechanisms within 'the international'. This is what Gramsci (1971: 243, Q13§7) referred to as the 'internal and international organisational relations of the state': i.e. movements, voluntary associations, and organisations, such as the Rotary Club, or the Roman Catholic Church, that had an 'international' character whilst being rooted within the state. Social-class forces may thus achieve hegemony within a 'national' order as well as through world order, by ensuring the promotion and expansion of a mode of production. Hegemony, then, can operate at two levels: by constructing a historical bloc and establishing social cohesion *within* a form of state as well as by expanding a mode of production *internationally* to project hegemony through the level of world order. Whilst political space is not reduced to state territoriality in this conception, there is nevertheless awareness of how 'place-specific conditions still mediate many production and trade relationships' (Agnew 2005: 166). A position to be developed in more detail in the next chapter, on the global political economy of uneven development, is that the 'national' point of departure as a *nodal* point in the spatiality of capitalist development remains vital. It is within a particular historical bloc and form of state that hegemony is initially constructed. Yet, beyond this initial consolidation, as hegemony begins to be asserted internationally, it is also within other different countries and particular forms of state that struggles may develop as a result of the introduction of new modes of production.

For instance, in Gramsci's time, this was born out by the expansion of Fordist assembly plant production beyond the United States, which would lead to the growing world hegemony and power of 'Americanism and Fordism' from the 1920s and 1930s (see Chapter 4). To draw on John Agnew (2005: 124),

> this involved projecting at a global scale those institutions and practices that had already developed in the United States, such as Fordist mass production/consumption industrial organisation, electoral democracy, limited state welfare policies, and government economic policies directed toward stimulating private economic activities.

As Gramsci explained, the way in which such world hegemony may consolidate itself is locally within a nodal national setting: 'It is in the concept of hegemony that those exigencies which are national in character are knotted together . . . A class that is international in character has . . . to "nationalise" itself in a certain sense' (Gramsci 1971: 241, Q14§68). Thus, as Kees van der Pijl (1989: 12; 1996: 307) notes in relation to this passage, the struggle for hegemony involves 'translating' particular interests, from a particular form of state, into forms of expansion that have universal applicability across a variety of different states. Usually, it is within this nodal 'national' context that hegemony is initially constructed, prior to outward expansion on a world scale, and it is within this point of departure that struggles unfold in contesting hegemony. Hence the importance of stressing 'interlinking hegemonies' within forms of state and across world order (Gills 1993: 190).

Pax Americana and Globalisation

It has been one of Cox's key objectives to explain additional processes of structural change, particularly the change from the post–Second World War order to globalisation. Cox argues that a US-led hegemonic world order, labelled *pax Americana*, prevailed until the early 1970s. It was maintained through the Bretton Woods system of fixed exchange rates and institutions such as the World Bank and the International Monetary Fund (IMF). Moreover, it was based on the principle of 'embedded liberalism', which allowed the combination of international free trade with the right of governments to intervene in their national economy in order to ensure domestic stability via social security and the partial redistribution of economic wealth (Ruggie 1982) – although here it should be recognised, as Hannes Lacher (1999: 348) shrewdly notes, that 'the postwar order may be better understood in terms of the dominance of a protectionist form of regulation of the market economy, than as a re-embedding of the market economy itself'. The corresponding form of state was the Keynesian welfare state, characterised by interventionism, a policy of full employment via budget-deficit spending, the mixed economy, and an expansive welfare system (Gill and Law 1988: 79–80). The underlying social relations of production were organised around a Fordist accumulation regime, characterised by mass production and mass consumption, and tripartite corporatism involving government–business–labour coalitions (Cox 1987: 219–30).[3] The forms and functions of US-led hegemony, however, began to alter following the world economic crisis of the 1970s and the collapse of the Bretton Woods system during a period of 'structural change' in the world economy in the 1970s. This overall crisis, both of the world economy and of social power within various forms of state, has been explained as being the result of two particular tendencies: the internationalisation of production and the internationalisation of the state, which led the thrust towards globalisation.

Since the erosion of *pax Americana* principles of world order in the 1970s, there has been an increasing internationalisation of production and finance, driven, at the apex of an emerging global class structure, by a 'transnational managerial class' (Cox 1981: 147; Cox 1987: 271). Taking advantage of differences between countries, there has been an integration of production processes on a transnational scale with transnational corporations (TNCs) promoting the operation of different elements of a single process in different territorial locations. This organisation of production and finance on a transnational level fundamentally distinguishes globalisation from the period of *pax Americana*. Following the neo-Gramscian focus on social-class forces, engendered by production as the main actors, the *transnational* restructuring of capitalism within globalisation is realised, which has led to the emergence of new social forces of capital and labour. Besides the transnational managerial class, other elements of productive capital (involved in manufacturing and extraction), including small- and medium-sized businesses acting as contractors and suppliers and import–export businesses, as well as elements of financial capital (involved in banking, insurance, and finance) have been supportive of this transnationalisation of production (Gill 1995a: 400–1). Hence there has been a rise in the structural power of transnational capital supported and promoted by forms of elite interaction that have forged common perspectives, or an 'emulative uniformity', between business, state officials, and representatives of international organisations, favouring the logic of capitalist market relations (Cox 1987: 298; Gill and Law 1989: 484). Significant contradictions are likely to exist between transnational social forces of capital and nationally based capital. The latter, engendered by national production systems, may oppose an open global economy, due to their reliance on national or regional protectionism against global competition. Parallel to the division between transnational and national capital, Cox identifies two main lines of division within the working class. First, workers of TNCs can be in conflict with workers of national companies, shadowing the split of capital. Second, and related to this, there may be a rift between established workers in secure employment, often within the core workforce of TNCs, and non-established workers in temporary and part-time positions at the periphery of the labour market (Cox 1981: 235). In other words, globalisation in the form of the transnationalisation of production has led to a fractionalisation of capital and labour into transnational and national social forces alike (Bieler 2006: 32–4).

During this period of structural change in the 1970s, then, the social basis across many forms of state altered as the logic of capitalist market relations created a crisis of authority in established institutions and modes of governance. As Craig Murphy (1998b: 159) has noted, 'adjustment to the crisis occurred at different rates in different regions, but in each case it resulted in a "neoliberal" shift in governmental economic policy and the increasing prominence of financial capital'. Whilst some have championed such changes as the 'retreat of the state' (Strange 1996), or the emergence of a 'borderless world' (Ohmae 1990, 1996), and others have decried the global proportions of such changes in production (Hirst and Thompson 1999; Weiss 1998), it is argued here that the internationalisation of production has profoundly restructured – but not eroded – the role of the state. After all,

> the state as an institutional and social entity . . . creates the possibility for the limitation of such structural power, partly because of the political goods and services which it supplies to capitalists and the institutional autonomy it possesses. The stance of the state towards freedom of enterprise . . . is at the heart of this issue. (Gill and Law 1989: 480)

The notion of the internationalisation of the state captures this dynamic by referring to the way transnational processes of consensus formation, underpinned by the internationalisation of production and the thrust of globalisation, have been transmitted through the policy-making channels of governments. The network of control that has maintained the structural power of capital has also been supported by an 'axis of influence', consisting of institutions such as the World Bank or the IMF that have ensured the ideological osmosis and dissemination of policies in favour of the perceived exigencies of the global political economy. As a result, as will be demonstrated in the chapter to follow, those state agencies in close contact with the global economy – offices of presidents and prime ministers, treasuries, central banks – have gained precedence over those agencies closest to domestic public policy – ministries of labour and industry or planning offices (Cox 1992: 31). Across the different forms of state in countries of advanced and peripheral capitalism, the general depiction is that the state has become a transmission belt for neoliberalism and the logic of capitalist competition from global to local spheres (Cox 1992: 31).[4]

From the Internationalisation of the State to Globalisation

Although the thesis of the internationalisation of the state has received much recent criticism, the work of Stephen Gill has greatly contributed to understanding this process as part of the changing character of US-centred hegemony in the global political economy, notably in his detailed analysis of the role of the Trilateral Commission (Gill 1990). Like Cox, Gill locates the global restructuring of production within a context of structural change in the 1970s. It was in this period that there was a transition from what Gill recognises as an *international historical bloc* of social-class forces, established in the post–Second World War period, towards a *transnational historical bloc*, not only forging links and a synthesis of interests and identities beyond national boundaries and classes but also creating the conditions for the hegemony of transnational capital. Yet Gill departs from Gramsci to assert that a historical bloc 'may at times have the potential to become hegemonic', thereby implying that a historical bloc can be established without necessarily enjoying hegemonic rule (Gill 1993b: 40). For example, Gill argues that the current transnational historical bloc has a position of supremacy but not hegemony: 'The use of the term "supremacy" is deliberate, intended to connote a form of rule based on economic coercion and the use – potential or actual – of organised violence as a means of intimidating and fragmenting opposition' (Gill 2004: 23). Drawing in principle on Gramsci, it is argued that supremacy prevails when a situation of hegemony *is not* apparent and when dominance is exercised through a historical bloc over split opposition (Gill 1995a: 400, 402, 412).

This politics of supremacy is organised through two key processes: the new constitutionalism of disciplinary neoliberalism and the concomitant spread of market civilisation. According to Gill, new constitutionalism involves the narrowing of the social basis of popular participation within the world order of disciplinary neoliberalism. It involves the hollowing out of democracy and the affirmation, in matters of political economy, of a set of macro-economic policies such as market efficiency, discipline and confidence, policy credibility, and competitiveness. It is 'the move towards construction of legal or constitutional devices to remove or insulate substantially the new economic institutions from popular scrutiny or democratic account-ability' (Gill 1991, 1992: 165). Economic and monetary union (EMU) within the European Union (EU) is regarded as a good example of this process (Gill 2001). New constitutionalism results in an attempt to make neoliberalism the sole model of development by disseminating the notion of market civilisation based on an ideology of capitalist progress and exclusionary or hierarchical patterns of social relations (Gill 1995a: 399). Within the global political economy, mechanisms of surveillance have supported the market civilisation of new constitutionalism in something tentatively likened to a global 'panopticon' of surveillance (Gill 1995b).

The overarching concept of supremacy has also been used to develop an understanding of the construction of US foreign policy towards the 'Third World' and the way in which challenges were mounted against the United States in the 1970s through the New International Economic Order (NIEO) (Augelli and Murphy 1988). It is argued that the ideological promotion of American liberalism, based on individualism and free trade, assured American supremacy throughout the 1970s and was reconstructed in the 1980s. Yet this projection of supremacy did not simply unfold through domination. Rather than simply equating supremacy with dominance, Augelli and Murphy (1988: 132) argue that supremacy can be maintained through domination *or* hegemony. As Murphy (1994: 295n.8) outlines, in a separate study of industrial change and international organisations, supremacy defines the position of a leading class within a historical bloc and can be secured by hegemony as well as through domination. Gramsci (1971: 57, Q19§24) himself states, 'the supremacy of a social group manifests itself in two ways, as "domination" and as "intellectual and moral leadership"'. Where the former strain of supremacy involves subjugation by force, the latter involves leading allied groups. Shifts or variations in hegemony therefore characterise conditions of supremacy, which may reveal the limits of organising the balance between passive and active consent relative to coercion within world order.

An important intervention by Kees van der Pijl (1998) further expands the possibility of using class struggle as an analytical device for the analysis of confrontations beyond those concerned with purely material interests. He distinguishes three areas of capitalist discipline and exploitation: (1) original, or primitive, accumulation and resistance to it, mainly relevant during the early history of capitalism (see Chapter 3); (2) the capitalist production process, referring to the exploitation of labour in the workplace; and (3) the extension of exploitation into the sphere of social reproduction, submitting education and health to capitalist profit criteria and leading to the destruction and exhaustion of the environment. It is the latter form of capitalist discipline that has become increasingly relevant during neoliberal globalisation. Resistance to it, whether by progressive social movements or by populist, nationalist movements, can be understood as class struggle as much as the confrontation between capital and labour at the workplace (van der Pijl 1998: 36–49).

In addition to the neo-Gramscian perspectives discussed so far, there also exists a diverse array of similar perspectives analysing hegemony in the global political economy. This includes, among others, an account of the historically specific way in which mass production was institutionalised in the United States and how this propelled forms of American-centred leadership and world hegemony in the post-Second World War period (Rupert 1995a). Extending this analysis, there has also been consideration of struggles between social forces in the United States over the North American Free Trade Agreement (NAFTA) and globalisation (Rupert 1995b, 2000). Moreover, there have been numerous analyses of European integration within the context of globalisation and the role of transnational classes within European governance (van Apeldoorn 2002; Bieler, 2000; Bieler and Morton 2001b; Bohle 2006; Cafruny and Ryner 2003; Holman, Overbeek and Ryner 1998; Ryner 2002; Shields 2003). Despite this output, commentaries and textbooks on European governance from mainstream and constructivist backgrounds still refrain from any serious engagement with their historical materialist counterparts (those most recently remiss in this area would include Christiansen, Jørgensen and Wiener 2001; Rosamond 2000; Wiener and Diez 2003). Elsewhere, the internationalisation and democratisation of southern Europe, particularly Spain, within the global political economy has been analysed (Holman 1996), as well as international organisations, including the role of gender and women's movements (Lee 1995; Stienstra 1994; Whitworth 1994). There has also been a recent turn to understanding forms of US foreign-policy intervention within countries of peripheral capitalism. This has included analysing the promotion of polyarchy, defined as 'a system in which a small group actually rules and mass participation in decision-making is confined to leadership choice in elections carefully managed by competing elites' (Robinson 1996: 49). Polyarchy, or low intensity democracy, is therefore analysed as an adjunct of US hegemony through institutions such as the US Agency for International Development (USAID) and the National Endowment for Democracy (NED) in the particular countries of the Philippines, Chile, Nicaragua, and Haiti, and is tentatively extended with reference to the former Soviet bloc and South Africa. Other recent research has similarly focused on the promotion of 'democracy' in southern Africa (Taylor 2001) as well as the construction and contestation of hegemony linked to democratisation processes in Mexico (Morton 2003c; Morton 2005c). Furthermore, aspects of neoliberalism and cultural hegemony have been dealt with in a study of mass-communications scholarship in Chile (Davies 1999). There are clearly a variety of neo-Gramscian perspectives dealing with a diversity of issues linked to the analysis of hegemony in the global political economy. The next section outlines some of the criticisms levelled against such perspectives and, in conclusion, indications are given about the directions along which current debates are proceeding.

Welcome Debate: Controversies Surrounding Neo-Gramscian Perspectives

In broad outline, neo-Gramscian perspectives have been criticised as too unfashionably *marxisant* or, alternatively, as too lacking in Marxist rigour. They are seen as unfashionable because many retain an essentially historical materialist position as central to analysis – focusing on the 'decisive nucleus of economic activity' (Gramsci, 1971: 161, Q13§18). Hence the accusation that analysis remains caught within modernist assumptions that take as foundational the structures of historical processes determining the realms of the possible (Ashley 1989: 275). However, rather than succumbing to this problem, the fallibility of all knowledge claims is accepted across neo-Gramscian perspectives. A minimal foundationalism is therefore evident, based on a cautious, contingent and transitory universalism that combines dialogue between universal values and local definitions within historically specific circumstances (Cox 1995b: 14; Cox 2000: 46).

Other commentators have alternatively decried the lack of historical materialist rigour within neo-Gramscian perspectives. According to Peter Burnham (1991), the neo-Gramscian treatment of hegemony amounts to a 'pluralist empiricism' that fails to recognise the central importance of the capital relation and is therefore preoccupied with the articulation of ideology. By granting equal weight to ideas and material capabilities, it is argued that the contradictions of the capital relation are blurred, which results in 'a slide towards an idealist account of the determination of economic policy' (Burnham 1991: 81). Hence, the categories of state and market are regarded as opposed forms of social organisation that operate separately in external relationship to one another. This leads to a supposed reification of the state as a 'thing' in itself standing outside the relationship between capital and labour (Burnham 1994).

In thinking about these criticisms, it was explained earlier how the social relations of production are taken as the starting point for understanding world order and the way in which they engender configurations of social-class forces. By thus asking what modes of social relations of production within capitalism have been prevalent in particular historical circumstances, the state is not treated as an unquestioned category. Indeed, in a way that is rather closer to Burnham's own position than he might admit, the state is treated as an aspect of the social relations of production, so that questions about the *apparent* separation of politics and economics or states and markets within capitalism are promoted. Although a fully developed theory of the state is not evident, there clearly exists a set of at least implicit assumptions about the state as a form of social relations through which capitalism and hegemony are expressed (Bieler and Morton 2003). This has led to a significant debate, concentrating on the social constitution of the economy and practices intrinsic to identity and interest formation as expressions of class power within and between states in the global political economy (Bieler et al., 2006). Moreover, ideas in the form of intersubjective meanings are accepted as part of the global political economy itself. Yet, in contrast to Burnham's claim, they are not regarded as an additional independent variable next to material properties. Turning to E.P. Thompson (1975: 261), it is clear that forms of power such as 'the law' may be seen as *both* an instrument through which definitions of property are imposed or maintained *and* an ideology in active relationship to social norms through which class relations are mediated. Productive relations are therefore in part meaningful in terms of their very definition in law. Hence the importance of Gramsci's principal emphasis, discussed in Chapter 4, on the 'material structure of ideology', and his awareness of the ideological mediations of the state through law, the family, as well as publishing houses, newspapers, journals, libraries, schools, and prisons right up to architecture, street layouts, and street names (Gramsci 1995: 155–6, Q3§49).[5] With regard to the latter, it is imperative to remember that it was not until after 1848 that certain governments in Europe began to replan cities in order to facilitate the operation of troops against revolutionaries (Hobsbawm 1962: 129). The archetypal example here was the hiring of Georges-Eugène

Haussmann (1809–92) by Napoleon III to 'modernise' Paris in the 1860s with the building of *grande boulevards* to accommodate new street cafés and single-function urban development. Richard Sennett (1977: 134–5) has summarised this as the transferance of an ecology of *quartiers* into an ecology of classes. Or, as Eric Hobsbawm (1975: 211) has stated in support:

> For the city's planners the poor were a public danger, their potentially riotous concentrations to be broken up by avenues and boulevards which would drive the inhabitants of the crowded popular quarters they replaced into some unspecified, but presumably more sanitary and certainly less perilous locations.

It is, then, through a 'material structure of ideology', involving architecture, street planning and layout, that a particular constellation of social-class forces may establish 'historically organic ideologies' that sustain validity within the consciousness of people's 'common sense' (Gramsci 1971: 376–7, Q7§19; see Bieler 2001; Bieler and Morton forthcoming). In Gramsci's own words, only those ideas can be regarded as 'organic' that 'organise human masses, and create the terrain on which men move, acquire consciousness of their position, struggle, etc.'. These are contrasted with ideas that are merely 'arbitrary, rationalistic, or "willed"', based on extemporary polemics (Gramsci 1971: 376–7, Q7§19). As explained in Chapter 4, this indicates an appreciation of the links intellectuals may have, or the wider social function they perform, in relation to the world of production within capitalist society. It is therefore an appreciation of how ideas and intellectual activity can 'assume the fanatical granite compactness of . . . "popular beliefs" which assume the same energy as "material forces"' (Gramsci 1971: 404, Q11§62).

A different series of criticisms has separately centred on the thesis of globalisation and the internationalisation of the state proposed by neo-Gramscian perspectives. In particular, Leo Panitch has argued that an account unfolds which is too top-down in its expression of power relations and assumes that globalisation is a process that proceeds from the global to the national or the outside in. The point that globalisation is authored by states is thus overlooked by using the metaphor of a transmission belt from the global to the national within the thesis of the internationalisation of the state (Panitch 1994, 2000). Abandoning the metaphor of the state as 'transmission belt', in preference for a focus on the interscalar articulation of 'national' and 'international' factors relevant to the uneven development of neoliberalism in the global political economy, will be stressed later, in Chapter 6. For the present, it has been added that this metaphor is a one-way view of internationalisation that generally: overlooks reciprocal interaction between the global and the local; overlooks mutually reinforcing social relations within the global political economy; or ignores class conflict within national social formations (Baker 1999; Ling 1996; Moran 1998). The role of the state, following Panitch's (1994: 74) argument, is still determined by struggles among social forces located within particular social formations, even though social forces may be implicated in transnational structures.

In response, it will be recalled from the above discussion that the point of departure within a neo-Gramscian approach could equally be changing social relations of production *within* forms of state *or* world order and that this is echoed within the unravelling of Gramsci's recognition of the scalar manner within which the 'national' was *nodal* rather than *dominant* in relation to 'the international' (see Chapter 3). Indeed, Cox's focus has been on historical blocs underpinning particular states and how these are connected through the mutual interests of social classes in different countries (Cox 1981: 153n.26). Further, following both Gramsci and Cox, the 'national' context is the only place where a historical bloc can be founded and where the task of building new historical blocs, as the basis for 'counter'hegemony to change world order, must begin. Gill too, although he tends to take a slightly different tack on the application of notions such as historical bloc and supremacy, is still interested in analysing attempts to constitutionalise neoliberalism at the national, regional and global levels (Gill 1995a: 422). Therefore, there is a focus on transnational networks of production and the way in which national governments have lost much autonomy in policy making, but also on how states are still an integral part of this process.

Extending these insights, it might also be important to recognise that capital is not simply something that is footloose, beyond the power of the state, but is represented by classes and fractions of classes within the very constitution of the state (Bieler and Morton 2003: 487–8). The phenomenon now recognised as globalisation, represented by the transnationalisation of production, therefore induces the reproduction of capital within different states through a process of *internalisation* between various fractions of classes within states (Poulantzas 1975: 73–6). Seen in this way, globalisation and the related emergence of transnational social forces of capital and labour has not led to a retreat of the state. Instead, there has unfolded a restructuring of different forms of state through an internalisation within the state itself of new configurations of social forces expressed by class struggle between different (national and transnational) fractions of capital and labour (see Morton 2003c, 2005c). This stress on both internalisation *and* internationalisation is somewhat different from assuming that various forms of state have become simple 'transmission belts' from the global to the national (see Bieler et al., 2006). Finally, Cox (1992: 30–1, 2002: 33) has made clear that the internationalisation of the state and the role of transnational elites (or a *nébuleuse*) in forging consensus within this process remain to be fully deciphered and need much more study. Indeed, the overall argument concerning the internationalisation of the state was based on a series of linked hypotheses suggestive for empirical investigation (Cox 1993/1996: 276). The overall position adopted on the relationship between the 'national' and 'the international', or between hegemony, supremacy, and historical bloc, may differ from one neo-Gramscian perspective to the next, but it is usually driven by the purpose and empirical context of the research.

Further criticisms have also focused on how the hegemony of transnational capital has been overestimated and how the possibility for transformation within world order is thereby diminished by neo-Gramscian perspectives (Drainville 1995). For example, the focus on elite agency in European integration processes by Gill and van Apeldoorn would indirectly reinforce a negative assessment of labour's potential role in resisting neoliberalism (Strange 2002). Analysis, notes André Drainville (1994: 125), 'must give way to more active sorties against transnational neoliberalism, and the analysis of concepts of control must beget original concepts of resistance'. It is therefore important, as Paul Cammack (1999) has added, to avoid overstating the coherence of neoliberalism and to identify materially grounded opportunities for 'counter'hegemonic action. All too often, a host of questions related to 'counter'hegemonic forms of resistance are left for future research, although the demonstrations during the 'Carnival Against Capitalism' (London, June 1999), mobilisations against the World Trade Organization (Seattle, November 1999), protests against the IMF and the World Bank (Washington, April 2000 and Prague, September 2000), 'riots' during the European Union summit at Nice (December 2000) as well as the G-8 meeting at Genoa (July 2001), and the annual World Social Forums (since 2001) and European Social Forums (since 2003), all seemingly further expose the imperative of analysing globalisation as a set of highly contested social relations. Overall, while the point about a lack of empirical investigation into concrete acts of resistance is correct in many instances, it should not be exaggerated either. It has to be noted that an analysis of the current power configuration of social forces does not by itself strengthen this configuration nor does it exclude an investigation of possible resistance. Rather, the analysis of hegemonic practices can be understood as the absolutely essential first step towards an investigation into potential alternative developments; and resistance can only be successfully mounted if one understands what precisely needs to be resisted. Moreover, several neo-Gramscian attempts dealing with issues of resistance have now been formulated and provide fertile avenues for further exploration (see Bieler and Morton 2004; Cox 1999; Gill 2000, 2001; Morton 2002). The primary task of critical scholarship is therefore to clarify resistance to neoliberal globalisation, which is the task in this book of Chapter 7.

The final and most recent criticisms have arisen from the call for a much needed engagement by neo-Gramscian perspectives with the writings of Gramsci and thus with the complex contextual issues that embroiled the Italian thinker (Germain and Kenny 1998). To overlook the latter could leave scholars open to the accusation of 'searching for gems' in the *Prison Notebooks* in order to 'save' IPE from a pervasive economism (Gareau 1993: 301). Due to the focus on historicising Gramsci earlier in the book (Chapter 2), there is no need to repeat the deliberation of these issues. It should suffice to indicate that by remaining engaged with Gramsci's thought and practice, a method can be established that is relevant to the history of ideas, acknowledging the role played by both past forms of thought and previous historical conditions in shaping subsequent ideas and existing social conditions. This method pushes one to consider what might be historically relevant as well as limited in a theoretical and practical translation of past ideas in relation to alternative conditions.

Conclusion: the Future of Hegemony?

To summarise, this chapter has introduced an alternative approach to structural issues of hegemony and world order to that in mainstream debates in IR. Notably, a case was made for a critical theory of hegemony that directs attention to relations between social interests in the struggle for consensual leadership rather than concentrating solely on state dominance. With a particular historical materialist focus and critique of capitalism it was therefore shown how various neo-Gramscian perspectives provide an alternative critical theory route to hegemony. As a result, it was argued that the conceptual framework developed by such neo-Gramscian perspectives rethinks prevalent ontological assumptions in IR due to a theory of hegemony that focuses on social-class forces engendered by changes in the social relations of production, forms of state, and world order. The account highlighted how this route to hegemony opens up questions about the social processes that create and transform different forms of state. Attention is thus drawn towards the *raison d'état*, or the basis of state power, that includes the social basis of hegemony or the configuration of social forces upon which power rests across the terrain of state–civil society relations. With an appreciation of how ideas, institutions, and material capabilities interact in the construction and contestation of hegemony, it was also possible to pay attention to issues of intersubjectivity. Therefore a critical theory of hegemony was developed that was not equated simply with dominance. As established in the focus on the political relation of hegemony, in Chapter 4, understanding the theory and practice of hegemony involves going beyond a theory of the 'state-as-force' to reappraise the front of cultural struggle (Gramsci 1995: 357, Q10I§12).

In a separate section, further developments by diverse, yet related, neo-Gramscian perspectives were outlined. Subsequently, a series of criticisms of the neo-Gramscian perspectives was also discussed. Analysis can be pushed into further theoretical and empirical areas by addressing a number of features. The first, in terms of further research directions, would be more direct consideration of the role of organised labour in contesting the latest agenda of neoliberal globalisation (Bieler 2003, 2005; Strange 2002).[6] Linked to this, second, would be greater reflection on the importance of the lack of value theory in tracing the competitive struggle between capitals in the above discussion, and thus whether there is detriment in neglecting a value-theoretic approach to the relation between appropriators and producers (Hampton 2006). Further work might therefore be done in recovering from Gramsci's writings concepts such as the tendency of the rate of profit to fall and the manner in which surplus value is appropriated from producers within the global political economy. This would entail focusing on the vertical capital–labour relation *as well as* the more common appreciation of horizontal relations between capitals (or inter-capitalist rivalry) (on the latter see van Apeldoorn

2004). After all, to cite Gramsci (1971: 402, Q7§18), 'in economics the unitary centre is value, alias the relationship between the worker and the industrial productive forces'. Third, it was also acknowledged at the outset of this chapter that any attempt to link the structural and historical characteristics of imperialism to the contemporary hegemonic phases of world order would be beyond the scope of the current study. In this regard it would be important to take up debate, in a future study, on the current dynamics of the 'new imperialism', and whether US hegemony is in a *structural* period of crisis or a *conjunctural* shift between coercion and consent in maintaining the extant world order. Suffice it to observe that militarism has long been characteristic of patterns of capital accumulation, albeit that current debate on the 'crisis' in US hegemony and/or the 'new imperialism' will have to address the mismatch between the *geographical* expression of capital accumulation within the global political economy and the *territorial* basis of governance within world order (Agnew 2005: 229; Harvey 2003: 26–31). Whilst these lines of discussion are necessarily beyond the scope of the present book, the remaining chapters will attempt to further debate on the geopolitics of globalisation by raising and contesting conjecture about whether there remains a link between globalisation and the state as a specific territorial expression of uneven development (Chapter 6). Once again it will transpire that Gramsci's role in acknowledging the scalar manner within which the 'national' was *nodal* rather than *dominant* in relation to 'the international' becomes pivotal in debates on uneven development in the contemporary global political economy. Or, put differently, how there is 'the existence within every state of several structurally diverse territorial sectors, with diverse relations of force at all levels' (Gramsci 1971: 182, Q13§17). Finally, it is also important to problematise the tactics and strategies of resistances to neoliberalism, which in Chapter 7 will entail giving further thought to subaltern social classes in mounting a critique of social–power relations within forms of state and the broader conditions of world order. Overall, what matters in this enterprise 'is the way in which Gramsci's legacy gets interpreted, transmitted and used so that it [can] remain an effective tool not only for the critical analysis of hegemony but also for the development of an alternative politics and culture' (Buttigieg 1986: 15).

6 The Global Political Economy of Uneven Development

> The construction of a national state is only made possible . . .
> by the exploitation of factors of international politics.
> — Antonio Gramsci (with Palmiro Togliatti),
> 'The Lyons Theses' (1925)

One of the themes touched on throughout this study has been the scalar manner in which Antonio Gramsci envisaged the relationship between the 'national' point of departure and 'the international'. Following Edward Said, it can be argued that Gramsci developed a critical consciousness that was geographical and spatial in its fundamental coordinates, to the degree that he situated class struggle over hegemony within 'unequal geographies'. This reveals a spatial grasp of world history rooted in social relations and geographies of complexly uneven development (Said 2000: 467–70). 'Gramsci was extremely sensitive to issues of scale, scalar hierarchies of economic, political, intellectual and moral power, and their territorial and non-territorial expressions', adds Bob Jessop (2006a: 31). This has been articulated as taking the 'national' point of departure as *nodal* rather than *dominant* when analysing processes of state formation within 'the international' (see Chapters 3 and 4). Given that the purpose of the book is to unravel the historical and contemporary relevance of Gramsci's thought and action, this chapter will dwell on such relevance by teasing out his contribution to understanding the geopolitics of globalisation, with specific reference to debates on the uneven development of neoliberalism. This will entail tackling an area of debate missing from the previous chapter, which is the extent to which globalisation marks an epoch in the history of capitalism that entails not only the rise of transnational capital but also the constitution of a transnational state. The scholarship of William Robinson has extensively asserted how current national and regional accumulation patterns reflect certain spatial distinctions specific to an integrated global capitalist configuration of power and production (see, *inter alia*, Robinson 2003, 2004a). It is precisely this configuration that he sees as bringing together a *transnational* capitalist class and a *transnational state* that is transcending the state-centrism and territorially bounded politics of space, place, and scale. In his words, 'the state as a class relation is becoming transnationalised' (Robinson 2004a: 99–100).

In this chapter, the thesis of the transnational state will be analysed in detail to argue the case for the relevance of a theory of passive revolution that encompasses the interscalar articulation of 'national' and 'international' factors relevant to understanding conditions of uneven development in the global political economy. As Bob Jessop (2006a: 38–9) counsels, this is not to argue for the simple re-scaling of concepts such as passive revolution from the 'national' to 'the international' (or transnational). Instead, it involves internalising the method of interscalar articulation encapsulated in the theory of passive revolution in order to appreciate the reciprocal influence of specific spatial scales in understanding the dynamics of global capitalism. This involves accepting *neither* the dominant fixity of state-centrism *nor* the dominant merger of transnational structures and class forces within a transnational state apparatus. Concurrently with Hannes Lacher (1999: 357), it is argued that 'national' economies are not simply governed by the political will of territorially defined constituencies but, at the same time, nor should one suppose that the imperatives of the world market alone are simply imposed on societies. By unravelling Gramsci on such subject matter in this chapter it will be possible to consider conditions of hegemony and passive revolution in relation to the continued uneven development of neoliberalism within the global political economy rather than accept the homogenisation implied in transformations toward a transnational state. As John Agnew has noted, one needs to avoid *both* the territorial trap of accepting the assumption of fixed state territoriality *and* the view that territoriality is becoming transformed into a globally undifferentiated transnational state. The critical issue, as he puts it, is 'the historical relationship between territorial states and the broader social and economic structures and geopolitical order (or form of spatial practice) in which . . . states must operate' (Agnew 1994: 77). Drawing from an earlier chapter on the history of modern state formation (Chapter 3), it will be argued that the theory of passive revolution promotes an understanding of states as 'nodes' grounded in space and situated in time. This perspective on nodal spatiality has the promise of emphasising how different scales between places relate to one another differentially over time (Agnew 2003: 13). The theory of passive revolution captures such dynamics whilst also highlighting the continued relevance of uneven development as a framing of social divisions in world order. The structure of the chapter falls as follows.

First, the theory of the transnational state and global capitalism as proposed by William Robinson will be detailed, and a critique elaborated. The latter involves developing three core problems within the theory of global capitalism and the transnational state. These are the problems of understanding: (1) the historical relationship between territorial states and capitalism; (2) the relationship between globalisation and uneven development; and (3) the spatial expression of capitalism and territoriality. On the basis of the criticisms offered, a second section will reiterate briefly the relevance of the theory of passive revolution to combining a focus on the world-historical context of uneven development and the connection to the formative influence of states. This section links to the extensive coverage of state formation and passive revolution in Chapter 3. It is at this stage of the discussion that the argument will turn to demonstrating how 'capital remains a force that by preference seeks to occupy the interconnections between separate political jurisdictions' (van der Pijl 2006: 15). A third section will therefore demonstrate the utility of a 'nodal' analysis of state transformation in relation to 'the international' by considering the rise of neoliberalism within a specific form of state. Following Robert Cox's focus on analysing social forces and relations of production, the point of departure taken to explain the historical process is the form of state in dialectical relation to world order (Cox 1981: 153n.6; see Chapter 5) – hence a concentration in this section on an empirical context of passive revolution in the history of modern Mexico that will trace how social class forces within the form of state in Mexico *authored* the globalisation of neoliberal restructuring (Panitch 1994). Put differently, the agency of particular social-class forces in constituting and reproducing the globalisation of neoliberalism is realised within the conditions of uneven development. This assists in avoiding the assumption that states are mere transmission belts in the transformation towards a transnational state (see Chapter 5). A detailed analysis of resistance movements to such neoliberal globalisation is beyond the purview of the present chapter. However, the subsequent chapter will demonstrate how the notion of passive revolution encompasses *both* the restructuring of capitalism, or the 'counter-attack of capital' organised by ruling social-class forces, *and* the articulation of 'anti-passive revolution' strategies of resistance (Buci-Glucksmann 1979: 223, 232). What might be historically *limited* in such a theoretical and practical translation of Gramsci's ideas to present conditions will then be picked up in the concluding chapter, thereby fulfilling the second ambition behind the book, namely unravelling Gramsci's approach to hegemony and passive revolution by revealing his limitations.

Contesting the Transnational State

Leslie Sklair has defined the term transnational as referring to 'forces, processes, and institutions that cross borders but do not derive their power and authority from the state'. Further, he argues that the term represents a decisive break from state-centrism by appreciating the globalising practices of a transnational capitalist class regarded as the main driver of the global capitalist system (Sklair 2001: 2–3). Taking this cue, Robinson has detailed a 'global capitalism' thesis based on the view that 'globalisation represents a new stage in the evolving world capitalist system that came into being some five centuries ago' (Robinson 2004a: 2). Globalisation therefore represents a qualitatively new epoch in the world history of capitalism 'characterised by the rise of transnational capital and by the supersession of the nation-state as the organising principle of the capitalist system' (Robinson 2003: 6). At first blush, there is much here in common with the theorising on hegemony and world order discussed in the previous chapter. Recall that Robert Cox (1981: 147) clearly indicated that 'it becomes increasingly pertinent to think in terms of a global class structure alongside or superimposed upon national class structures' (see Chapter 5). Various contributions have therefore traced the role of class fractions extant in global capitalist structures to suggest transnational class formation processes (Apeldoorn 2002, 2004; Bieler 2000, 2006; Overbeek 2004; van der Pijl 1998; Ryner 2002). The singular feature of the 'global capitalism' thesis, though, is the bold argument that 'in the emerging global capitalist configuration, transnational or global space is coming to supplant national space', with the attendant view that nation-state institutions are becoming superseded by transnational structures leading to the emergence of a transnational state (Robinson 2003: 19–20). Globalisation, it is argued, marks the rise of transnational capital *and* the supersession of the nation-state as an axis of world development *and* the interstate system as the framework of capitalist development (Robinson 2001a: 532; Robinson 2003: 12). The nation-state is no longer considered to be a 'container' for the processes of capital accumulation, class formation, or development (Robinson 2001a: 533; Robinson 2004a: 89). In its stead is the constitution of a transnational state, defined as 'a particular constellation of class forces and relations bound up with capitalist globalisation and the rise of a transnational capitalist class, embodied in a diverse set of political institutions' (Robinson 2003: 43).

> The globalisation of production has entailed the fragmentation and decentralisation of complex production chains and the worldwide dispersal and functional integration of the different segments in these chains. Yet this worldwide decentralisation and fragmentation of the production process has taken place with the *centralisation* of command and control of the global economy. (Robinson 2004a: 15 original emphasis)

A key feature, it is argued, of the epoch of globalisation is therefore not only the transformation of the state but its *supersession* as an organising principle of capitalism by a transnational state apparatus consisting of transnational class alliances involving everything from transnational corporations (TNCs); to the expansion of foreign direct investment (FDI); to cross-national mergers, strategic alliances, capital interpenetration, interlocking directorates, worldwide subcontracting, and resourcing; to the extension of special economic zones and other forms of economic organisation (Robinson 2003: 39). Local and regional accumulation patterns are assumed to reflect spatial distinctions shaped by an increasingly integrated global capitalist arrangement (Robinson 2006: 173). The transnational state, then, 'is a particular constellation of class forces and relations bound up with capitalist globalisation and the rise of a transnational capitalist class embodied in a diverse set of political institutions' (Robinson 2004a: 99). There are three main ancillary claims attached to the theory of global capitalism and the transnational state that need to be highlighted prior to examining three different lines of critique that were outlined in the introduction to this chapter.

First, the assumption about the emergence and consolidation of transnational state practices affirms the view that states act as mere transmission belts for the diffusing aspects of global capitalism. Recall here the discussion from Chapter 5 that across the different forms of state in countries of advanced and peripheral capitalism, Robert Cox generally depicted the state as a transmission belt for neoliberalism and the logic of capitalist competition from global to local spheres

Same as Cox

(Cox 1992: 31).[1] National states are rather similarly and somewhat uncritically endorsed by Robinson as transmission belts, or 'filtering devices', acting as proactive instruments in advancing the agenda of global capitalism (Robinson 2003: 45–6; Robinson 2004a: 109). Stated directly, 'national states remain important, but they become transmission belts and local executors of the transnational elite project' (Robinson 2003: 62). By way of example, so-called 'transitions' to democracy are held to be one such feature of adjustments in the political structures of state forms to the economic changes wrought by capitalist globalisation (Robinson 2003: 54). The somewhat hollow process of democratisation is here understood as the *promotion of polyarchy*, referring to 'a system in which a small group actually rules and mass participation in decision-making is confined to leadership choice in elections carefully managed by competing elites' (Robinson 1996: 49). Much heralded 'transitions' to democracy are thus 'a political counterpart to the project of promoting capitalist globalisation, and . . . "democracy promotion" and the promotion of free markets through neoliberal restructuring has become a singular process in US foreign policy' (Robinson 2000: 313). Transitions to 'polyarchy', to follow the argument, are therefore characteristic of states acting as transmission belts of capitalist globalisation. In any given case, the goal is 'to organise an elite and to *impose* it on the intervened country through controlled electoral processes' (Robinson 1996: 111, emphasis added).

Path breaking as such scholarship is on the paradigm of democratic transition and the promotion of polyarchy, the problem here is that such claims become too broad when reflecting on specific cases of the *internalisation* of democratisation and associated class struggles within forms of state (Morton 2005c). The passive diffusion of transnational capital and polyarchic political structures needs to be considered critically in relation to struggles over the restoration and contestation of class power in specific forms of state. At the centre of the argument for the state as transmission belt, then, is a disaggregation of politics and economics, so that 'class relations (and, by implication, struggle) are viewed as external to the process of [global] restructuring, and labour and the state itself are depicted as powerless' (Burnham 2000: 14). This leads to the identification of external linkages between the state and globalisation, while the social constitution of globalisation within and by social classes in specific forms of state is omitted (Bieler et al., 2006: 177–8). It is not possible to examine fully how this impacts on theories of the state, but suffice it to say that a stress on the *internalisation* of class interests within the state, through the transnational expansion of social relations, is different from assuming that various forms of state have become simple 'transmission belts' from the global to the national level (see Chapter 5). A theory of the state can therefore be presented in the very constitution and reproduction of the social relations of production as founded on the perpetuation of class contradictions (see Bieler and Morton 2003: 481–9; Bieler et al., 2006: 155–75).

The second ancillary assumption linked to the thesis of the transnational state is that global class restructuring is leading to the accelerated proletarianisation of peasant communities. This is the process by which peasants lose access to land and become workers, leading to the creation of new rural and urban working classes (Robinson 2004a: 8). Eric Hobsbawm has long heralded 'the death of the peasantry' as the most dramatic and far-reaching social change to mark the twentieth century, resulting from transformations in agricultural production. In his trilogy on the 'long nineteenth century' (from the 1780s to 1914), he argued that the peasantry as a social class were destined to fade away, a possibility that had become more actual by the late twentieth century (Hobsbawm 1994: 289–91). Whilst problems with this argumentation will be detailed in the next chapter (Chapter 7), for Hobsbawm the epochal significance of this transformation is clear, indicating that the peasantry for all practical purposes as a class has disappeared. Stemming from this, the impact of globalisation in Latin America is felt to further the proletarianisation of the peasantry in light of the restructuring of traditional agricultural production towards non-traditional agricultural exports (NTAE), such as fruits, cut flowers, ornamental plants, winter vegetables, and spices (Robinson 2003: 252–8). Again, though, in the case of de-peasantisation, the priority is granted to the project of capitalist transformation and integration of agriculture into *global structures*, to the extent that 'the structural power of the global economy is exercised through NTAE global commodity chains as a market discipline resulting in an intensified subordination of agricultural producers to transnational capital' (Robinson 2003: 189). To be sure, there are developments that have led the UN Food and Agriculture Organization (FAO), at the annual Regional Conference for Latin America and the Caribbean, to state that the rural population in the region is doomed to disappear (*Latinamerica Press*, 7 September 2005: 12, www.lapress.org). What these broad claims tend to neglect, though, is precisely the constitution and reproduction of peasantries through the dynamics of capital accumulation. Whilst the trend at the heart of claims about the 'death of the peasantry' may be evident, there is, at least, a twofold neglect in the assumption about de-peasantisation. First, of the processes of class formation evident in the transformation of the peasantry within state forms through which a range of productive activities are combined; and, second, of the purposeful agency articulated by the peasantry as a subaltern class linked to their (re)constitution within the changing dynamics of capital accumulation (Bernstein 2000). The action of groups like the Ejército Zapatista de Liberación Nacional (EZLN) in Mexico and similar agrarian-based movements, such as the Movimento dos Trabalhadores Rurais Sem Terra (MST) in Brazil calling for agrarian reform, would seemingly challenge the thesis about the inevitable demise of the peasantry (see Chapter 7).[2] Contemporary features of these rural movements in Latin America, whilst resonating with familiar motifs of peasant movements in earlier transitions to capitalism, raise new issues about the old 'agrarian question' (Brass 2002), which are neglected in the totalising assumption of de-peasantisation at the hub of the transnational state thesis.

Finally, amongst the ancillary assumptions on the emergence, consolidation, and diffusion of transnational state practices is the contention that the transnational model of development is *ending* conditions of primitive accumulation (Robinson 2003: 158). Globalisation is held as the culmination of capitalism's extensive enlargement, to the degree that 'capitalist production relations are replacing what remains of precapitalist relations around the globe. The era of the primitive accumulation of capital is coming to an end' (Robinson 2004a: 7). Yet this assumption belies Ernest Mandel's (1975: 46, original emphasis) point that:

> Primitive accumulation of capital and capital accumulation through the production of surplus-value are . . . not merely *successive* phases of economic history but also *concurrent* economic processes. Throughout the entire history of capitalism up to the present, processes of primitive accumulation of capital have constantly coexisted with the predominant form of capital accumulation through the creation of value in the process of production.

Hence the need to distinguish between two separate moments in the history of primitive accumulation: (1) primitive accumulation whose historical origins in constituting propertyless producers divorced from their means of subsistence go back to the genesis of the capitalist mode of production; and (2) the distinct situation that defines processes of primitive accumulation that already occur within a capitalist world market (Mandel 1975: 47). Ongoing primitive accumulation of capital is therefore a persistent feature of capitalist processes of production. There is unevenness to such processes of primitive accumulation of capital that are combined with processes of capitalist and pre-capitalist modes of production, which contribute greatly to shaping state sovereignty and economic development in postcolonial states, as will be explained in more detail in the next main section of this chapter. For the present discussion, issues of state territoriality and class formation within specific state forms are elided within the account of global capitalism and the somewhat passive diffusion of transnational capital at the heart of the transnational state thesis. The task of critique will now turn to covering three additional dimensions that further undermine the transnational state argument. These focus on the historical relationship between territorial states and capitalism; the relationship between globalisation and uneven development; and the spatial expression of capitalism and territoriality.

State Territoriality and Capitalism

'The nation-state system', Robinson argues, 'is a relatively fixed set of historical structures whose foundations were laid in the seventeenth century' (Robinson 2004a: 90). Territorial state sovereignty is presumed to have emerged as a consequence of the 1648 Peace of Westphalia *prior* to the subsequent unfolding of primitive accumulation of capital throughout the world. A case is then made that capitalism was a *necessary condition* for the development of the interstate system (Robinson 2004a: 102): 'The nation-state, or interstate, system is a historical outcome, the particular form in which capitalism came into being based on a complex relation between production, classes, political power and territoriality' (Robinson 2004a: 90). It is this form of the state that is then presumed to be superseded by transnational capitalism 'and with it the supersession of the interstate system as the institutional framework of capitalist development' (Robinson 2004a: 92). But, in Hannes Lacher's words, 'the sovereign state . . . was *never* truly a container of society, and modern social relations always included crucial global dimensions' (Lacher 2003: 523, original emphasis).[3] As detailed elsewhere in this book (see Chapter 3), capitalism was born into an anterior international system of state territoriality. Therefore changing configurations in the spread of the capitalist world market have had to adapt in specific ways to the international states-system that *preceded* the emergence of capitalism as a social totality (Lacher 2002: 161). The existence of territorial sovereign states and the presence of a system of states thus shaped the subsequent geopolitical expression of capitalism. 'The "modern" states, together with "modern" conceptions of territoriality and sovereignty', argues Ellen Meiksins Wood (2002c: 22), 'emerged out of social relations that had nothing to do with capitalism.' That is why Lacher (2002: 159) argues that 'capitalism came to exist politically in the form of an international system for reasons not directly driven by the nature of capital'. The geopolitical presence of capitalism was thus organised politically through the medium of a system of states (see Teschke 2003).

Understanding the historical emergence of the geopolitical structure of capitalist political space is therefore advanced best through a methodology that can address the fragmentation of the capitalist polity into a states-system that structures relations between classes *both* nationally *and* transnationally (Lacher 2002: 160). By contrast, the argument that globalisation marks an epoch in the history of capitalism that entails not only the rise of transnational capital but also the constitution and diffusion of a transnational state fails to adequately develop a history of capitalism, or to substantively historicise the relationship between the state and capitalism. In this sense, statements such as 'the nation-state and the interstate system are not a constitutive component of world capitalism . . . but a (the) historical form in which capitalism came into being' must surely be inaccurate (Robinson 2004a: 143–4). By extension, the transnational state thesis claims that there exists 'a "deterritorialisation" of the relationship of capital to the state' and that this results in 'the "pure" reproduction of social relations, that is, a process not mediated by fixed geo-political dynamics' (Robinson 2001b: 191; 2004a: 141; 2004b: 149). The overall problem, as Philip McMichael (2001: 203–5) notes, is that there is an absence of a historical theory of capitalism that prevents a realisation of how geopolitical relations are embedded in the states-system and how global relations are immanent to capitalism.

Globalisation and Uneven Development

Whilst, within the transnational state thesis, there is an emphasis on the geographical expression of global capitalism as a condition of uneven development, at the same time the unitary effect of capitalism is assumed to involve worldwide progression towards and diffusion of the presence of a transnational state. Rather than highlighting the *lack* of homology, then, between capitalism's effects through conditions of uneven development, it is argued that there is a transition toward transnational state formation. Stated most clearly, the 'particular spatial form of the uneven development of capitalism is being *overcome* by the globalisation of capital and markets and the *gradual equalisation of accumulation* conditions this involves' (Robinson 2004a: 99, emphases added). Behind this view of the gradual equalisation of accumulation conditions lies the core weakness at the heart of the transnational state thesis. It is one that collapses into an assumption about the 'homoficence of capitalism', meaning the unitary diffusion and impact of capitalism across different regions, and that overlooks the contradictions of uneven development expressed through the varied relations of capital in divergent state-formation processes (Foster-Carter 1977: 57–8, 65). The transnational state thesis assumes that capitalism is having a unidirectional impact on diverse historical and geographical state and class relations. The stress on gradual equalisation, furthermore, posits conditions of *evened development* rather than the contradictions of differential developmental conditions.[4] The consequence is that conditions of *un*even development are flattened out by the assumptions of the transnational state thesis. This leads to the omission of uneven development and the particularities of primitive accumulation and state formation in specific locations through the 'levelling' of transnational capital (Kiely 2005: 34–8).

> The new locus of development is emergent transnational social space. There is no theoretical reason to posit any necessary affinity between continued uneven development and the nation-state as the particular territorial expression of uneven development. (Robinson 2001a: 558)

A realisation of the contradictions of uneven development is thereby lost, as are expressions of class struggle inhering across different state and geopolitical spatial scales. This is despite the fact that statements such as 'the uneven development of the transnationalisation process is an important source of conflict' are made, for here the driver of uneven development should surely be the contradictions of capitalism itself rather than transnationalisation (Robinson 2004a: 134). The latter is more consequence than cause of uneven development. This confusion is itself the upshot of the problematic conception, outlined above, of the historical relationship between the rise of a territorial states-system and capitalism that is at the centre of the transnational state thesis.

The Spatial Expression of Capitalism and Sovereign Territoriality

Finally, as a consequence of the argument that nation-states are no longer relevant 'containers' of economic, social, political, and cultural processes it is also held that 'transnational or global space is coming to supplant national spaces' (Robinson 2004a: 89, 92). In the transnational state thesis, moreover, the contention is that states 'are no longer the point of "condensation" of sets of social relations. They are no longer *nodal points*' (Robinson 2004a: 143, emphasis added). The significant problem here, though, is the lack of appreciation of the articulation of capitalism through multi-scalar relations. Capitalism does not simply supplant one spatial scale for another but instead works across spatial scales located within state forms and through geopolitics. The point is not to assume the supplanting of one spatial scale for another – or to take the dominance of one spatial scale over another as a given – but to appreciate the manner in which capitalism operates through nodal rather than dominant points. This means appreciating states as political nodes in the global flow of capital, whilst eschewing claims that the global system can be reduced to a struggle between states (Bieler et al., 2006: 162, 191). Instead, according to Robinson (2004a: 123), 'decision-making and regulatory mechanisms emanating from supranational agencies and from local contingents of the transnational bourgeoisie are superimposed on national states, which themselves become absorbed into the emergent transnational state apparatus'. The focus on non-governmental organisations (NGOs) is significant here, with such networks situated within a structure linking local, national, and transnational space but transposed onto a very strict top-down vertical hierarchy. What this presents is a series of 'out-of-scale' transnational images that are supposed to be reorienting political processes whilst lacking discriminate contents (Said 1990: 8). The transnational state thesis therefore offers a *flattened ontology* that removes state forms as a significant spatial scale in the articulation of capitalism, levels out the spatial and territorial logics of capital accumulation, and elides the class struggles extant in specific locations.

In contrast to the transnational state thesis that produces out-of-scale transnational conceptions of social development, it will be argued that the theory of passive revolution provides a latent method of analysis that combines an appreciation of 'the international' causal dynamics shaping state formation processes as well as the relevance of 'national' class forces. What is pivotal to this theory of passive revolution is the very causal presence granted to 'the international' within a historical methodology that can account for the specific contexts of state formation. Building on the discussion in the earlier part of the book (see Chapter 3), it will be recalled that Gramsci traced 'how the complex problem arises of the relation of internal forces in the country in question, of the relation of international forces, and of the country's geo-political position' (Gramsci 1971: 116, Q10II§61). In Chapter 3, three dimensions of the causal presence of 'the international' and its relation to the 'national' were detailed through the theory of passive revolution. To recap, these involved a focus on uneven development represented through analysis of the colonial subjection of the global politico-economic system to Anglo-Saxon capitalism; the questioning of Fascism as a response to the intervention of Anglo-American capital in Italy; and a focus on the internationalism of Woodrow Wilson as a class doctrine of liberalism and modern capitalism. The logic of this theorising, then, was an appreciation of the different scales between geography, territory, place, and space. It reflects the need to identify a hierarchy of scales at which different policies might serve to anchor geopolitical priorities within specific spatial and geographical territorial forms. Like more recent spatially-informed approaches to world politics, my argument is that this is a historical approach to geopolitics that can recognise the complex, intersecting effects of geographical representations and the spatial distribution of material conditions on political practices (Agnew 2001; Agnew 2005). The production of spatial configurations is an active moment in the dynamic of capital accumulation to the extent that 'there is . . . no "spatial fix" [such as a transnational state] that can contain the contradictions of capitalism in the long run' (Harvey 1982: 442). The theory of passive revolution is therefore a nodal approach to the spatial division of geopolitics that throws into relief certain factors of state formation related to the emergence and transformation of the international system, thus contributing to our very understanding of 'the international' in conditioning state formation. Pulling together specific aspects outlined earlier in the book (Chapter 3), the relevance of this theory of passive revolution to geopolitical relations is illustrated in Figure 6.1.

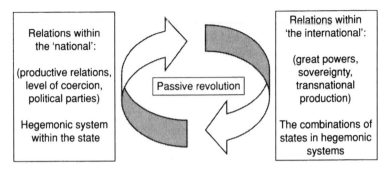

Figure 6.1   Geopolitical relations and 'the international'

After all, as Gramsci explained, the way in which world hegemony may consolidate itself is locally within a nodal national setting:

> It is in the concept of hegemony that those exigencies which are national in character are knotted together . . . A class that is international in character has – in as much as it guides social strata which are narrowly national (intellectuals), and indeed frequently even less than national: particularistic and municipalistic (the peasants) – to 'nationalise' itself in a certain sense. (Gramsci 1971: 241, Q14§68)

Relating this to Figure 6.1, the manner in which the rule of capital is maintained is thus advanced best through a nodal appreciation of state formation processes (or *relations within the 'national'* that are constitutive of hegemonic systems within states) that, in turn, are embedded within geopolitical conditions (or *relations within 'the international'* that are constitutive of states in hegemonic systems of world order). A theory of passive revolution is able to encapsulate the processes of capital accumulation shaping state forms that are embedded in the geopolitical patterning of world order.

The Passive Revolution of Capital

The notion of passive revolution captures the political rule of capital and the way in which processes of state formation are embedded in the geopolitical circumstances of uneven and combined development. The theory places emphasis on those progressive aspects of historical change during revolutionary upheaval that become undermined, resulting in the reconstitution of social relations but within *new forms* of capitalist order. It is an account of historical change that concentrates on the restoration of the social relations of capitalist development within a crisis period of modern state formation whilst also emphasising the class strategy of a ruling group. As detailed earlier (see Chapter 3), the concept of passive revolution was developed to directly refer to the Risorgimento movement, which culminated in the unification of Italy in 1860–61. Yet Gramsci also extended the term through a historical methodology to refer to nineteenth-century liberal–constitutionalist movements as a whole; to the post-Napoleonic restoration (1815–48); as well as to the restorations following the social upheaval of the First World War that culminated in the rise of Fascism. Within conditions of passive revolution 'the important thing is to analyse more profoundly . . . the fact that a state replaces the local social groups in leading a struggle of renewal' (Gramsci 1971: 105–6, Q15§59). Such a situation unfolds when the ruling class is unable to fully integrate the people through conditions of hegemony, or when 'they were aiming at the creation of a modern state . . . [but] in fact produced a bastard' (Gramsci 1971: 90, Q19§28). The thesis of passive revolution thus refers to a general principle of historical research, as we saw in Chapter 3.

Building on this, distinct processes of state formation and associated forms of sovereignty have emerged within a global division of labour shaped by the expansion of capitalism and the uneven tendencies of development characterised by a combination of capitalist, pre-capitalist and semi-capitalist relations, particularly in the postcolonial world. Following Mandel (1975: 46–81, 85–103), this process of uneven and combined development – involving uneven processes of primitive accumulation alongside combined processes of capitalist and pre-capitalist modes of production – has contributed greatly to shaping state sovereignty and economic development in postcolonial states. As discussed above, the uneven tendencies of development wrought by processes of primitive accumulation unfolded within the framework of an already existing world market and international states-system. This means that the international growth and spread of capitalism in postcolonial states occurs through ongoing processes of primitive accumulation. The latter classically entails the displacement of 'politically' constituted property by 'economic' power, entailing a 'historical process of divorcing the producer from the means of production' and generating propertyless individuals compelled to sell their labour (Marx 1887/1996: 705–6). Yet, due to the presence of a territorialised state framework, processes of primitive accumulation

in the postcolonial world became heavily reliant on the state as the
locus of capital accumulation. 'Much has therefore depended on
how the state has been constituted and by whom, and what the
state was and is able or prepared to do in support of or in opposition
to processes of capital accumulation' (Harvey 2003: 91). As Mandel
(1975: 54) has pointedly put it, in these instances, the state acts as
the 'midwife of modern capitalism'.

It is within this context of uneven and combined development
and through the specific class conflicts ascribed to processes of
capital accumulation that the history of state formation and
passive revolution can be related. In the postcolonial context, state
formation unfolds in a world-historical context of uneven and
combined development with a formative influence on political
structures being the international system of states (Halliday 1987:
220, 226). Imitative behaviour within such states coping with social
crises generated by the circumstances of uneven and combined
development therefore entailed attempts to create a modern state
as the necessary precondition for the furtherance of capitalism. This
means that the universal rule of capital through passive revolutions
– or state-led attempts at developmental catch-up – often resulted in
a 'bastard birth' of 'strikingly incomplete' achievements besides the
construction of a modern state (Anderson 1992: 115). Frequently in
such cases, state formation literally became a process of *étatisation*
involving transplanted political structures introduced, sometimes
by force, as an imported form of political centralisation (Badie and
Birnbaum 1983: 74, 97–9). As Fred Halliday (1992: 458–9) has put it,
the result was a 'pathos of semi-peripheral escape' within which the
emergence of capitalism required a state to impose its reproduction
over a specific territory. Or, recalling Eric Hobsbawm's (1975: 73,
166) elaboration, mentioned in Chapter 3, in underdeveloped parts
of the world, state formation processes were often mimetic of mid-
nineteenth-century European national unifications, as 'countries
seeking to break through modernity are normally derivative and
unoriginal in their ideas, though necessarily not so in their practices'.
In sum, according to Partha Chatterjee (1986: 43), the strategy of
'passive revolution becomes the historical path by which a "national"
development of capital can occur without resolving or surmounting
those contradictions' of capital. It represents not only the type
of class strategy undertaken in establishing and maintaining the
expansion of the state but also the ways in which capitalism is
forced to revolutionise itself *whenever* hegemony is weakened or a

social formation cannot cope with the need to expand the forces of production.

'To sharpen it', continues Chatterjee (1986: 30), 'one must examine several historical cases of "passive revolutions" in their economic, political and ideological aspects.' It is not possible here to develop a complete historical sociology of modern state formation in Mexico, which is rightfully the subject of a separate study.[5] However, the next section develops one such phase in the history of modern state formation and uneven development in Mexico, within which the rise of a strategy of neoliberal capitalist accumulation is situated, whilst highlighting the reciprocal influence of the 'national' *and* 'the international' in a scalar manner within which the form of state as a point of departure is taken as *nodal* rather than *dominant*. As Marx (1894/1959: 25) himself noted, there is a need to 'locate and describe the concrete forms which grow out of the movements of capital as a whole' so as to 'approach step by step the form which they assume on the surface of society in the action of different capitals upon one another', which is the task of the next section.[6]

The History of Mexico Seen as a Struggle of 'Passive Revolution'?

One way of examining the social constitution of neoliberalism in Mexico, and the social bases of the state, meaning the specific configuration of class forces that supports the basic structure of state–civil society relations, is to distinguish *analytically* between an accumulation strategy and a hegemonic project. Following Jessop (1990: 198–9, 207–8), an accumulation strategy defines a specific economic 'growth model', including the various extra-economic preconditions and general strategies appropriate for its realisation. The success of a particular accumulation strategy relies upon the complex relations among different fractions of capital as well as the balance of forces between dominant and subordinate classes, hence the importance of a hegemonic project. This involves the mobilisation of support behind a concrete programme that brings about a unison of different interests. An *accumulation strategy* is primarily oriented towards the relations of production and thus to the balance of class forces, whilst *hegemonic projects* are typically oriented towards broader issues grounded in not only the economy but the whole sphere of state–civil society relations. These are not to be regarded as separate realms, but as two aspects of political action grounded in the same social relations of production (see Bieler et al.,

2006: 164–72). As Jessop (1990: 201) indicates, 'the crucial factor in the success of accumulation strategies remains the integration of the circuit of capital and hence the consolidation of support within the dominant fractions and classes', i.e. the struggle over hegemony. My argument is that the uneven development of neoliberalism in Mexico, as an expression of capitalist world development, can be understood within these terms (see also Morton 2003c). The conflicts of interest that eventually culminated in the accumulation strategy of neoliberalism, reflected especially in the presidency of Carlos Salinas de Gortari (1988–94), were pursued whilst reconfiguring the hegemonic project of the once-ruling Institutional Revolutionary Party (PRI). This resulted in fragmentation, leading to a contemporary crisis of authority in Mexico. It now remains to give an account of the context within which the conflicts of interest between class forces took place that led to changes in the form of state in Mexico, before considering more contemporary circumstances.

The Rise of a Neoliberal Accumulation Strategy in Mexico

In order to account for the period that Mexicans refer to as the 'tragic dozen' (1970–82), the determinant factor for the transition from an import substitution industrialisation (ISI) strategy of accumulation to that commonly referred to as the neoliberal strategy of *salinismo* has been seen as a set of institutional changes *within the organisation of the state* (Centeno 1994: 41). The crucial phase that laid the basis for this shift in accumulation strategy in Mexico was the period in the 1970s that set the stage for subsequent developments (Dussel Peters 2000: 45).

By the 1970s, during the *sexenio* (six-year term) of Luis Echeverría (1970–76), the government needed to revive its deteriorating legitimacy and responded with a neo-populist programme of political and social reforms. Hence the Echeverría administration embarked on a macroeconomic strategy of 'shared development' within a supposed *apertura demócrata* (democratic opening) to forge a populist coalition between national industrialists, peasants, urban marginals, disillusioned labour sectors, students, and the middle classes. Yet, faced by pressure from internationally linked industrialists, Echeverría was unable to implement sufficient tax increases to support public spending directed towards national industry and the working- and middle-class sectors. The inability to implement tax increases on internationally linked capital resulted in foreign borrowing becoming the major source of financing for development policies (Davis 1993: 55). Also, due to expanded state intervention in the economy and the increasingly anti-private-sector rhetoric, the government began to lose the support of significant sectors of capital. Such state intervention increasingly alienated the private sector and as a result 'the alliance that ha[d] existed between state and national capital was severely strained' (Centeno 1994: 69). An indication of this was the rise of the private sector in vocally articulating its opposition, notably with the founding of the Business Co-ordinating Council (CCE) in 1975, which for the first time proposed economic policies in opposition to the government, following the impact of the oil crisis of 1973 on Mexico's economic performance. It is important to note that whilst neoliberalism had *not* taken hold at this time, crucial cleavages within the organisation of the state were developing that would lead to shifts in capitalist accumulation.

Pivotal in preparing the conditions for such changes was the Mexican financial crisis of 1976. As James Cockcroft (1983: 259) has put it, 'capital flight, noncompetitiveness of Mexican products, dollarisation of the economy, and IMF pressures forced a nearly 100 per cent devaluation of the peso in late 1976, almost doubling the real foreign debt . . . as well as the real costs of imported capital goods – to the detriment of nonmonopoly firms and the advantage of the TNCs'. Yet the financial crisis can be seen to be as much related to the expansionary public-sector expenditure policies driven by the crisis of the PRI as to the macroeconomic disequilibria, driven by structural change in the globalising political economy linked to US inflation. Whilst the IMF certainly imposed austerity measures and surveillance mechanisms on Mexico, it has been argued that these were less violatory than feared – although they did have a strong impact in altering the internal distribution of power between social classes in Mexico (Whitehead 1980: 846–7, 851).

At almost the same time, large oil reserves were also discovered, estimated by 1982 at 72 billion barrels, with probable reserves at 90–150 billion and potential reserves at 250 billion, amounting to the sixth largest reserves in the world (Cockcroft 1983: 261). Hence the political economy of Mexico became dependent on petroleum-fuelled development under the administration of José López Portillo (1976–82), whilst attempts were made to balance the tensions between competing social classes. However, a coherent course, capable of satisfying the interests of national and internationally linked capital in Mexico, was not set. By the time world oil prices dropped in

1981, leading to reduced oil revenues, accelerating debt obligations, and a surge in capital flight, Mexico faced another financial crisis, which initially led to the nationalisation of the banks on 1 September 1982. This was a 'last-ditch effort' to recoup revenues for the public sector and reassert some form of state autonomy, but it resulted in reinforcing private-sector opposition, capital flight, inflation, and balance of payments problems (Davis 1993: 61).

As with the earlier crisis, the result of the 1982 debt crisis was a combination of mutually reinforcing factors, both within the globalising political economy and the form of state in Mexico.

> The crisis was precipitated by the world oil glut, a world economic recession, and rising interest rates in the United States, but its root causes were domestic: excessively expansionary monetary and social policies, persistent overvaulation of the peso, over-dependence of the public sector on a single source of revenue (oil exports), a stagnant agriculture sector (at least that part which produced basic foodstuffs for domestic consumption), an inefficient and globally uncompetitive industrial plant, excessive labour force growth . . ., a capital-intensive development model that made it impossible to create an adequate employment base, endemic corruption in government, and resistance by entrenched economic and political interests to structural reforms. (Cornelius 1985: 87–8)

This resulted in another IMF austerity programme – involving reductions in government subsidies for foodstuffs and basic consumer items, increases in taxes on consumption, and tight wage controls targeted to control inflation – that the Mexican administration implemented by exceeding planned targets. Therefore, the crisis arose as a result of a conjunction of factors that also included the rise of technocrats – under way throughout the 1970s – which led to the ascendancy of the accumulation strategy of neoliberalism. Consistent with the thesis on the internationalisation of the state detailed in the previous chapter, a crucial issue at this time was the institutional career paths of the elite, which began to alter, so that ministries associated with banking and finance planning provided the career experience likely to lead to the upper echelons of government. What eventually unfolded in Mexico were specific transnational fractions of capital that would come to fuse the concerns of state managers, sectors of the business elite, large conglomerates tied to the export sector such as the *maquila* (in-bond) strategy of export-led industrialisation, and sectoral reform of agricultural production. Notably this was the context within which the Ministry of Programming and Budget (SPP) came to rise to institutional predominance as a pivotal *camarilla* (clique) within the organisation of the state.

The SPP was created in 1976 and culminated the process of taking economic policy making away from the Ministry of the Treasury and Public Credit (SHCP). Overall, not only was direct control secured over the most important resources of information for plans and projects in the bureaucracy, but competing factions within the PRI could also be circumvented. Significantly, the three presidents before president Ernesto Zedillo (1994–2000) all originated from agencies related to these changes, with López Portillo (1976–82) heralding from SHCP and Miguel de la Madrid (1982–88) and Carlos Salinas (1988–94) from SPP. By 1983 almost 60 per cent of all cabinet-level appointees had started their careers in these sectors and over 80 per cent had some experience within them, whilst in the Salinas cabinet 33 per cent had experience in SHCP and 50 per cent had worked in SPP (Centeno and Maxfield 1992: 74). The rise of such technocrats, in line with the framework for understanding state transformation described in Chapter 5, ensured that precedence was accorded to ministries of finance like SPP that would subordinate other ministries and prioritise policies more attuned to transnational economic processes. The growing influence of neoliberal ideas in Mexico can therefore be linked to the existence of a transnational capitalist class connecting IMF analysts, private investors, and bank officials as well as government technocrats in and beyond the PRI. This is how the internationalisation of the state proceeded in Mexico. To cite Gramsci, it was a process whereby 'in the political party the elements of an economic social group get beyond that moment of their historical development and become agents of more general activities of a national and international character' (Gramsci 1971: 16, Q12§1).

A pivotal factor in the formation of this transnational capitalist class in Mexico was the move during the Echeverría presidency after the oil boom of 1975–76 to expand scholarships to foreign universities as a method of integrating dissidents radicalised by the massacre of students at Tlatelolco on 2 October 1968 (Berins Collier 1992: 66). Thus, throughout the 1970s, not only was there a dramatic increase in the educational budget *within* Mexico, leading to a 290 per cent increase in the number of university students between 1970 and 1976, but the number of scholarships for study

abroad increased even more dramatically (Centeno 1994: 152n.25).
It can therefore be argued that the dissemination of foreign ideas in
Mexico increased as a direct result of the oil boom. This led to many
tecnócratas adopting a more conservative ideology whilst becoming
dependent on the president for their subsequent governmental
position – hence resulting in the crucial rise of *camarillas* that shifted
institutional loyalty from a particular ministry or subgroup within the
bureaucracy to close political and personal links with the president.
It was this technocratic elite that took for granted the exhaustion
of the previous ISI development strategy and engendered a degree
of social conformism favouring the adoption of an accumulation
strategy of neoliberalism. Yet it was hardly questioned to what extent
such structural problems were not just intrinsic to ISI but related
also to a series of exogenous shocks, such as the oil crisis, combined
with erroneous decisions made in the 1970s following the oil boom.
Overall, though, the overriding significance of the above changes was
that the rise of *tecnócratas* (or the 'cult of technocracy') in Mexico
was advanced by links with transnational capital within the form
of state during a period of structural change in the 1970s (Cockcroft
1983: 217).

For example, during this period of structural change or the
'reformation of capitalism' in Mexico, fractions of a transnational
capitalist class became influential in shaping the *maquila* (in-bond)
strategy of export-led industrialisation fuelled by foreign investment,
technology, and transnational capital (Sklair 1993: 13–14). Whilst
the *maquila* industry has its roots in the Border Industrialisation
Programme (BIP), introduced in 1965 after the United States ended
the Bracero Programme (which provided a legal basis for labour
migration from Mexico to the United States), it was not until the
1970s that economic promotion committees began to bring to fruition
the earlier visions of border industrialisation. The latter particularly
proceeded under the auspices of the Secretariat of Commerce and
Industrial Development (SECOFI), the industry ministry, within de la
Madrid's administration. Between 1979 and 1985 *maquilas* increased
by 40 per cent and employees almost doubled (Sklair 1993: 70).

At an early stage in this transformation, the interests of private
capital were represented by organisations within the National
Chamber of Manufacturing Industries (CANACINTRA). Along with
other capitalist groups – such as the Confederation of Chambers of
Industry (CONCAMIN), the Confederation of National Chambers of
Commerce, Services and Tourism (CONCANACO) and the Employers'

Confederation of the Republic of Mexico (COPARMEX) – the major fractions of large and medium-sized manufacturers co-ordinated and consolidated capital's influence over the state. This influence proceeded further when such capitalist organisations regrouped in 1975 through the Business Co-ordinating Council (CCE), to represent the interests of large-scale monopoly capital within the state. The *maquila* industry was thus promoted, nurtured, and supervised by fractions of a transnational capitalist class in Mexico, but through processes of carefully managed state–labour–business relations within the form of state that later developed into a full-blown export-led strategy of industrialisation (Sklair 1993: 227). However, the interests of transnational capital also reached beyond the *maquila* industry to gradually secure the integration of Mexico into the global political economy. Hence, 'the official agricultural policies of the Díaz Ordaz and Echeverría periods [also] promoted transformations which deepened the integration of local farmers into a transnational system of agricultural production' (Gledhill 1996: 183). One consequence of this effort to reproduce the accumulation strategy of neoliberalism in Mexico was the 1992 reform of collective *ejido* landholdings enshrined in Article 27 of the Mexican Constitution, undertaken as a prelude to entry into the North American Free Trade Agreement (NAFTA) in 1994 (Craske and Bulmer-Thomas 1994). This led to the increased capitalisation of land – involving changing property relations and shifts from rank-based social ties and communal commitments of civil–religious hierarchies to cash derived from wage labour – that would impact on forms of resistance such as the Ejército Zapatista de Liberación Nacional (EZLN) (see Chapter 7).

An additional feature that also became crucial in the struggle over the neoliberal accumulation strategy was the introduction of the Economic Solidarity Pact (PSE) in 1987. The PSE was initially a mixed or 'heterodox' programme that aimed to tame the current account deficit and inflation based on a commitment to fiscal discipline, a fixed exchange rate and concerted wage and price controls. It has been heralded as instrumental in achieving a successful renegotiation of external debt following the debt crisis of 1982, in line with the Baker (1985) and Brady (1989) Plans, and further radicalising the import liberalisation programme following Mexico's entry into the General Agreement on Tariffs and Trade (GATT) (Urquidi 1994: 58).

Overall, three components of the PSE were crucial: the government's pledge in favour of the acceleration of privatisation and deregulation; the centrality awarded to the CCE; and the use of large retailers' market power to discipline private firms and further ensure the participation of business elites (Heredia 1996: 138). The CCE – itself formed from a forerunner of big-business private-sector groups within the capitalist class known as the Mexican Businessmen's Council (CMHN) – became pivotal in initiating and implementing the PSE (Whitehead 1989: 210). As indicated earlier, the class interests of the CCE became centred around a 'transnationalised' segment of national capital, including direct shareholders of large conglomerates tied to the export sector, with experience in elite business organisations (Luna 1995: 83). Subsequently, many of the CCE leaders became more closely linked with the PRI via committees and employers' associations in order to increase interest representation within the state. Little wonder, therefore, that the class interests represented by the CCE had a huge impact on the policies implemented by the PRI, including increased privatisation (Ugalde 1994: 230). One commentator has gone so far as to argue that the relationship between the private sector and the political class became part of a narrow clique exercising a 'private hegemony', so that

> it would be no exaggeration to say that this alliance was based on a carefully thought-out strategy to bring public policy in line with private sector demands, to effect a global reform of the relationship between the state and society, and hence to redesign Mexico's insertion into the emerging neoliberal global order [of uneven development]. (Ugalde 1996: 42)

As a consequence, there was a shift in the PSE from a commitment to state–labour corporatist relations to a disarticulation, but not severing, of the state–labour alliance in favour of the overriding interests of capital. This has been variously recognised as a form of 'new unionism' or neo-corporatism, 'an arrangement involving the reduction of centralised labour power and the participation of labour in increasing productivity' (Teichman 1996: 257). The privatisation of the Mexican Telephone Company (TELMEX) in 1990, one of the pinnacles of the privatisation programme, particularly reflected the strategy of 'new unionism'. This not only involved manipulation of the Mexican Telephone Workers' Union (STRM), one of the key labour organisations used to secure privatisation; it also entailed Salinas permitting the leader of STRM, Hernández Juárez, to create an alternative labour federation, the Federation of Goods and Services Unions (FESEBES), to further facilitate privatisation. Hence labour became more dependent on the PRI during the privatisation of TELMEX, which generated new resources for corruption and clientelism and lessened union democracy within STRM (Clifton 2000). What is important here, then, is that the accumulation strategy associated with neoliberalism did not involve a wholesale retreat of the state nor did the state act as a simple conduit or 'transmission belt' for neoliberal globalisation. As Centeno (1994: 195) has commented, 'the pacto [PSE] demonstrated that the *técnocratas* were not generic neoliberals who applied monetarist policies indiscriminately but were willing to utilise a variety of mechanisms to establish control over the economy'. What the case of Mexico does exhibit, though, is precisely the internalisation of certain transnational class interests conducive to a specific reorganisation of production relations and changes in the form of state. The analysis now turns from discussing the details of how the neoliberal strategy of accumulation privileged particular social relations of production in Mexico to address how the interlinked hegemonic project of the PRI was also altered and undermined.

The Changing Circumstances of PRI Hegemony

Intrinsically linked to changes in the social relations of production stemming from the 1970s was an increase in the sources of political instability in Mexico. 'Political struggles over national economic policy began in the early 1970s when problems associated with import-substituting industrialisation began to mount' (Cook, Middlebrook and Horcasitas 1994: 18). These struggles were manifest in the *sexenios* of Echeverría (1970–76) and López Portillo (1976–82) to the extent that the PRI faced problems involving an erosion of political legitimacy following the Tlatelolco massacre in 1968, a discontented urban middle class, disaffection with the ISI accumulation strategy, the emergence of new opposition movements outside the officially recognised party system, the additional emergence of urban and rural guerrilla movements, and the declining ability of the PRI to compete with registered opposition parties (Middlebrook 1993).

For instance, the National Coordinating Committee of Educational Workers (CNTE), founded in 1979, came to challenge, particularly in the peasant communities of Chiapas, the state-imposed and privileged position of the National Education Workers' Union (SNTE), established in 1943 (Foweraker 1993). This was also the period when independent unions articulated a so-called *insurgencia obrera* (labour insurgency) to question the lack of autonomy and democracy of official unions and to articulate demands across a variety of sectors beyond purely economic concerns (Carr 1991: 136–9). Yet, as a harbinger of reforms under the neoliberal accumulation strategy, the López Portillo administration coercively suppressed many of these opposition movements and implemented economic reforms in favour of the private sector as a prelude to introducing the Law on Political Organisations and Electoral Processes (LOPEE) in 1977. Between 1976 and 1979, the dynamism of the *insurgencia obrera* faded and became dominated by the themes of economic crisis and austerity (Carr 1991: 137). At the same time, the LOPEE became an attempt to manage political liberalisation within the current of the *apertura democráta* (democratic opening) by enlarging the arena for party competition and integrating leftist political organisations whilst inducing them to renounce extra-legal forms of action. The measures, for example, involved the Mexican Communist Party (PCM) obtaining its *official* registration as a political party that in 1979 led to its first legal participation in elections since 1949. Subsequently, in 1981, the PCM merged with four other left-wing parties to establish the Unified Socialist Party of Mexico (PSUM) (Carr 1985). Thus the PCM, the oldest communist party in Latin America at that time, effectively dissolved itself whilst attempting to compete electorally within the parameters of the LOPEE reform (Cockcroft 1998: 265). The reform, therefore, was more than a simple co-optation measure. It was designed to frame and condition the very institutional context of opposition movements and constituted the construction of a specific legal and institutional terrain that was capable of containing popular demands by defining the terms and fixing the boundaries of representation and social struggle (Foweraker 1993: 11–12). It thus epitomised the structures of passive revolution shaped by the unevenness of economic and social development: an attempt to introduce aspects of change through the state as arbiter of social conflict. In the words of Echeverría the political reform strived to 'incorporate the majority of the citizens and social forces into the *institutional* political process' (as cited by Pansters 1999: 241, original emphasis). As Kevin Middlebrook (1995: 223–4) has argued, this was a limited political opening that was essential at a time of severe social and political tension in order to balance stringent economic austerity measures with policies designed to diffuse widespread discontent. The capacity of labour to articulate an alternative vision for Mexican economic and social development through either official or independent unions, evident in the 1970s, thus declined throughout the 1980s to become scarcely evident a decade later (Cook 1995: 77–94).

What was evolving in the form of state at this time in Mexico, therefore, within the context of structural change in the global political economy, was a shift in the hegemonic influence of the PRI. More accurately, the attempt at political reform in the 1970s was an indication of the ailing class hegemony of the PRI. No longer capable of representing class-transcending interests, the PRI began to reorient the social relations of production towards a new hierarchy in favour of particular class forces. As a result it is possible to perceive the fraying and unravelling of PRI hegemony in the 1970s. The LOPEE political reform was a clear indication of an attempt to balance the competing demands of subaltern classes with those of the private sector and transnational capital in Mexico. It was a response to the erosion of support for the basic structure of the political system.

Yet it is not easily explained as the exercise of 'normal' hegemony as outlined in Chapter 4. Hegemony in this sense relies on the organic equilibrium of a relationship between leaders and led, rulers and ruled, based on consent. Instead, the PRI became increasingly unable to conceal its real predominance and relied on more coercive measures. 'Between consent and coercion', Gramsci (1971: 80n.49, Q19§24) notes, 'stands corruption/fraud (which is characteristic of certain situations when it is hard to exercise the hegemonic function, and when the use of force is too risky).' This is a situation in which the party turns 'into a narrow clique which tends to perpetuate its selfish privileges by controlling or even stifling opposition forces' (Gramsci 1971: 189, Q13§36). It can then entail a shift in the threshold of power from consensual to coercive means indicative of state crisis and the disintegrative elements of catastrophic equilibrium. As a counterpart to the neoliberal accumulation strategy, the PRI increasingly began to reflect these traits of passive revolution throughout the 1980s.

For example, during the Salinas *sexenio*, attempts were particularly made to reconstruct history in order to naturalise radical neoliberal changes to the political economy (Salinas de Gortari 2002). As a result, neoliberalism came to represent a 'hegemonic shift' in the attempt to dismantle the nationalism of the Mexican Revolution linked to ISI and displace its political symbolism as a focal point of national consciousness (Powell 1996: 40). Yet the government's ideological use of the legacy of the Mexican Revolution was not merely a straightforward foil for neoliberalism but, instead, was adapted to specific conditions in Mexico. This fundamental reconstruction of the hegemony of the PRI and transformation of state–civil society relations within Mexico was particularly exhibited through projects like the National Solidarity Programme (PRONASOL).

Following the continued crisis of representation facing the PRI and the tenuous majority Salinas received from the electorate in 1988, a significant attempt was made to try to maintain hegemony. A notable feature in this effort was PRONASOL, a poverty alleviation programme combining government financial support and citizen involvement to design and implement community development and public works projects. As the PRI had changed from an inclusive party designed to cover all segments of society to an exclusive one in which only some sectors were represented, PRONASOL was emblematic of the attempt to shore up the loss of hegemonic acquiescence (Centeno 1994: 224). It combined material and institutional aspects, focusing on social services, infrastructure provision, and poverty alleviation in order to rearrange state–civil society relations and the coalitional support of the PRI (Cornelius, Craig and Fox 1994: 3). There were three main objectives of PRONASOL. First, it attempted to adapt the state's traditional social role to new economic constraints and to redefine the limits of its intervention in the context of a neoliberal strategy of accumulation. Second, it attempted to diffuse potential social discontent through selective subsidies, accommodate social mobilisation through 'co-participation', and undermine the strength of left-wing opposition movements. Third, it attempted to restructure local and regional PRI elites under centralised control (Dresser 1991: 1–2). PRONASOL was clearly a targeted attempt to buttress both the accumulation strategy of neoliberalism and the hegemony of the PRI that was under threat from those very changes.

Emanating from the Salinas *camarilla* that had dominated the SPP, PRONASOL was officially described as an attempt to modernise, pluralise, and democratise state–civil society relations in Mexico as part of the doctrine of 'social liberalism': 'a mode of governance that ostensibly seeks to avoid the worst excesses of both unfettered, free market capitalism and heavy-handed state intervention-ism, by steering a careful middle course between these "failed" extremes' (Carlos Salinas, as cited by Cornelius, Craig, and Fox 1994: 4). Usurping the language and mobilising role of grassroots organisations, PRONASOL was itself portrayed as a 'new grassroots movement', empowering citizens through 'an experience of direct democracy', whilst also redefining members of traditional corporatist organisations as 'consumers' of electricity, improved infrastructure, and educational scholarships (Carlos Salinas, as cited by Cornelius, Craig, and Fox 1994: 6–7). This new style of thinking amongst state officials 'was reinforced by ideas recommending the involvement of the poor and NGOs in anti-poverty projects promoted by many international actors, including international financial institutions such as the World Bank and the Inter-American Development Bank, the United Nations, and international donors and development specialists' (Piester 1997: 473). Between 1989 and 1993, the World Bank directly lent PRONASOL US$350 million to improve rural service provision and to support regional development in four of Mexico's poorest states – Oaxaca, Guerrero, Hidalgo, and Chiapas – whilst the Bank also supported a health and nutrition pilot project (Cornelius, Craig, and Fox 1994: 16).

Despite the rhetoric, though, PRONASOL preserved and even reinforced presidential rule and complemented the established bureaucracy. As Denise Dresser (1991: 2) states, 'the politics of PRONASOL sheds light on why hegemonic parties like the PRI can survive even when threatened by powerful alternative organisations, and why the party has apparently been able to revive after a period of crisis and decline'. Essentially, PRONASOL was crucial to maintaining the lagging effect of the PRI's hegemony, because it provided the political conditions for sustaining the neoliberal accumulation strategy, notably through a modernisation of populism and traditional clientelist and corporatist forms of co-optation. This was carried out through a process of *concertación*, understood as the negotiation of co-operative agreements between social movements and the state involving division and demobilisation. The *concertación* strategies espoused by PRONASOL represented a convergence of interests between those of the popular organisations and the technocratic sectors within the PRI and the government (Dresser 1991: 32). Thus, whilst the Salinas administration presented neoliberalism as a hegemonic project in Mexico, it used PRONASOL to create a sense of inclusion and a durable base of support within civil society. This objective was also fulfilled within PRONASOL by denying the existence of class antagonisms whilst at the same time claiming to transcend class differences (Dresser 1994: 147).

By the time PRONASOL became institutionalised within the Ministry of Social Development (SEDESOL), in 1996, it was clear that the programme had been successful in sustaining the passive revolution of neoliberalism (Soederberg 2001): meaning that it was intrinsic in changing the correlation of class forces in Mexico – to supervise the 'counter-attack of capital' through passive revolution – within which there was a transformation of the elite from arbiter of class conflict to ruling in its own interests (Hodges and Gandy 2002a: 246). PRONASOL incorporated potentially threatening leaders, alternative programmes, and ideas by nullifying substantive differences. Hence, despite the neoliberal accumulation strategy making it increasingly difficult to conceal the real predominance of its narrow basis of interest representation, the PRI still managed to exert some form of dwindling hegemony albeit relying more on coercion than on true leadership. The increasing prevalence of coercion throughout the late 1980s and 1990s, particularly reflected in impunity towards human rights violations evident in the rise in the number and profile of political assassinations and kidnappings, bears this out. As Wil Pansters (1999: 256, original emphasis) puts it, 'the combined result of neoliberal economic adjustment, institutional malfunctioning and the decomposition of personalistic networks and loyalties [wa]s . . . an increase in violence *at all* societal levels.'

Hence the view that there was a worsening crisis of hegemony in Mexico throughout the phase of neoliberal restructuring in the 1980s and 1990s. It was a situation when 'the ruling class has lost its consensus, i.e. is no longer "leading" but only dominant, exercising coercive force alone'; it meant 'precisely that the great masses ha[d] become detached from their traditional ideologies, and no longer believe[d] what they used to believe previously' (Gramsci 1971: 275–6, Q3§34). As the prominent intellectual Carlos Fuentes expressed it at the time: 'It is as though the PRI has gone out to kill itself, to commit suicide. There are Priístas killing Priístas. . . . What we see is the internal decomposition of a party, which has, in effect, completed its historic purpose' (*Mexico and NAFTA Report*, 8 December 1994).[7] The PRI, to summarise in Gramsci's words, became a party that increasingly existed as 'a simple, unthinking executor . . . a policing organism, and its name of "political party" [became] simply a metaphor of a mythological character' (Gramsci 1971: 155, Q14§70). Social order was increasingly regressive, to the extent that the party was 'a fetter on the vital forces of history', so that it had 'no unity but a stagnant swamp . . . and no federation but a "sack of potatoes", i.e. a mechanical juxtaposition of single units without any connection between them' (Gramsci 1971: 155, Q14§70; 190, Q13§36).

As a result, the changes inaugurated in Mexico that led to the promotion of neoliberalism can be understood as an expression of passive revolution operative within a conjuncture of capitalist world development. Neoliberalism continued to reflect the incomplete process of state and class formation in Mexico that was never truly settled after the Mexican Revolution (Hodges and Gandy 2002b; Morton 2006b). It represented a furtherance of particular path-dependent responses to forms of crisis and thus a strategy developed by the ruling classes to signify the restructuring of capitalism, or the 'counter-attack of capital', in order to ensure the expansion of capital and the introduction of 'more or less far-reaching modifications . . . into the economic structure of the country' (Gramsci 1995: 350, Q10I§9). Neoliberalism, therefore, can be summarised as less 'tightly linked to a vast local economic development, but . . . instead the reflection of international developments which transmit their ideological currents to the periphery' (Gramsci 1971: 116, Q10II§61). In Mexico, hegemony became limited to privileged groups and was based on a central core of elite and exclusionary decision making that enacted rhetorically 'revolutionary' changes in the social relations of production, through the neoliberal accumulation strategy alongside engineered social and political reform. Needless to say, as the contradictions of neoliberalism become more apparent, the 'path-dependent legacies of neoliberal errors' will also need to be addressed (Jessop 2002: 169).

However, it should not be presumed on the basis of the above argument that both the accumulation strategy and the hegemonic project of neoliberalism entailed the erosion of state power or the conversion of the state into a 'transmission belt' for transnational capital. Neoliberalism in Mexico did not involve the dismantling, or retreat, of the state, but the rearrangement of social relations into a new hierarchy. As Dresser (1994: 155) has commented,

> Even though neoliberal policy currents underscore the importance of reducing the economic power of the state, the Mexican case reveals that the imperatives of political survival will often dictate the need for continued state intervention through discretionary compensation policies.

The modernisation, rather than dismantling, of the state through PRONASOL was thus based on a 'neo-corporatist' arrangement that was pivotal in bolstering the accumulation strategy *and* hegemonic project of neoliberalism (Craske 1994). Such nuances in the transformation of the Mexican state are revealed through a focus on the form of state, which is taken as a 'nodal' point of departure in assessing the geopolitical relations of neoliberal capitalist accumulation in the context of uneven development.

Conclusion: the Shifting Sands of Hegemony

One of the contentions of this chapter has been that the process of historically specific interest representation and class struggle reflected in the transition from ISI to neoliberal capitalist accumulation is grasped better by a focus on how the agenda of neoliberalism was constituted, or *authored*, by particular social class forces within the form of state. The theory of passive revolution reveals the different scales of power and production under capitalist accumulation processes, whilst prompting one to take as 'nodal', rather than dominant, the 'national' point of departure in tracing the geopolitics of capitalist uneven development. The analysis of the passive revolution of capital linked to the rise of neoliberal capitalist accumulation in Mexico bears out David Harvey's (2006: 33–4, 102–4) claim that the progression of neoliberalism within conditions of uneven development has proceeded more from the diversification, innovation and competition between different scales of national and regional fractions of capital than the straight diffusion of 'global capitalism' via a transnational state. As Ernest Mandel (1975: 332–3) affirmed some time ago, 'the counteracting force of the uneven development of capital prevents the formation of an actual global community of interest for capital'. A focus on new trends in the uneven development of capital accumulation, through the multiscalar focus on the passive revolution of capital in specific state forms within global accumulation processes, assists this realisation. It is on this basis that the adequacy of the transnational state thesis has been challenged as a suitable account of the relationship between space and development. Whilst it is acknowledged that a specification of the relationship between issues of space and territory is difficult (Robinson 2003: 326), my argument has challenged three crucial conventions about the transnational state thesis. Namely, the problematic conception of the historical connection between state territoriality and capitalism; the assumption that global capitalism is having a unidirectional impact on conditions of uneven development, referred to as positing the homoficence of capitalism and evened development; and the ontological assumption of a transnational state that flattens out the spatial and territorial logics of capital accumulation, eliding class struggles extant in specific locations. The thesis of the transnational state fails to avoid a depiction of the passive diffusion of transnational capital to different spatial and territorial places and scales. Future advances in debate on the uneven development of the global political economy would most likely have to square the differences between a theory of uneven and combined development and earlier arguments about the development of underdevelopment, which have been presently overlooked. 'The essential difference between the two theories', notes Ronald Chilcote (2000: 227), 'is the latter's association of capitalism with the conquest of the Americas and the former's assumption that the capitalist mode of production did not fully establish itself even in Europe until the eighteenth century.' These, stated succinctly, have been the arguments that animated this chapter.

As a result, it was possible to trace the shifting sands of hegemony linked to the rise of the accumulation strategy of neoliberalism in Mexico, especially reflected in the era of *salinismo*, which seriously eroded the historical basis of the PRI. This bears out the view that granting priority to the accumulation function of the state can undermine its legitimation function and thus weaken hegemony (Cox 1982: 54). The demise of ISI and the rise of neoliberalism were accompanied by the exhaustion of PRI hegemony. With the phase of structural change in the 1970s, the historical and social basis of PRI hegemony began to alter and seriously erode. Throughout the 1980s and 1990s, the PRI increasingly resorted to forms of dominance and coercion, reflecting an increasingly dwindling form of class hegemony. It is within this era of structural change that a crisis of hegemony unfolded.

> In every country the process is different, although the content is the same. And the content is the crisis of the ruling class's hegemony. . . . [Hence] a 'crisis of authority' is spoken of: this is precisely the crisis of hegemony, or general crisis of the state. (Gramsci 1971: 210, Q13§23)

By thus tracing these shifting sands of hegemony it was argued that the PRI was hegemonic only in a very narrow sense and it continued to lose a large degree of internal coherence and legitimacy from the 1970s onwards. Whilst the lagging effects of such class hegemony were evident during the restructuring of state–civil society relations within the accumulation strategy of neoliberalism, the historic purpose of the PRI was ended by the victory of Vicente Fox on 2 July 2000. It is beyond the scope of this chapter to determine whether a cohesive form of hegemony can be refashioned within the second generation of neoliberalism in Mexico (see Middlebrook 2004; Charnock 2006). Yet it was possible through the theory of passive revolution to emphasise variations or lags in hegemony and how forms of hegemony have been discernible but recessive over the period under consideration in the decades since the 1970s. This helps to avoid either assuming that hegemony is switched on and off like a light switch or indulging in crude dichotomies between coercion and consent in understanding the role and influence of the PRI within the conditions of passive revolution and recurring crisis.

More generally, the above analysis of neoliberalism in Mexico also highlighted how social-class forces engendered common perspectives on the importance of fiscal discipline and market-oriented reforms between technocratic elites of a common social background. Put differently, building on the framework established in Chapter 5, attention was drawn to an unfolding process of class struggle brought about by the expansion of capital and the *internalisation* of class interests between various fractions of classes within state–civil society relations. This involved focusing on how social relations within the form of state in Mexico were actively and passively implicated in transnational structures of the global political economy. The discussion of the PSE and PRONASOL, two coexisting measures both introduced to offset political instability resulting from the neoliberal accumulation strategy and the reconfigured hegemonic project of the PRI, exemplify this process of struggle.

The final point that the argument has raised is that the case of Mexico does not signify the straightforward reproduction of a uniform 'model' of neoliberalism. Instead, the dissemination and acceptance of neoliberal values in Mexico has meant an adaptation of social relations to culturally specific conditions. To be sure, this may result in resemblances with similar processes elsewhere in the global political economy but, as the development of policies in Mexico displays, there is a certain peculiarity to local tendencies in response to changes in world order. It would be inappropriate to assume therefore that the social constitution of neoliberalism in Mexico was brought about in a manner that matched the view of the state as a simple 'transmission belt' for global restructuring purposes. The next chapter raises the importance of further considering 'anti-passive revolution' strategies of resistance to the constitution of neoliberal capitalist development (Buci-Glucksmann 1979: 232). Again, the significance of a nodal focus on the 'national' point of departure will be raised within the causal conditioning of 'the international'.

7   Globalisation and Resistance: The Power of the Powerless

> No one can be expected to imagine new things; but one can expect
> people . . . to exercise fantasy so as to round out the full living
> reality on the basis of what they know.
> — Antonio Gramsci, letter to Tatiana Schucht (25 April 1927)

Having discussed in the previous chapter constitutive elements in
the uneven development of neoliberalism, it becomes important
to consider forms of agency that might be contesting practices
of hegemony and passive revolution within the global political
economy. To date, the analysis of social forces engendered by
changes in the social relations of production, outlined in Chapter
5, has been criticised for prioritising the study of neoliberalism at
the expense of the potential for resistance. This chapter attempts to
address this gap by proposing a general methodological approach
to the study of resistance and by drawing upon this in specifically
analysing a concrete case of resistance within the contemporary
global political economy.

It will do so by asserting a Gramscian way of thinking about the
socio-cultural interplay of ruler and ruled within struggles over
hegemony and passive revolution, leading to various avenues along
which domination and resistance can be analysed. Most pivotal here
is the importance of recognising what has been broadly referred to
as 'the power of the powerless': the everyday modest expressions of
volition that often remain anonymous but whose political impact
often transcends individual revolt to transform consciousness and
structure purposeful agency (Havel 1985: 64–5). Whilst hegemonic
power is expressed through the habitualisation and internalisation
of social practices – organising and dividing subjectivities – it also
provokes acts of resistance. The aim of this chapter is to retrace
and represent a novel method to understanding forms of political
agency and thus the power of the powerless linking globalisation
and resistance.

Connecting with the ambition that animates this book as a whole,
the first section of the chapter introduces a specific approach to

considering the 'power of the powerless' by unravelling Antonio Gramsci's own methodological criteria in understanding the history of *subaltern classes* and their pivotal role in exposing and contesting material relations of power. What is significant about this focus on subaltern practices of resistance, though, is the centrality accorded to issues of class struggle. Certain studies claiming a focus on forms of resistance have consciously excluded an examination of class solidarities from other forms of collective agency (Amoore 2005a). The result is a deep ambivalence towards ascribing collective identities to global resistances. As Louise Amoore (2005b: 7) asks, 'can collective agencies be mapped onto class solidarities, or do they more closely mirror ethnic, gendered or racial identities?' Yet it would be mistaken, as in this case, to draw a binary line between class solidarities and ascriptive collective identities. My argument, instead, is that global resistances are understood better as local responses to the uneven development of neoliberalism linked to class struggle over the exploitation of the natural and social substratum, which has to be grasped in terms of novel and purposeful forms of subaltern agency (see Bieler and Morton 2004; van der Pijl 1998: 46–8).

Concretely, unravelling Gramsci's methodological criteria for understanding the history and practice of subaltern classes can be linked to various forms of resistance. Whilst the diversity of such forms is described, the specific structure of the chapter will shift from outlining broad conceptual issues to a particular consideration of the case of the Ejército Zapatista de Liberación Nacional (EZLN) in Chiapas, Mexico, linked to transformations in property relations within the context of the restructuring of capital and the rise of neoliberalism on a global scale. Hence, in the second section of the chapter, the response of the EZLN is situated within the era of *structural change* in the 1970s (a period detailed in the two previous chapters), during which the logic of capitalist social relations shifted towards neoliberal policy priorities. The roots of the rebellion are therefore analysed by focusing on the changing forms and relations of production in Chiapas during the 1970s (see Ross 1995), which led to a growth of radical peasant organisations that would influence the formation of the EZLN. As a result of this analysis, issues arise concerning the intersection of class-based and indigenous forms of identity asserted by the EZLN. This shows how the movement is situated within the recomposition of class struggle in Mexico (Veltmeyer 1997, 2000).

In the third section, the immediate context of the rebellion is discussed in relation to the restructuring of capital represented by the rise of neoliberal globalisation, understood as the expansion of the interests of capital accumulation on a global scale through policies favouring market-imposed discipline, monetarism, and the logic of competitiveness (as detailed in Chapter 5). The latter is most significantly epitomised by the implementation of the North American Free Trade Agreement (NAFTA) in Mexico. In the fourth section, the innovative methods of struggle developed by the EZLN are analysed within the context and categories of 'counter'hegemonic forms of resistance developed by Gramsci, thereby unravelling a further dimension to his contemporary relevance. The forms of political representation developed by the EZLN in resisting neoliberal restructuring are thus analysed in terms of how they pressed claims and asserted autonomy within a critique of social power relations in Mexico. Understanding how all of the above issues have emerged and developed is best promoted by taking the 'national' point of departure as *nodal* in the analysis of wider global transformations; the approach that has been central throughout this book. Thus the point is sustained that 'the line of development is towards internationalism although the point of departure is "national" – and it is from this point of departure that one must begin. Yet the perspective is international and cannot be otherwise' (Gramsci 1971: 240, Q14§68). The following account will therefore encompass both specific changes to production relations that affected the rise of the EZLN, whilst embedding these within the global political economy of uneven development. What emerges, in conclusion, is an appreciation of the peasantry as a subaltern class that in the case of the EZLN also focuses on the subjective implications of political consciousness; processes of agency, or the power of the powerless, in contesting neoliberalism; and, therefore, the role that subaltern classes play in constituting and contesting the modern world.

A Methodological Approach to Analysing Subaltern Classes

Through an emphasis on the socio-cultural interplay between ruler and ruled, Gramsci advocated a focus on struggles over hegemony and passive revolution within which both domination *and* resistance might be analysed. It is an emphasis also shared by Walter Benjamin, in wanting to draw attention to history that was written less from the standpoint of the 'victor' and more from that of the class struggle and 'anonymous toil' of their contemporaries (Benjamin 1940/1970: 246–8). Here, Gramsci's own criteria on the history of subaltern classes are useful as a point of departure to analyse alternative historical and contemporary contexts (Gramsci 1971: 52–5, Q25§2, Q25§5). According to Gramsci, the specific history of subaltern classes is intertwined with that of state–civil society relations more generally. It is therefore important to try to unravel such contestations.

One way of doing so is to identify the 'objective' formation of subaltern social classes by analysing developments and transformations within the sphere of production (Gramsci 1971: 52, Q25§5). This advances an understanding of the 'decisive nucleus of economic activity', but without succumbing to expressions of economism (Gramsci 1971: 161, Q13§18). As detailed in Chapter 3, historical and contemporary research needs to incorporate, as much as possible, a consideration of the mentalities and ideologies of subaltern classes, their active as well as passive affiliation to dominant social forms of political association, and thus their involvement in formations that might conserve dissent or maintain control (Gramsci 1971: 52, Q25§5). Additionally, such a method entails focusing on the political formations which subaltern classes themselves produce that press claims or assert autonomy within the existing conditions of hegemony. Questions of historical and political consciousness expressed by subaltern classes can then be raised with the ultimate aim of appreciating the common terrain dialectically occupied by both structure and agency (Bieler and Morton 2001b). 'The history of subaltern social groups is necessarily fragmented and episodic', writes Gramsci, to the extent that 'subaltern groups are always subject to the activity of ruling groups, even when they rebel and rise up' (Gramsci 1971: 54–5, Q25§2). This method of analysis, also discussed in a historical context in Chapter 3, can be useful in tracing contemporary subaltern class practices and forms of agency by thinking in a Gramscian way about such issues.

For instance, a focus on the political formations that subaltern classes themselves produce in contesting hegemonic practices could equally range across a whole series of different expressions of collective agency. These political formations might include the variety of different organisational trade unions, workers' co-operatives, peasant associations, or social movements that organise to contest developments within the sphere of production. The identification of class identity, however, does not imply that interests and political strategies are simply determined by the location of subaltern-class forces in production processes. Production is only determining, in the first instance, in that it prevents some strategies and enables others, as detailed in Chapter 5. 'Whether any such possibilities are realised, and in what particular ways, depends upon open-ended political struggles in which the power relations of capitalism will necessarily be implicated' (Rupert 2003: 183). This focus on the different political formations produced by subaltern agency, in contesting hegemonic practices, ensures that other forms of identity involved in struggle – such as ethnic, nationalist, religious, ecological, and gender forms – are included in the framework in terms of their class relevance (Cox 1987: 353).

What emerges, then, is a methodology of subaltern class analysis – whether that be in the form, *inter alia*, of trade unions, workers' co-operatives, peasant associations, or social movements – embedded within a historical materialist political strategy of transformation (Green 2002: 19–20). Detailed studies can then proceed by: (1) analysing the complex origins of political and organisational forms of specific subaltern class agency; (2) linking the emergence of such origins to subsequent consciousness-raising efforts and identity formation; and (3) demonstrating how subaltern classes attempt to press claims or assert autonomy within the existing conditions of hegemony and passive revolution through material transformation. The diversity of subaltern classes, though, means that not all forms of agency are automatically progressive in resisting neoliberal restructuring. As demonstrated in a recent case study of the European Social Forum (ESF), resistance can embody a whole range of established trade unions: new, radical unions; social movements of direct action and extra-parliamentary resistance; single-issue alliances; social democratic movements; or anarchistic forces (Bieler and Morton 2004). More broadly, there are also nationalist, right-wing social movements, which attempt to protect a perceived cultural and ethnic superiority at the national level against all types of transnational pressures and subversions (Rupert 2000: 94–118). In sum, there are sources of both democratic subaltern activism and anti-democratic impulses, which reflect in part the transformations of capitalism. Whilst the diversity of these routes to assessing the relevance of subaltern-class agency is important, the above methodological approach will be deployed in the next section in tracing the combination of developments that exacerbated the agrarian landscape in Chiapas, precipitating the social mobilisation that led to the EZLN.

The action of groups like the EZLN in Mexico or similar agrarian-based movements, such as the Movimento does Trabalhadores Rurais Sem Terra (MST) in Brazil, or regional peasant movements such as Via Campesina, with its ties to 'anti-globalisation' fora, are important precisely because they expose and challenge the thesis about the inevitable demise of the peasantry. As we saw in the previous chapter, the historian Eric Hobsbawm has for some time heralded 'the death of the peasantry' as the most dramatic and far-reaching social change to mark the twentieth century, resulting from transformations in agricultural production (Hobsbawm 1987: 137; Hobsbawm 1994: 289–91; Hobsbawm; 1999: 219–22). Stemming from this, it has been assumed that the specific variety of subalternity, poverty, exploitation, and oppression encapsulated by the peasantry and their relation to land and production would lead to the gradual political disintegration of their class identity. As also noted in Chapter 6, it is this assumption that is at the heart of the 'global capitalism' thesis, leading to the view that there is a complete proletarianisation of the peasantry resulting from the restructuring of traditional agricultural production by transnational capital (Robinson 2003: 252–8; see also Cammack 2002: 126–7). Yet, in contrast to the straightforward 'death of the peasantry', the EZLN is significant in highlighting the very constitution and reproduction of peasantries through the dynamics of capital accumulation, to reveal processes of subaltern-class formation and forms of purposeful agency. Contemporary features of these rural movements in Latin America are notably still shaped by enduring conditions of uneven and combined capitalist development, 'combined because capitalism forms a system on a world scale . . . [and] uneven because development is not linear, homogenous, and continuous' (de Janvry 1981: 1). At the same time, however, as these features resonate with familiar motifs of peasant movements in earlier transitions to capitalism, they also raise new issues about the old 'agrarian question' (Brass 2002; Bernstein 2002).

Subaltern Class Agency and Changes to the Social Relations of Production

The agrarian-based EZLN movement is significant for at least three main reasons. First, it was itself cognisant of the historically uneven development of capital accumulation in Mexico and the way in which this has impacted on regional conditions in the southern state of

Chiapas, to be discussed below. This context of uneven development has an enduring contemporary significance given that, throughout the period 1994–2003, foreign direct investment in Chiapas came to no more than US$8.94 million, tiny in comparison to the US$127,000 million that entered Mexico in the same period (Villafuerte Solís 2005: 476). It would therefore be erroneous to assume that transnational capital is simply transforming the rural landscape in Chiapas. Second, the crisis in the rural economy has witnessed the exodus of peasants to labour markets in the north of Mexico and the United States, with remittances close to US$500 million per year in 2004–05, comparable to the value of basic grains and the local state's three principal export commodities (coffee, bananas, and mangoes) (Villafuerte Solís 2005: 478–9). It would be a mistake, though, to assume that this exodus is simply leading to the proletarianisation of the peasantry, given that peasants in Chiapas have responded to the changing dynamics of capital accumulation with a range of productive activities and novel forms of agency, as detailed shortly. Third, the focus on the EZLN is all the more important in revealing what was referred to in Chapter 6 as 'anti-passive revolution'[1] strategies of resistance to the hegemony of transnational capital, thereby explicitly attempting to challenge the uneven development of neoliberalism within the global political economy.

Chiapas as a region has been inserted into relations of uneven development affecting Mexico as a whole at least since the Mexican Revolution (1910–20). Following the 1920s, land reform in Chiapas forged political compliance among indigenous highland communities, which engendered exploitation of the peasantry and promoted dependent capitalism. Once the original claims of redistribution made by Emiliano Zapata in Morelos had been invalidated by the policies of Álvaro Obregón, land reform was undertaken in the name of the state (Collier 1987: 95). Across Mexico, land reform was regarded as an instrument to pacify rebellious *campesinos* and create communities of cheap workers near commercial farm operations (Barry 1995: 20). At the local level in Chiapas, the institutionalisation of clientelistic practices formed the basis for an authoritarian state, assuring the concentration of land and capital by private owners.

In Chiapas, then, even during the administration of Lázaro Cárdenas (1934–40), agrarian reform left almost intact the power of the regional elite, to the extent that redistribution did not disguise the capacity of large landowners to resist many of the 'revolutionary' programmes (Serrano 1997: 78). By the 1940s, the process of penetrating and willingly binding Indian communities in Chiapas to the reformist party–state was complete. As Jan Rus (1994: 281, emphasis added) comments: 'By the time the PRM [Partido de la Revolución Mexicana] became the PRI . . . in the mid-forties [1946], the former self-defensive, closed communities of the Chiapas highlands had become *integral parts* of the party's local machine.' This situation was maintained by a series of ties connecting dominant family elites in Chiapas and bilingual indigenous *caciques* (power-brokers) in the region, known as *scribe-principales*, who positioned themselves between class fractions of the Institutional Revolutionary Party (PRI) and local elites. As a result, Chiapas has been described as an internal colony providing the rest of Mexico with oil, electricity, timber, cattle, corn, sugar, coffee, and beans. Up to the 1980s, whilst only having 3 per cent of the total population, the region as a whole produced 54 per cent of the country's hydroelectric power, 13 per cent of Mexico's maize (corn), 13 per cent of the country's gas, 5 per cent of the timber, 4 per cent of the beans, and 4 per cent of its oil (Collier with Quaratiello 1994: 16). Despite changing political climates, Chiapas has been aptly described as a rich land consisting of poor people (Benjamin 1996).

Changing Forms and Relations of Production: Structural Change in Chiapas

It was from the 1970s onward that a conjunction of several factors proved particularly crucial in precipitating social mobilisation in Chiapas. A combination of migrant flows influenced by changes in production and land demands, the expansion of cattle-ranching forcing the relocation of peasants, ambitious state projects negatively impacting on peasant subsistence, an energy boom skewing peasant and commercial agriculture, and the subsequent impact of neoliberal policies on state programmes and policies of support, all exacerbated the agrarian landscape in Chiapas. Therefore, rather than peasants being unaccustomed to change, communities underwent constant readjustment during this period, which led to a crucial local social re-organisation (Rus 1995: 71–89). Such reaction to the dynamics of capitalism, and fundamental changes to the way of life for certain communities in Chiapas, also posed challenges that undermined the institutionalised control of social conflict organised through the PRI, with peasant movements experiencing a greater degree of autonomy.

During the 1950s and 1960s agrarian reform laws began to promote an influx of indigenous immigrants into eastern areas in Chiapas, notably in the *Selva Lacandona* (Lacandon jungle), which were then followed by a second wave migration of cattle-ranchers from Tabasco and Veracruz (Nations 1994: 31–3). Certain areas, principally in the Lacandon jungle and Simojovel in the eastern parts of the state, became settlement or colonising frontiers so that, 'by the 1970s, immigrants from other areas of Mexico joined the flow of highland Indians into the east [of Chiapas] under Luis Echeverría's populist promotion of colonisation' (Collier 1994a: 372). According to George Collier (1994b: 110), around 57 per cent of land in the southeast of Mexico came to be held in the tenure of *ejidos*, or agrarian collectives, by the 1970s. Yet these were primarily marginal, rain-fed lands, leaving developed and irrigated lands relatively unaffected by agrarian reforms in the hands of private commercial agriculture. The distinction is important, because communities became dependent on migratory labour for economic survival, due to the very marginal nature of land titles, which increased their vulnerability to the series of crises that impacted on agriculture in Chiapas during the 1970s and 1980s.

It is with reference to energy development and the linked oil boom in the 1970s that material and social bases of community existence in Chiapas particularly began to alter. A crucial consequence of this form of development was the impact of the Organization of Petroleum Exporting Countries (OPEC) oil crisis on communities in Chiapas, which skewed production away from the fragile agricultural sector toward large-scale development projects (Rus 1995: 78). One of the roots of the Zapatista rebellion can therefore be linked to the pernicious impact the oil boom had in restructuring social relations of production in Chiapas.

> After the OPEC oil crisis in 1972, Mexico borrowed internationally to expand oil production for export and to finance ambitious projects of development. During the resulting development boom, Mexico's agriculture declined from 14% of GDP in 1965 to just 7% of GDP in 1982, as resources for production flowed into other sectors. Mexico, propelled by energy development, became more and more oriented towards foreign markets and away from food self-sufficiency. (Collier 1994c: 16)

A feature of this was an expansion of Gulf coastal and inland oil production facilities in Tabasco, Campeche, and adjacent areas to Chiapas, whilst huge hydroelectric dam projects were added along the Grijalva river basin at Las Peñitas, La Angostura, and Chicoasén. The populist promotion of agricultural policies during the Luis Echeverría administration (1970–76) was succeeded by the oil-led boom of the Lopez Portillo administration (1976–82) so that Chiapas became the productive source of 50 per cent of Mexico's electric power and most of its petroleum (Collier, Mountjoy, and Nigh 1994: 398–407). Significantly, the Mexican Petroleum Company (PEMEX) became responsible for 45 per cent of all government expenditure in Chiapas in 1975; an amount which itself was three times the level all branches of government had spent in Chiapas in 1970 (Cancian and Brown 1994: 23).

These state-led projects of development had several consequences in the central highlands of Chiapas, principally drawing peasants into off-farm wages and entrepreneurial opportunities in transport and commerce, linked to the energy industry, or out of agriculture and into wage work as unskilled labourers in construction (Collier 1994b: 115). These changes in the social relations of production resulted in distinctions being drawn between subsistence-producing peasants and those involved in wage labour. In particular, productive relations became more class-based, whilst gender and generational differences were also heightened by new meanings associated with work. This change in the social relations of production in Chiapas signified a move away from the politics of rank-based forms of organisation, based on community hierarchies, to the politics of class-based forms of organisation (Collier 1994d). It was a process of class formation, to draw from E.P. Thompson (1978), whereby particular communities experienced new structures of exploitation and identified new points of antagonistic interest centred around issues of class struggle; even though forms of class-consciousness – involving a conscious identity of common interests – may not have immediately emerged.

In Chiapas, these issues of class struggle arose when peasant communities sought to resolve antagonisms less through the rank-based social ties and communal commitments of civil–religious hierarchies and more through cash derived from wage work or through factions associated with political parties (Collier 1994d: 9–16). Yet this transformation did not simply equate with the death of the peasantry as a social class and thus as a form of political agency. Instead the situation was a mix of agricultural petty commodity production alongside the exchange of wage labour and other economic activities (Kovic 2003: 61). For instance, the attractiveness of wage work over peasant agriculture during the 1970s did draw communities in Chiapas into a capitalist social division of labour, but this became an especially vulnerable and acute situation after the collapse of Mexico's oil-fuelled development in 1982, discussed in Chapter 6. This meant that peasants then had to return to agricultural production alongside developing a mix of economic activities within the context of growing class-stratification and changing processes of capitalist accumulation. Hence the importance of recognising how class content 'subsists' in the mobilisation of social movements along with other identities (Foweraker 1995: 40; Hellman 1995: 170–1).

As peasants became further excluded from processes of capitalist accumulation and detrimentally affected by rapidly changing social relations of production they began to embrace new forms of political organisation. These increasingly began to emerge outside the institutional presence of the PRI. Hence the importance of analysing the increasingly class-based conflict represented by the growth of new peasant organisations in the 1970s, which was also crucially constituted through radical consciousness-raising efforts, prior to the appearance of the EZLN.

Consciousness-raising and the Growth of Radical Peasant Organisations

It has been argued that the formation of the EZLN movement is only intelligible if related to the pastoral and community work of Bishop Samuel Ruiz García (MacEoin 1996: 19).[2] Ruiz was the bishop of San Cristóbal diocese from 1960 to 1999 and cultivated contacts with French and Italian intellectual priests, clerical sociologists, and anthropologists of development throughout the 1960s (Womack 1999: 27–8). As a result, there were efforts in Chiapas to promote forms of social action and consciousness-raising within the diocese. According to John Womack (1999: 23) an emphasis was placed on *tomar conciencia*: a form of critical reflection that involved taking cognisance and questioning received faith, wisdom, and conventions, as a move towards becoming active subjects in response to changing material circumstances. At first, this approach in Chiapas reproduced vertical or top-down power relations based on the pedagogical position of lay preachers or catechists (Harvey 1998: 72). However, due to the central importance placed on constant reflection, there was a dialectical relation between the raising of a critical consciousness amongst the people of Chiapas and the very role of lay preachers or catechists (MacEoin 1996: 29). As Samuel Ruiz himself described the transformation, 'I came to San Cristóbal to convert the poor, but they ended up converting me' (as cited by Womack 1999: 27). It was a situation whereby, following Gramsci (1971: 350, Q10II§44), 'every teacher is always a pupil and every pupil a teacher'. What emerged, therefore, was a different, more reciprocal and participatory, relationship between leaders and led.

Importantly, the consciousness-raising efforts carried out by catechists in Chiapas operated within the overall context of liberation theology and the growing influence of *comunidades eclesiales de base* (Christian Base Communities) across Latin America. Gaining impetus from the organisational work of the Medellín Council of Latin American Bishops (Colombia, 1968), there followed a rise in indigenous deacons in Chiapas throughout the 1970s, which created community leaders who inspired new forms of collective political and economic action targeted toward land and political rights (Harvey 1998: 73–6). Within this context, the pivotal role played by Bishop Samuel Ruiz in shifting peoples' ideas about the changing social situation can be understood as the agency of an organic intellectual. As detailed in Chapter 4, this refers to the action of somebody organically connected to social-class forces at the grassroots level with the task of 'systematically and patiently ensuring that this force is formed, developed, and rendered ever more homogeneous, compact and self-aware' (Gramsci 1971: 185, Q13§17). The connectedness or 'organic quality' of Samuel Ruiz broke with a conventional understanding of the role of the priesthood as a separate caste or that of a 'traditional intellectual' detached from the people (Gramsci 1996: 173–4, Q4§33). Instead, an awareness amongst the people of the exploitative nature underpinning social relations linked to changes in production was actively constructed and brought about through education and the development of a critical consciousness, in an attempt to overcome everyday taken-for-granted attitudes. Indicative of this have been Ruiz's ethical reflections on the causes of uneven development in Chiapas. For example:

The objectives of the global economic system, and in particular the excesses committed under its processes of production, are causing irreparable damage to natural resources and must be transformed. This problem has emerged in Chiapas not because of anything particular to Chiapas, but because the uprising took place as concern was growing about the concrete global threat created by the productive system. (as cited by Rosen and Burt 1997: 43)

Equally crucial at the time was the invitation Ruiz extended to Maoist groups to carry out community organising in Chiapas in the 1970s, which then further consolidated social and autonomous forms of radical peasant organisation outside the institutional control of the PRI (La Botz 1995: 34). It was from within the complex waxing and waning of such peasant organisations throughout the 1970s and 1980s that the EZLN would eventually emerge (see Harvey 1995: 39–73; Harvey 1990).

Overall, new peasant networks progressed with a less centralised structure and a more critical stance toward the role of conventional political parties, whilst rejecting dependency on the leadership of particular individuals (Harvey 1988: 299–312). It was also a trend that was emblematic of a reconfiguration of state–civil society relations across Mexico in the light of a crisis of authority experienced by official legal and institutional forms of political expression (see Chapter 6). 'As mobilisation and land invasions increased, so did repression. The decade of the 1970s was dominated by forced eviction of invaded land, overt repression, massive arrests and assassination of agrarian leaders' (Serrano 1997: 90). The formation of radical peasant organisations within the context of changing forms of social relations of production in the 1970s also began to experience the assault of neoliberal restructuring in the 1980s. Hence, rather than a simple expression of fluctuating *conjunctural* events, resembling a coincidence of spontaneous or occasional responses, it is possible to situate the rise of the EZLN within a series of *organic* developments linked to the emergence of a neoliberal strategy of capitalist accumulation. The distinction is important because conjunctural movements stem from immediate circumstances, organic developments from enduring predicaments.

> Conjunctural phenomena . . . do not have any far-reaching historical significance; they give rise to political criticism of a minor, day-to-day character, which has as its subject top political leaders and personalities with direct governmental responsibilities. Organic phenomena on the other hand give rise to socio-historical criticism, whose subject is wider social groupings – beyond the public figures and beyond the top leaders. (Gramsci 1971: 177–8, Q13§17)

Hence the importance of considering the significance of the 'far-reaching socio-historical criticism' expressed by the EZLN of the accumulation strategy of neoliberalism.

The Accumulation Strategy of Neoliberalism and Agrarian Reform

During the administration of Carlos Salinas de Gortari (1988–94) in Mexico a new phase of capitalist accumulation proceeded that involved neoliberal restructuring of the social relations of production. Efforts to reconstitute and redefine social consensus included undercutting the old basis of hegemony maintained by the PRI and reconstructing, but not dismantling, the previous form of state in Mexico (Nash and Kovic 1996). This particularly involved attempts at reconstituting populist and clientelist forms of co-optation through targeted social programmes such as the National Solidarity Programme (PRONASOL), as discussed in Chapter 6. Therefore, the recomposition of capital on a global scale under the rubric of neoliberal restructuring proceeded in Mexico along lines that involved attempts to rearticulate a hegemonic project through a material and political discourse known as *salinismo* (see Salinas de Gortari 2002). The EZLN rebellion on 1 January 1994 was thus a response both to the global strategy of neoliberal capitalist accumulation and to the specific discourse of *salinismo* in Mexico, which peaked with the implementation of NAFTA (Zermeño 1997). Hence NAFTA was announced by the Zapatistas as 'the death certificate for the ethnic peoples of Mexico' and Subcomandante Marcos declared that the rebellion, 'isn't just about Chiapas – it's about NAFTA and Salinas's whole neoliberal project' (Ross 1995: 21, 153). It was therefore no coincidence that the EZLN rebellion was orchestrated on the very same day that NAFTA came into effect.

One of the principal measures of neoliberal restructuring in Mexico was reforming the agrarian sector. During the 1970s increases in state revenues from petroleum exports helped to sustain agricultural subsidies, which became embodied within the Mexican Food System (SAM) in 1980. However, although annual subsidies stimulated national maize production among peasant producers, the international market for oil prices and the debt crisis eliminated the financial base of SAM and the attempt to implement redistributive food policies (Fox 1993). During the administration of Miguel de la Madrid (1982–88), rather than public programmes to stimulate maize production, marketing and consumption,

the Mexican government reaffirmed its commitment to meet its international financial obligations, thus committing a major proportion of the federal budget to debt servicing, and began a process of crisis management, oriented toward markedly reducing

the level of subsidies and cutting back social services, selling off
state-owned enterprises and postponing investment in the physical
infrastructure of the country. (Hewitt de Alcántara 1994: 8)

Between 1987 and 1989 the price of maize plummeted contributing
to a deepening recession in the countryside, whilst the proportion of
maize producers operating at a loss increased from 43 to 65 per cent
between 1987 and 1988 (Hewitt de Alcántara 1994: 12). Within the
context of neoliberal restructuring there was, then, an overhaul of
the agricultural sector that involved the privatisation of state-owned
enterprises and the withdrawal of price supports and subsidies, in
accordance with World Bank demands (Gilly 1998: 290). Notably
the state-owned Mexican Coffee Institute (INMECAFÉ), established
in 1958, was also dismantled under the privatisation policies of
salinismo, which meant a withdrawal from purchasing and marketing
functions and the reduction of technical assistance. The collapse
of world coffee prices by 50 per cent in 1989 compounded this
withdrawal and exacerbated the plight of rural communities, with
smallholders in the areas of Ocosingo, Las Margaritas, and Los Altos
in Chiapas abandoning production between 1989 and 1993. The
restructuring of the state and the reconfiguring of the hegemonic
project of the PRI, which was analysed in Chapter 6 as part of the
rise of the accumulation strategy of neoliberalism, therefore also
included fundamental reform of the agricultural sector. Among other
issues, this reform involved altering the pivotal status of collective
ejido landholdings.

This entailed reforming Article 27 of the Mexican Constitution
of 1917, which enshrined the *ejido* as central to collective land
ownership. Yet the *ejido* also ensured a form of political and organisational state control, because it became the principal vehicle for
state regulation of peasant access to land and therefore helped to
maintain political control over the peasantry. However, under the
ejido reform, lands could be legally sold, bought, rented, or used
as collateral for loans; private companies could purchase lands;
new associations between capitalist developers and *ejidatarios* (*ejido*
owners) were allowed; and provisions for peasants to petition for
land redistribution were deleted, formally ending the process of land
distribution, with primacy given to private property relations (Harvey
1996: 194–5). Yet conclusions asserting the wholesale destruction of
rural communities on the basis of changes to the *ejido* agrarian code
should be muted. The collective status of such landholdings was

more apparent than real as there was an ongoing capitalisation of rural production even before the reform of Article 27. The symbolic break, though, with past agrarian reform was pivotal and destroyed any future hope of land redistribution among the peasantry (Harvey 1998: 188). This loss of hope would be compounded by the realisation that reform of the agrarian code would *accelerate* the capitalist transformation of agricultural productive relations (Collier 1994b: 124). The gradual elimination of restrictions on maize imports initiated over a 15-year period under NAFTA – with average yields of maize in Mexico at 1.7 tons/hectare compared to 6.9 tons/hectare in the United States – would tend to support this view and thus agricultural land would become increasingly abandoned by smallholders (Dewalt and Ress with Murphy 1994: 56).

One result of this neoliberal restructuring of the agrarian sector was that social and institutional bases of peasant representation linked to the *ejido* system were fundamentally altered (de Janvry, Gordillo, and Sadoulet 1997). This meant that, as the privatisation of communal *ejido* landholdings proceeded, alternative institutional organisations had to be constructed in an attempt to re-establish and redefine the broader hegemonic process. Yet this proved increasingly difficult as more autonomous forms of peasant mobilisation in Chiapas, discussed earlier, developed outside the institutional organisation of the PRI. In response, the PRI resorted to attempts to define and limit the conditions within which peasant associations could emerge, to ensure their continual absorption, disaggregation, and neutralisation. With such aims in mind, as a consequence of the gradual elimination of price subsidies within NAFTA, a new support programme for the Mexican agricultural sector, known as the Direct Rural Support Programme (PROCAMPO), was announced in 1993. As the first disbursements were initiated just prior to the 1994 national elections it became clear that PROCAMPO subsidies were really only a palliative. They not only resulted in benefiting local merchants and private intermediaries rather than rural producers but they also, over the medium to long term, excluded small peasant producers (Harvey 1998: 183). At the same time, PRONASOL funds were also allocated for similar purposes, amounting to some US$15 billion throughout the whole period of the Salinas *sexenio* (Cornelius 1996: 59). Notably, Chiapas itself was targeted with more PRONASOL funds than any other state, receiving US$192 million in 1993 (Cornelius 1995: 148). However, such funds were diverted by the clientelistic politics of state Governor Patrocinio González Garrido (1988–92).

During this neoliberal phase of restructuring, conflicts between and within peasant groups in the highland communities of Chiapas were also encouraged, especially during the governorships of Absalón Castellanos (1984–88) and Patrocino González Garrido (1988–92) (García de León 1995: 10–13). This indicated that the old basis of hegemony maintained by the PRI was being increasingly undercut by neoliberal restructuring to the agrarian sector (see Chapter 6). Hence there was a growing absence of hegemonic rule as the social and institutional bases of peasant control were altered. Although there were attempts to redefine the broader hegemonic process through the implementation of policies such as PRONASOL and PROCAMPO, recourse to violent repression at this time was indicative of the coercion that backed the lack of consensus. A policy of impunity to human-rights violations also emerged in Mexico, particularly during the 1980s and 1990s.[3] Between 1994 and 1996 this manifested itself in Chiapas with the assassination of over 100 activists linked to the centre-left Party of the Democratic Revolution (PRD) (Kampwirth 1998: 47n.11). Estimated troop deployments in Chiapas since 1994 have ranged from 12,000 to 74,000 with the latter representing at least a third of the total Mexican Federal Army.[4] This resulted in the militarisation of over one-third of Chiapas, including 17 major military barracks, 44 semi-permanent military installations, and the deployment of one soldier for every three or four inhabitants of every community (Stephen 1997: 10–11). One report put together by a group of human rights organisations in Chiapas, including the Fray Bartolomé de las Casas Human Rights Centre established by Samuel Ruiz in San Cristóbal in 1989, noted that the annual cost of this deployment was conservatively estimated to be US$200 million. The report also raised suspicion about nightly low-level flights to spread marijuana seeds in the conflict area as a pretext for justifying an escalated military campaign against narco-trafficking.[5] The result was a stark increase in paramilitary activity, involving groups such as Los Chinchulines, Tomás Munster, Movimento Indígena Revolucionario Anti-Zapatista, Máscara Roja, Fuerzas Armadas del Pueblo, and, the largest, Paz y Justicia. A local PRI deputy, Samuel Sánchez Sánchez, admitted to being the spokesperson and leader of Paz y Justicia, whilst the Movimento Indígena Revolucionario Anti-Zapatista had reported links to PRI federal deputy Norberto Santiz López.[6] The participants of such paramilitaries were commonly young men with no land or reliable means of subsistence, the product therefore of the government's agricultural policies of neoliberal restructuring (Aubry and Inda 1998: 9).

Notably, it was this climate of violence and the problems of internal divisions within excluded communities that came together in the massacre of 45 people in Acteal in the highlands of Chiapas, twelve miles north of San Cristóbal, on 22 December 1997. These people belonged to a group called Sociedad Civil las Abejas who had close links to Samuel Ruiz. They were non-violent EZLN sympathisers who had fled the nearby Zapatista bulwark of Chenalhó in an effort to escape paramilitary violence (Nadal 1998a: 18–25). Following the Acteal massacre the official state justifications for a policy of coercion were shifted from a 'war on drugs' to preventing further acts of 'inter-ethnic war' (Gall 1998: 531–44). 'From this point onwards', Antonio García de León (2005: 520) has explained, 'the state was no longer able to control Chiapas without a strong policy of militarisation, which made it impossible to sustain the electoral triumph of the PRI in the region.' As Luis Hernández Navarro (1998: 8) has added, 'within the logic of counterinsurgency, the massacre also serves as exemplary punishment for those who dare to challenge the local and national hegemony of the ruling party'. This was coupled with the arbitrary exclusion of foreign citizens, a policy known as 'political cleansing'. Between 1996 and 1997 immigration authorities expelled 60 foreigners, with a further 141 being 'invited' to leave, whilst in January 1998 the International Committee for the Red Cross (ICRC) was ordered to cease operations in Chiapas (Nadal 1998b: 20–2). These expulsions included the director of Mexico Solidarity Network (MSN), Tom Hansen, and Michel Chanteau, the former French Catholic priest of the Tzotzil community of Chenalhó, who was expelled after 35 years service in the community.

Several issues emerge from this discussion that are worth highlighting before the strategies of resistance of the EZLN are analysed. Most significantly, the specific struggle in Chiapas signifies generally the degree of conflict and coercion present at the level of sub-national politics that has entailed hardline Priísta leaders exercising impunity to ensure their tenure (Cornelius 1999: 11). It is difficult, therefore, to argue that the PRI articulated 'normal' conditions of hegemony 'characterised by the combination of force and consent, which balance each other reciprocally, without force predominating excessively over consent' (Gramsci 1971: 80n.4, Q19§24). As discussed in various chapters in the first part of this book, there is a clear lack of intellectual and moral leadership here expressive of such 'normal' conditions of hegemony. Rather than an organic equilibrium based on a relationship between leaders and led, rulers and ruled, the PRI became increasingly unable to conceal its real predominance and relied on more coercive measures. The situation reflected more the traits of passive revolution, a period during which a 'crisis of authority' was evident, meaning that the social basis supporting the basic structure of the political system was undermined, resulting in a breakdown of social consensus (see Chapter 4). 'As soon as the dominant social group has exhausted its function', within such conditions of passive revolution, 'the ideological bloc tends to crumble away; then "spontaneity" may be replaced by "constraint" in ever less disguised and indirect forms' (Gramsci 1971: 60–1, Q19§24). As the Mexican intellectual Carlos Fuentes (1990: 29) wrote in one of his novels: 'The obvious truth about Mexico . . . is that one system is falling apart on us, but we have no other system to put in its place.'[7]

The resistance of the EZLN is therefore embedded in the history of passive revolution linked to processes of state formation and the conditions of uneven and combined development in Mexico, as also detailed in the preceding chapter. It is a reflection of the limited or *fractured hegemony* marking modern state formation in Mexico (Van der Haar 2005: 493–6). The EZLN rebellion is thus best inserted within a history of passive revolution in Mexico marked by the attempts of developmental catch-up and the incomplete achievements of modern state formation (see Chapter 6). As Luis Hernández Navarro (1998: 9) put it at the time, the crisis in Mexico resulted from 'contradictions between a set of political institutions based on top-down corporatist and clientelist relations on the one hand, and an increasingly mature civil society which seeks full participation on the other'. It is within this crisis period that social-class forces in Chiapas attempted to forge a counterhegemonic movement by publicly emerging on 1 January 1994 as the EZLN with a mass base of support and a well-organised army. It was this force of over 3,000 initial combatants that occupied the towns of San Cristóbal, Ocosingo, Las Margaritas, Altamirano, Chanal, Oxchuc, and Huixtán with demands for work, land, housing, food, health, education, independence, freedom, democracy, justice, and peace. Whilst the decision to resort to armed conflict did not draw a consensus from within the EZLN movement, it nevertheless prevailed as a final option. 'We spoke out, but there was no echo', Samuel Ruiz stated: 'It took a suicidal peasant insurrection for anyone to pay attention.'[8] The following section highlights 'counter'hegemonic aspects of the EZLN to unravel it further in relation to Gramsci's strategic thinking and practice.

Aspects of 'Counter'hegemonic Struggle and the Power of the Powerless

'The ethnic identity of an oppressed people – the Maya – is embraced proudly', observes Bill Weinberg (2000: 193), 'but not exalted to the exclusion of common class concerns.' At a time when utopias across Latin America were declared by Jorge Castañeda (1994) as unarmed, the EZLN initiated a military offensive on 1 January 1994 against the above processes of neoliberal restructuring, which raised new questions about the options and innovative techniques open to resistance movements. Almost immediately there was a mobilisation of different weapons, fusing the materiality of armed struggle with the symbolic importance of particular images and discourses. Within 'counter'hegemonic forms of resistance a combination of strategies is available. Specifically, Gramsci differentiated between those based on a 'war of manoeuvre' and those involving a 'war of position', although these should not be regarded as different extremes or mutually exclusive options but, rather, possibilities located on a continuum (see also Chapter 4). A 'war of manoeuvre' is analogous to a rapid assault targeted directly against the institutions of state power, the capture of which would only prove transitory. Alternatively, a 'war of position' is comparable to a form of trench warfare involving an ideological struggle on the cultural front of civil society: to overcome the 'powerful system of fortresses and earthworks', requiring a concentration of hegemonic activity 'before the rise to power' in an attempt to penetrate and subvert the mechanisms of ideological diffusion (Gramsci 1971: 59, Q19§24; 238, Q6§138). Thus the initial military assault by the EZLN begun in January 1994 was a transitory phase in a 'war of manoeuvre', reflected in the 'First Declaration of the Lacandon Jungle' that declared the intention to advance onto the capital of the country and defeat the Mexican Federal Army (Marcos 1995: 53). Since this phase, although the armed option has been present but limited, it has been possible to highlight the strategy of a shifting 'war of position' conducted by the EZLN. This has involved asserting intellectual and moral resistance to confront both the ideological apparatus of the PRI, but also wider material social-class interests in Mexico that have subsequently been supportive of the accumulation strategy of neoliberalism. Hence 'while Marcos has never declared himself a Gramscian, it is impossible to believe that he has had no exposure to Gramsci' (Bruhn 1999: 44). Within this war of position, various novel features have been adopted by the EZLN to articulate 'anti-passive revolution' struggle, with five standing as particularly noteworthy: (1) the activation of national and international civil society; (2) the aim to address and establish indigenous rights; (3) the appeal to collective interests beyond the ascriptive identities of ethnicity; (4) the campaign for wider democratisation; and (5) the constant goal of innovation through new forms of governance within the communities of Chiapas.

First, with regard to the activation of civil society, the EZLN has promoted various forms of mobilisation and new forms of organisation to gain wider national appeal. This initially included calling for a National Democratic Convention (CND), in the 'Second Declaration of the Lacandon Jungle', which was part of the strategy of building up an overall 'counter'hegemonic project within civil society. As a result, the CND was organised between 6 and 9 August 1994 in San Cristóbal and at a place in the Lacandon jungle renamed Aguascalientes, where more than 6,000 delegates were brought together to deliberate on the need for a transitional government and strategies to promote democracy and develop a co-ordinated national project (Stephen 1995: 88–99). Despite ultimate failure in influencing the outcome of the national elections on 21 August, this was a clear effort to mobilise civil society as a site of popular antagonism, to try to develop a solidarity of interests as the basis for a 'counter'hegemony.

Similarly, the aim of activating civil society has had both a national *and* an international dimension, represented for example by the attempt on 1 January 1996 to form an additional political force called the Zapatista National Liberation Front (FZLN), which aimed to support the EZLN as an urban counterpart organisation through a wider, more organic structure based on common consent. A crucial feature of both fronts was the continued emphasis on links between leaders and led, which drew on the earlier practices of social mobilisation within the indigenous communities. Globally, the impact of the EZLN has also been noted in terms of inspiring the broad round of recent 'anti-capitalist' resistance movements. As Luca Casarini, the main spokesperson of autonomist resistance active within the ESF, has indicated, the recent practical activities of 'anti-capitalist' resistance in Europe and elsewhere unfolded in the wake of the EZLN (see Hernández Navarro 2004: 3–4). Various international meetings convened by the EZLN, both in Mexico (July–August 1996) and in Europe (Spain, July–August 1997), known as intercontinental meetings against neoliberalism, demonstrated the insertion of such resistance within the global conditions of neoliberalism. Albeit with modest outcomes, the EZLN became a backstop for the global justice movement and set precedents for the 'anti-capitalist' movement, leading to the subsequent targeting of initiatives such as the Free Trade Area of the Americas (FTAA). There are now over 80 EZLN solidarity communities in Europe and approximately 50 such communities in the United States that have supported the autonomous municipalities in Mexico whilst simultaneously campaigning closer to home against neoliberalism. Many of the characteristics of anti-globalisation resistance are thus seen as debuting in the rebellion of the EZLN in Mexico, with the latter consistently demonstrating an ability to mediate between the particular and the universal to forge a global consciousness of solidarity (Olesen 2004). The EZLN has thus witnessed many of its vocal claims being echoed in the activities of the global social justice movement (Olesen 2005: 102–26).

The second area of importance in the expression of resistance has been the EZLN's involvement in peace talks and the assertion of indigenous rights at San Andrés Larráinzar, a small town in Chiapas, with two intermediaries in dialogue with the state, the Commission of Concord and Pacification (COCOPA) and the National Mediation Commission (CONAI). The peace process hoped to address a series of issues revolving around indigenous rights and culture, negotiations on democracy and justice, land reform, and women's rights. It resulted in the San Andrés Accords on Indigenous Rights and Culture, signed on 16 February 1996, which laid the groundwork for significant changes in the areas of indigenous rights, political participation and cultural autonomy. Concretely, this inspired the founding of the National Indigenous Congress (CNI) in 1996 as representative of Mexico's indigenous peoples, who make up between 10 and 14 per cent of the country's population. Whilst, again, advances such as the CNI and the San Andrés Accords should be seen as limited in terms of securing substantive gains for the indigenous communities in Mexico, they should not be totally discounted. For instance, some have swayed towards the former stance by drawing a comparison between talks with the EZLN and the overall process of electoral reform in Mexico. 'Everyone agrees the dialogue must be pursued, there is a broad consensus regarding the worthiness of the cause', averred Jorge Castañeda (1995: 258), 'but few are terribly excited either about the outcome itself or its urgency. As long as the process continues, there is little concern about its results, or absence thereof.' Thus it can be agreed that little progress has been made since the San Andrés Accords were signed on 16 February 1996. However, presaging a continuation of resistance after the national elections on 2 July 2000 – which witnessed the defeat of the PRI and the presidential victory of Vicente Fox backed by the centre-right National Action Party (PAN) – the EZLN have embarked on renewed forms of resistance to assert indigenous rights. On 21 March 1999 both the EZLN and FZLN organised a strategically important 'Consulta for the Recognition of the Rights of the Indian Peoples'. This was a mobilisation of 5,000 Zapatista delegates consisting of teams of two people – one male, one female – visiting every municipality across Mexico to promote participation in a referendum on the peace 'process' and the future of the EZLN. The consulta resulted in some 3 million votes, with 95 per cent of the participants voting in favour of honouring the San Andrés Accords, recognising Indian rights, and supporting military withdrawal from Chiapas. The Zapatistas also subsequently set the date of 25 February 2001 for the 'March of Indigenous Dignity' to leave San Cristóbal in Chiapas, to cross through various states, and arrive in Mexico City on 6 March, in order to promote support for their latest demands. This was designed to mount increasing pressure in support of the fulfilment of the San Andrés Accords and the bill on indigenous rights that followed the original COCOPA legislative proposal. Between 28 April and 2 May 2001, Congress approved a watered-down version of the original COCOPA bill on indigenous rights and culture. This failed to recognise communities as legal entities or their rights to natural resources or to hold communal property, which could have threatened the property rights of landowners. Hence the conservative view that there will be a return to the *status quo ante bellum* in Chiapas.[9] Although the outcomes might seem disappointing, the endeavour constantly to innovate, with new forms of political mobilisation and expression in the name of indigenous rights, is itself significant.

What these tactics have meant in practice is, third, an endeavour to appeal to various forms of identity as the basis for a 'counter'hegemony linked through common points of convergence grounded in capitalist relations of exploitation.

The EZLN in Chiapas has created a counter-hegemonic discourse in Mexican national culture that draws on the past hegemonic culture of the revolution but radically reinvents it by invoking the mediating figure of Zapata as a bridge to current social issues. (Stephen 1997: 42–3; see also Stephen 2002)

Primarily, the ambiguities of identity have been embraced by constructing and mobilising ethnic identity whilst also maintaining a degree of anonymity through the wearing of masks. This helps to project issues of ethnicity whilst creating new social spaces within which alternative forms of identity coexist. At one level this has involved making an equation between indigenous identity and poverty, to recognise that socio-economic exclusion has an ethnic dimension (Nash 1995). At another level it has involved promoting indigenous identity within the context of Mexican nationalism and appeals to the workers' movement and trade union struggle in Mexico (Earle 1994: 26–30; Roman and Arregui 1997: 98–116). Additionally, there have been attempts to reinvent group identities by emphasising the struggle against gender inequalities and by affirming sexuality rights (Eber and Kovic 2003; Harvey 2000: 158–87; Hernández Castillo 2001; Rovira 2000). However, this does not mean that the new discourses and challenges to power relations have become part of everyday practice or that there is complete internal democratisation within the communities of Chiapas. Nor does it mean that struggle conducted on the basis of ethnic identity leads simply to inter-class conflict, since intra-class conflict between peasant producers in indigenous communities has also been evident (Brass 2005: 660–1). Nevertheless, the struggle initiated by the Zapatistas has transcended some of its particular aspects to engender a wider movement of Zapatismo in and beyond Mexico (Leyva Solano 1998). As Marcos himself has stated, explicitly critiquing neoliberal globalisation, the EZLN struggle is a search for 'a world in which there is room for many worlds. A world capable of containing all the worlds.'[10]

The fourth focus area that the EZLN has promoted since the beginning of the rebellion has been the rallying cry for democracy in Mexico. Initial communiqués in 1994 signalled the demand for work, land, housing, health, education, independence, freedom, democracy, and justice (Marcos 1995: 51–4). It has therefore been possible to witness the EZLN's contribution, along with other civil society organisations in Mexico, to the cleanliness of elections, the importance of electoral monitoring, the transparency of civil service practices, the need for independent media reporting, and the popularisation of civic participation (Gilbreth and Otero 2001). 'The PRD is a vote', the Mexican cultural critic Carlos Monsiváis has declared but, 'the Zapatistas are a cause' (personal interview, 20 March 1999, Mexico City). However, the historic defeat of the PRI and the victory of Vicente Fox seemingly drained some of the potency away from this demand, in terms of the official 'consolidation' of democratisation in Mexico. One needs to remain circumspect therefore about the formalistic degree of such 'democratic transition', the unspecified nature of such a hollow form of democracy, and the equation of democracy with the periodic circulation of elite classes (see Morton 2005c). Most significantly, the fact that neoliberalism can be upbraided as a thoroughly *un*democratic common denominator in both a national and an international context is significant. The Zapatista pursuit of democracy, then, may have resulted in a series of missed opportunities.

> Simply to call for the adherence on the part of the Mexican social formation to a systematically non-specific form of democracy, as the EZLN have done, without simultaneously calling into question the class structure which gives expression to the way in which (and for whom) political democracy operates within this wider context, negates their own demand for social justice in Chiapas. (Brass 2005: 670; see also Vilas 1996: 277–81)

In Chiapas itself, the election of a new state governor on 20 August 2000 led to the victory of Pablo Salazar, representing an eight-party 'Alliance for Chiapas', which again would seemingly detract from the EZLN cause of democratisation. The sanguine view is that these polls have been turning points in the Zapatista conflict because peace proposals – backed by a 'democratic' mandate – would be difficult to rebuff.[11] Likewise, Luis H. Alvarez, the co-ordinator of governmental peace efforts in Chiapas under the Fox administration, announced the partial withdrawal of the army in Chiapas in December 2000, although the army still maintains a large presence throughout the state alongside paramilitaries. Breaking their silence with the new administration, the Zapatistas embarked on a whole series of new initiatives from 2002 onwards, with new demands focusing on 'three signals'. These were: (1) fulfilment of the San Andrés Accords, following the COCOPA legislative proposal; (2) release of all Zapatista prisoners held at Cerro Hueco state prison in Chiapas and in the states of Tabasco and Querétaro; and (3) a large process of demilitarisation that would go beyond prevailing troop movements. Whilst there has been partial compliance with these 'three signals' – Chiapas state Interior Minister, Emilio Zebadúa, even acknowledged that the autonomous municipalities in Chiapas created by the EZLN represent legitimate aspirations that could be regularised through constitutional means – there are still major stumbling blocks to such negotiations. Not least of these is the fact that there are at least 20,000 refugees in Chiapas internally displaced by armed conflict. Conditions are exacerbated by the decision of the ICRC finally to close its office in 2004, leading to the ending of food distribution to 8,000 refugees in the communities of Pohlo and Chenalhó.

Yet, picking up the common national and international denominator of neoliberalism, the Zapatistas have also roundly criticised development proposals promoted by the Vicente Fox government, with Marcos stating that, 'although there is a radical difference in the way you came to power, your political, social and economic programme is the same we have been suffering under during the last administrations'.[12] Perhaps more ominously, Marcos went on to state in an interview with the national newspaper La Jornada, 'I don't know if our plans are terribly subversive, I don't believe so, but I do know that, if this isn't resolved, something terrible is going to explode, even without us.'[13] Fifthly and finally, therefore, the EZLN has continued to innovate with new forms of governance to challenge the Mexican state alongside pursuing tactics of land occupation. This initially led Richard Stahler-Stock (1998: 14) to observe that 'the real challenge to PRI hegemony lies in the Zapatistas' development projects, including collective agriculture, building local infrastructure, piping water from streams, training health promoters and starting up small enterprises'. Since the Zapatista uprising in 1994, land seized by various peasant organisations and indigenous communities has been estimated to be between 60,000 and 500,000 hectares, with government distribution in reaction to such seizures amounting to 180,000 hectares, although retaliation by landowners has reduced these figures (Barmeyer 2003: 133–4). More recently, since August 2003, the Zapatistas have expressed their resistance to the Mexican government through the creation of five caracoles (or 'spirals'), in the communities of Chiapas (La Garrucha, Morelia, Oventic, La Realidad, and Roberto Barrios) to replace the former autonomous municipalities that covered more than 30 townships. These caracoles are based on five Juntas of Good Government, in an attempt to further redefine and assert autonomy as well as to promote economic development. The caracoles cover the Guatemala border region, the southern and northern canyons, the northern zone and the highlands of Chiapas. They are responsible for carrying out legal, judicial, and economic policies across the range of education, health care, justice, and development. Further Zapatista communities have relocated from isolated communities in the Montes Azules bioreserve, to move to lands with easier access to the regional Juntas of Good Government to establish easier access to education and health care. Some Zapatista communities within the Juntas, throughout the state of Chiapas, have also implemented a strategy of raising income from coffee, by pushing up the price paid to peasant producers from 12.5 to 15 pesos per kilo (or US$0.54 to US$0.68 per pound). Whilst the EZLN has difficulty in protecting, defending, and expanding development initiatives and land redistribution in Chiapas it would again be precocious simply to dismiss such efforts. The autonomous communities no longer recognise government-imposed authorities, but democratically install their own community representatives. Within the newly created municipal structures, the Zapatista communities name their authorities and commissions for various spheres of duty, such as land management, education, health, justice, and women's rights (Barmeyer 2003: 135). It is for these endeavours that the achievements of the EZLN should be recognised, whilst it remains an open question as to what lasting effect it will have on the terrain of social struggle in Mexico.

All these novel features of 'anti-passive revolution' struggle were also present in the initiative launched on 1 January 2006, when a delegation of the EZLN departed from Chiapas to visit all Mexico's 32 states. This marked the first step in a new Zapatista political initiative known as the 'Other Campaign' (or *La Otra*), a proposal aiming to forge an 'anti-capitalist' alliance 'from below and to the left' in Mexico and beyond. The Other Campaign – timed to coincide with the 2006 Mexican presidential race, and including Subcomandante Marcos in a new role as Subdelegate Zero – aims to build a programme of struggle capable of constructing democracy from below along with national and international organisations resisting neoliberalism.

Conclusion: Subaltern Class Struggle and the Power of the Powerless

In 1910, a hacienda estate owner declared to the Zapatistas of the Mexican Revolution (1910–20), in the village of Anenecuilco, 'If that bunch wants to farm . . . let them farm in a flowerpot, because they are not getting any land' (see Womack 1968: 63). More recently, the EZLN have struggled to maintain the momentum for their rebellion over land, peasant autonomy through community development projects and, most significantly, in relation to the San Andrés Accords centred on indigenous rights. However, it would be too pessimistic to accord with Jorge Castañeda (personal interview, 9 and 13 March 1999, Mexico City), one-time secretary of foreign relations in the Vicente Fox administration, that 'despite having enormous international support and the emblematic aspects of a just cause, the movement has gone absolutely nowhere. The Zapatistas have been nowhere, gone nowhere and they are nowhere.' After all, as Gramsci (1996: 60–1, Q3§62) counselled:

> A realistic politics must not concern itself solely with immediate success . . . it must also create and safeguard those conditions that are necessary for future activity – and one of these is the education of the people. This is the issue. The higher the cultural level and the greater the development of the critical spirit, the more 'impartial' – that is, the more historically 'objective' – one's position will be.

The conclusions to draw from this chapter, then, centre on three dimensions related to the question of resistance within the global conditions of capitalist restructuring.

First, in terms of unpacking a sociology of power, due recognition has to be granted to the intertwined histories of hegemonic *and* subaltern-class resistance practices. This entails recognising the 'power of the powerless' or the modest expressions of human volition, the vast majority of which might remain anonymous but at the same time demand greater attention in order to understand structured agency. The case of the EZLN under analysis here highlights different dimensions of peasant-based agency and demands for control over land in Mexico – therefore vitiating claims about the disappearance of the peasantry as a meaningful social class engaged in active forms of resistance. Regardless of whether such agency results in repeated cycles of mass protest / negotiation / agreements / broken promises / mass protest (Petras and Veltmeyer 2002: 64–8), it is clear that the Zapatista rebellion has acted as a catalyst for wider resistance against the neoliberal project in and beyond Mexico. It resonates with Theodor Adorno's (1974: 151) view that knowledge must proceed less through a consideration of the 'fatally rectilinear' succession of victory and defeat and more through a reflection on those dynamics that fall by the wayside, the blind spots that escape the dialectic.

Second, the EZLN demonstrates that the existence and reproduction of indigenous identity largely depends on access to land, meaning that there is a class basis to their actions, due to the combination of their roles as peasant producers and wage labourers. As Gerardo Otero (2004) has outlined, class grievances and ethnic identity issues are important in the constitution of the peasantry within the EZLN movement, which shapes both their material interests and cultural aspects of identity set against the context of changing social relations of production. Issues of class struggle therefore matter. Whilst the EZLN itself is struggling to retain a presence in leading social movements in Mexico, the wider formation of class struggle through the intersection of labour and social movements in Mexico continues. Emblematic here is the forming of the Labour, Peasant, Social and Popular Front (FSCSP) – founded in 2002 by independent labour unions such as the National Union of Workers (UNT); the Permanent Agrarian Congress (CAP); and the Mexican Union Front (FSM) – to stand in opposition against the effects of the neoliberal agenda in Mexico. Demonstrations and work stoppages have thus far been organised through the FSCSP against the reform and privatisation of the social security system, the proposed reform of the Federal Labour Law to increase flexibilisation and employers' rights, and the privatisation of the energy sector in Mexico. The EZLN has been important in drawing attention to the transformation of class identities and forging links between labour and social movements. It has conducted its own understanding of class struggle, whilst aiming to establish 'the attainment of a "cultural–social" unity through which a multiplicity of dispersed wills, with heterogeneous aims, are welded together with a single aim, on the basis of an equal and common conception of the world' (Gramsci 1971: 349, Q10II§44). How such resistance mutates will therefore increasingly become an especially acute matter in the face of second-generation neoliberal reforms.

The third conclusion to draw in terms of the 'power of the powerless' relates to the politics of scale of such resistance. Linking in with the discussion in Chapter 6, at the heart of the spatial terrain of both hegemony and resistance is a combination of logics driven by transnational, regional, national, and local dynamics. One cannot afford to impute a singularly transnational logic to the domains of hegemony and resistance at the expense of local context and texture. 'Global solidarity activities', as Thomas Olesen (2004: 265) avers, 'in fact often originate at the local and national level and revolve around cultural and identity characteristics tied to these spaces.' Resistance initiatives are themselves embedded in the local experiences of wider capitalist processes. This demands due recognition of the different spatial scales of hegemony and resistance that work through transnational, state, and local power matrices without collapsing into a logic that privileges any single domain. Nevertheless it should be clear that how hegemony within 'the international' becomes translated and/or contested through local social formations is an intrinsic part of the picture of domination and resistance. This point should be at the forefront of analysis in the consideration of the second generation of neoliberal reforms in Mexico and Latin America, when further changes to property relations will reveal new social bases of discontent, resistance, and forms of class struggle articulated in the form of the power of the powerless. These are some of the principles at stake in questioning the conditions of hegemony and passive revolution within world order. These issues are summarised in the conclusion to the book, which also considers what is *limited* in the theoretical and practical unravelling of Gramsci's relevance to alternative socio-historical conditions and world power relations.

8 Conclusions *against* the *Prison Notebooks*

> The philosophy of praxis is precisely the concrete historicisation of philosophy and its identification with history.
> — Antonio Gramsci, *Quaderni del carcere*, Q11§22

Two principal tasks will be addressed in the conclusion to this book. First, there will be a return to the central contribution of the volume, which will provide the opportunity for a summary of the overall argument and all the main points that were raised throughout the preceding chapters. The basic contributions on the connection between hegemony and passive revolution within conditions of uneven development in the global political economy will be reiterated. Second, this conclusion will attend to a slightly different task, which requires a little more outline. In the Introduction (Chapter 1), it was emphasised how important it is to try to consider what might be historically *limited* in a theoretical and practical unravelling of Gramsci's way of thinking about hegemony and passive revolution to alternative social conditions of uneven development. After all, to engage with Gramsci not only requires empirical illustration but it also demands theoretical engagement *with* and *against* Gramsci (Nield and Seed 1981: 226). In some ways this involves taking the discussion beyond Gramsci. The second task, then, entails reflecting on some of the potential flaws in my own argument, which might even be thrown into relief by the analysis of different social conditions. Hence, four possible problems will be raised in the second section to this conclusion, all related to developing a Gramscian way of thinking about differing contexts of hegemony and passive revolution within conditions of uneven development. These possible problems, provocatively called conclusions *against* the *Prison Notebooks*, involve (1) querying the adequacy of Gramsci's notion of uneven development as a factotum of arguments about hegemony and passive revolution; (2) dealing with Gramsci's faith in the guiding role of the 'Modern Prince' (the Communist Party) and how this relates to present political conditions considered throughout the book; (3) considering to what extent problems may arise from a possible Leninist bias toward statism within Gramsci's framework; and (4) questioning whether one needs to be more reticent about the primary role attributed by Gramsci to social classes as the main agents of political change, and thus the extent to which there is a predetermined essentialist conception of human nature underpinning his analysis. As will be argued, the tactic of thinking in a Gramscian way about these potential problems – or conclusions 'against' the *Prison Notebooks* – will assist in providing the means for transcending such criticisms.

Summary of the Book

In analysing the class relationships, monetary systems, and international division of labour shaping the conditions of world economic crisis since 1929, Gramsci stated that 'the world is a unit, whether one likes it or not, and that all countries, when they remain in certain structural conditions, will pass through certain "crises"' (Gramsci 1995: 221, Q15§5). This book has argued that within the flux of geopolitical events that confronted Gramsci, he initiated a reconnaissance of the conditions of uneven development shaped both locally and on a world scale by questions of hegemony and passive revolution. On the basis of the exegetical stance established in Chapter 2, the themes of hegemony, passive revolution, and uneven development were expanded throughout the book by grasping the leitmotiv, or rhythm of thought, within Gramsci's theory and practice. This entailed detailing in subsequent chapters not only how Gramsci conceived capitalism as a world-historical phenomenon, within which states and groups of states with different levels of development were inserted, but also how these relationships on a world scale condition struggles over hegemony and passive revolution. Issues of state formation and passive revolution within 'the international' were therefore traced in Chapter 3, drawing on Gramsci's analysis of Renaissance Italy, the 'Southern Question' of uneven development, and the fractured hegemony shaping the passive revolution of the Italian Risorgimento. Pivotal here was the method of historical analogy deployed by Gramsci as an inter-pretative criterion for the study of state-formation processes. This historical sociological method grants explicative power in accounting for the causal sequencing of Italian state development within the wider history of the European states-system and the subsequent rise of capitalism. Unravelling Gramsci in this instance entailed presenting the theory of passive revolution as a major contribution to understanding the historical sociology of uneven development and the reciprocal influence of 'national' factors within 'the international' context of global capitalism. In Chapter 4, Gramsci's spatial awareness of the 'national' point of departure as nodal – passively and actively intertwined with 'the international' – was examined in relation to the articulation of hegemony. Whilst related to a set of wider issues, unravelling Gramsci on the construction and contestation of hegemony entailed delineating how the combination of both force and consent classically characterises the problem posed by hegemony and the historical basis of the modern state linking political society and civil society. This 'normal' condition of hegemony differs from the limited or fractured hegemony indicative of conditions of passive revolution based on an unstable equilibrium of compromises between social classes and the greater prevalence of fraud and corruption, if not bare coercion. In line with so much of Gramsci's thought, hegemony was considered by taking a 'national' point of departure, whilst also reflecting on the 'international' conditions of uneven development, most specifically with reference to 'Americanism and Fordism'.

In Part II of the book, the engagement and unravelling of Gramsci proceeded to consider conditions of hegemony and passive revolution within the uneven development of world order. Central to my argument here was that Gramsci's role in acknowledging the scalar manner of the 'national' point of departure as nodal in relation to 'the international' is crucial in attempting to unfold historical and contemporary trends of hegemony and passive revolution within the uneven development of the global political economy, as we saw in Chapter 5. In Chapter 6, the multiscalar focus on the passive revolution of capital within global accumulation processes, in the specific state form of Mexico, assisted this stance. Moreover, this approach helped to avoid the depiction of the passive diffusion of transnational capital through state forms, conceived as a simple 'transmission belt', commonly associated with the 'global capitalism' thesis. The inherent danger with the latter arguments about a transnational state is that class struggles extant in specific state forms become elided or flattened out by the attendant spatial and territorial assumptions of transnationalism. The politics of scale once again came to the fore in Chapter 7 in relation to questions of resistance, when the unravelling of Gramsci's understanding of 'counter'hegemonic strategies of structural transformation and subaltern class agency were deployed, once more in relation to the specific state form of Mexico. This chapter set about unravelling Gramsci on questions of resistance to neoliberalism and thus the very conditions of fractured hegemony and passive revolution constitutive of uneven development in Mexico. Overall, the book effectively meshes the two evaluative principles related to the unity of theory and practice outlined at the start of the study (see Chapter 2). Namely, (1) that theory is guided by an interest in understanding practical politics; and (2) that once a theory has advanced an understanding of an alternative concrete reality, it is expressive of the very conditions of that reality. Unravelling Gramsci throughout the book has therefore entailed both the concrete historicisation of philosophy and its identification with history.

Conclusions *against* the *Prison Notebooks*

In his early journalistic writings Antonio Gramsci reflected upon the Russian Bolshevik Revolution of 1917 and recognised it as the revolution *against* Karl Marx's *Capital*. By 'missing' a stage of 'bourgeois' capitalist development, the Russian Revolution revealed that the canons of historical materialism were not ironclad. Therefore, rather than following a rigid doctrine of dogmatic and unquestionable claims, people were 'living out' historical materialism, but without renouncing its deeper message of historical and political criticism (see Gramsci 1994c: 39–42). Later, in prison, Gramsci expanded on this line of thinking. A theory of historical materialism has to develop as a practical canon of historical study, he argued, rather than as a total conception of the world (Gramsci 1994a: 311). As James Joll (1977: 111) confirms, 'Gramsci wanted to write neither a handbook for revolutionaries nor a description of a future Utopia.'

With a similar emphasis and critical appreciation in mind, it is possible to reflect on some of the common problems associated with a Gramscian way of thinking about past and present social conditions in alternative contexts. The objective here is to consider what could be deemed problematic by *present* practical conditions of transformative politics (Davidson 1974: 142). A commitment to raising such problems is an important part of the reflexive enterprise that underpins the critical theoretical approach of this book. This entails reflection on the process of theorising as well as questioning those very assumptions and values that are accepted within a perspective. It is also an intrinsic part of a critical theory that is able to be critical of the world and of itself. Four problems are highlighted, as well as how the method of thinking in a Gramscian way might assist in transcending such pitfalls. After all, taking Gramsci's steer, 'Interpretations of the past, when one seeks the deficiencies and the errors . . . from the past itself, are not "history" but present-day politics *in nuce*' (Gramsci 2001, vol.5: 226, Q15§52).[1]

Beyond Uneven Development?

General conjecture on uneven development is faced with the metatheoretical critique that Marxist concepts have proved incapable of consistent application to the subject matter of development studies. Most controversially, this has been encapsulated in David Booth's overview of development sociology in the argument that the complex and challenging issues of development in postcolonial social formations cannot be sufficiently grasped in terms of the dynamics and differential spread of capitalism through uneven and combined development. The problem of 'picking off and lumping together' specific structures within 'national' state forms, which are pitched within the generality of laws of uneven development, it is argued, results in contorting state specificities to international causal factors of world capitalism (Booth 1985: 774; Booth 1994). The same argument about the suppression of different types and stages of development within postcolonial state forms – outside core states of the global economy – could also be extrapolated to those considerations of uneven development that similarly accord priority to international causal factors (e.g. Brenner 2003; Rosenberg 2005). The unfulfilled promise of theorisations on uneven development, then, is to combine an appreciation of the generality of capitalism with a historical sociology of transformations within specific forms of state. At issue here is whether theorisations of uneven development can capture the common and the distinct conditions that have faced the postcolonial state on a world scale, whether that be in relation, *inter alia*, to state corporatist, state capitalist, neo-patrimonialist, or developmentalist forms of state. This challenge could equally unravel the relevance of Gramsci's theorisation of uneven development to conditions of state formation. However, it should be clear from the argument throughout the book that one cannot presume uniform developments either within, or across, different regional state-formation processes. On the contrary, the pressures of uneven development are clearly mediated through different *forms of state* based on nationally specific configurations of class fractions and conditions of hegemony and/or passive revolution. By thinking in a Gramscian way about the specific peculiarities of state-formation processes, it is possible, then, to recover general tendencies, relevant to alternative historical and contemporary cases, within any diligent empirical account of uneven and combined development.

Similarly, one could also query whether Gramsci considered distinctive forms of hegemony and passive revolution within conditions of uneven development in a manner that effectively combined both a political dimension and a value-theoretic dimension. Does Gramsci's theory of hegemony, passive revolution, and uneven development avoid collapsing into 'soft economic sociology'?[2] Whether this charge is also evaded by wider historical-materialist considerations of uneven and combined development from a social property relations perspective is also open to debate. On this issue, the demarcation drawn by Gramsci between classical political economy and the 'critical economy' of historical materialism is significant (see Bieler and Morton 2003: 481–5). As Gramsci counsels, 'one must take as one's starting point the labour of all working people to arrive at definitions both of their role in economic production and of the abstract, scientific concept of value and surplus value' (Gramsci 1995: 168, Q10II§23). It is therefore significant that Gramsci identified Volume 3 of the 'critique of political economy' (or *Capital*) as being the central 'object of fresh study' in order to establish the organic importance of contradictions at the centre of the law of the tendential rate of profit to fall (Gramsci 1995: 431, Q10II§36; Gramsci 1971: 311–12, Q22§13; Marx 1894/1959: 211–66). Enter Gramsci, again:

> When can one imagine the contradiction reaching a Gordian knot, an insoluble pass requiring the intervention of Alexander with his sword? When the whole world economy has become capitalist and reached a certain level of development i.e. when the 'mobile frontier' of the capitalist world economy has reached its Pillars of Hercules. (Gramsci 1995: 429–30, Q10II§33)[3]

The reflections on absolute and relative surplus value, the study of the dynamic of socially necessary labour time, the observations on the law of the tendential rate of profit to fall within 'Americanism and Fordism', and thus the conception of value and surplus value, all evident within Gramsci's theorising of capitalism and uneven development, are thus still to be unravelled. Whether doing so would undermine Gramsci's theorisation of uneven development to conditions of state formation or contribute to thinking in a Gramscian way about such processes is substance for future debate.

Faith in the Guiding Role of the 'Modern Prince'?

In light of the analysis of resistance in Chapter 7, it would seem that faith in the guiding role of the 'Modern Prince' – the Communist Party – is fundamentally misplaced in today's social world. This assumption might stem from the series of novel features within the EZLN movement that pose challenges to ideas of political theory. Basing a reading of Gramsci on the political needs of *our* historical moment, then, faith in the guiding role of the 'Modern Prince' as an executant of political change stands as a historically limited and contingent element of Gramsci's problematic. If we are to seek conclusions beyond the plane of pure theory, we therefore need to consider why, how, and what present-day conditions are fostering concrete forms of political action. This could include considering in a Gramscian way the ways in which collective forms of political organisation still play a role. Some commentators, for instance, have considered a more nuanced theory of the party as a 'collective intellectual' relevant to forms of organisation within the global political economy. Such work has recognised the, at times, subtle understanding behind Gramsci's notion of the 'party' (Augelli and Murphy 1997: 31–2). Hence the importance of appreciating the way groups of newspapers or reviews (around which individual and collective interests could converge) were incorporated within Gramsci's notion of the 'party' (Gramsci 1971: 148–9, Q17§37). Accordingly, Gramsci recognised that capitalism could operate without a party as it found political representation in large newspapers (Gramsci 1977: 336). 'It is the newspapers, grouped in sets', wrote Gramsci (1992: 201, Q1§116), 'that constitute the real parties.' As a result, present-day analysis could proceed by focusing on the way research centres of global governance fulfil similar class (-related) functions in the global political economy. For example by analysing the roles of, among others, the World Bank, the United Nations Development Programme (UNDP), the World Trade Organization (WTO) or the World Economic Forum (WEF) as different 'parties' that shape world order (Murphy 1999: 289–304). This is one example of how conclusions ostensibly reached *against* the *Prison Notebooks* – rejecting a faith in the 'Modern Prince' – might then lead to a fruitful analysis of concrete issues by thinking in a Gramscian way about the present.

A further example could include the different ways in which state–civil society relations might be reconstructed by the co-ordination of popular movements through organic intellectuals linked to a 'postmodern' collective Prince (Cox 1999: 15; Gill 2000: 131–40). Indeed, this framing of the relationship between a 'party' and fundamental social-class forces is directly pertinent to the discussion of the EZLN in Chapter 7. Therefore, because the EZLN presents itself as an anti-party, but also binds together intellectual and political leaders with a mass base, it would be worthwhile considering within future research the nature of the EZLN as a 'party', or collective intellectual, in line with the critical approach outlined above. This could also help to raise questions about whether Gramsci was preoccupied with forms of modernity that have little contemporary relevance (Martin 1998: 169–71), which would include going beyond the notion of the party as creator of a new state.

A Leninist Bias toward Statism?

Additionally, it has been argued by some that there remains a Leninist bias toward statism within Gramsci's emphasis on forging collective interests into a political movement. He is part of an endeavour to 'change the world through the state' that has configured much of revolutionary thought in the twentieth century (Holloway 2002: 11–18). This commonly results, so the judgement goes, in achieving and/or contesting state power encompassing political communities (Nimni 1994: 193). There is certainly support for this interpretation, not only from those theoretical and practical activities conducted by Gramsci, but also within commentaries on such work (Day 2005). It has been remarked, for instance, that there is an authoritarian touch evident in Gramsci's conception of politics that might not be supported by contemporary tastes (Clark 1972: 496). Similarly, the drive toward unity that was implied in Gramsci's struggle has been highlighted as a key weakness, because it risks becoming, in the pejorative sense, totalitarian (Bellamy and Schecter 1993: 166).[4] It is supposed that the creation of an alternative form of state could not have been implemented in anything but a totalitarian manner (Bellamy 1987: 140; Bates 1976: 115–31).

To be sure, there is a conception of collective action that does not largely depart from a centralist focus on the political party and is thus essentially Leninist in perspective (Forgacs 1984: 95–6). Yet the approach Gramsci developed towards the party and the construction of a national–popular movement has to be seen as part of a dialectical tension. This involved the different but linked approaches between Gramsci's leadership of the Communist Party of Italy (PCd'I) and that of his predecessor Amadeo Bordiga (PCd'I leader, 1921–23). The Bordiga–Gramsci tension as we saw in Chapter 4, revolved around maintaining a rigid party (*à la* Bordiga) whilst propagating more 'molecular' and organic tendencies (*à la* Gramsci). These tendencies are part of a complex whole rather than a simple opposition (Williams 1975: 175–84). In this sense it is not possible simply to counterpoise Gramsci's authoritarian and democratic credentials. What is evident, though, is that Gramsci's credentials are not identifiable with the normative concerns of liberal-democratic pluralism. It should therefore be no surprise that they fail to satisfy the interests of those individuals who have an attachment to the tenets of liberal democracy. Yet, rather than leading one to develop conclusions that would entail the outright rejection of the *Prison Notebooks*, the invitation to think in a Gramscian way about such potential problems affords rich alternative avenues of enquiry.

One such avenue is evident, for example, in Gramsci's stress on grassroots forms of social change and political organisation. This is particularly supported by his theoretical and practical concerns, not only in prison but also during his pre-prison involvement in the Factory Councils movement of Turin. Although great emphasis was placed on a disciplined and organised party, there are clear indications that this activity was also conceived as 'anti-state' (Gramsci 1977: 58, 80). Such activity was also, importantly, regarded as separate from trade union forms of political organisation. Although trade unions could become tools of revolution, they were regarded as part of the reformist and bureaucratic structures that labour took as a commodity within capitalist societies (Gramsci 1977: 109–13, 265; Gramsci 1994c: 249–50). 'The trade union has an essentially competitive, not communist, character', Gramsci (1977: 99) argued; 'It cannot be the instrument for a radical renovation of society.'

In contrast, as outlined in Chapter 4, Gramsci sought for the emancipation of labour through the institution of Factory Councils during the period in Italy known as the *biennio rosso* (1919–20). These Factory Councils attempted to stand outside the realm of industrial legality and the political relations of the 'democratic' state. Albeit at times ambiguously, the Factory Councils aimed to destroy old hierarchies and build new 'state-like' organisations to replace the institutions of the democratic–parliamentary state (Gramsci 1977: 73–8, 340–3; Gramsci 1994c: 173–7). This amounted to an attempt to cultivate grassroots mechanisms of democracy, a revolution from below, which is distinguishable from a Leninist bias toward statism. It was part of 'a dynamic, democratic movement from below incompatible with any image of authoritarian control from above' (Femia 1998: 113; see also Martinelli 1968–69).

It can therefore be argued that Gramsci favoured forms of organic and democratic political organisation based on movement from below rather than authoritarian and bureaucratic control from above (Gramsci 1971: 185–90, Q13§36). Linking with the theme raised immediately above on the guiding role of political parties, Gramsci's fidelity towards Leninism did not express itself simply through an attachment to the vanguard party, nor did it collapse into a voluntarist presentation of revolutionary politics.

What Gramsci outlined was neither an anarchistic spontaneous mass movement nor an elite party that would be the exclusive repository of consciousness, but a synthesis of the two – an organic linkage between elite and mass, the organised and spontaneous, the planned element and the vital impulse. (Boggs 1976: 109)

But what does all this mean for present-day political practice? In terms of Gramsci's own thinking, one has to be clearly aware of the dialectical tension between authoritarian and democratic tendencies. Therefore, by acknowledging tensions in Gramsci's theory and practice, like the problematic issue of a Leninist bias toward statism, it might be possible to work through and remain attentive to such contradictions. This would be another advantage gained from thinking in a Gramscian way about alternative political conditions and internalising his method of enquiry about present political realities. This then throws up other issues that could act as pointers to future research. For example, is the way Gramsci envisaged emancipatory social mobilisation – outside the realm of conventional state institutions – relevant to contemporary politics? Is the fact that social movements today have developed their aims outside the realm of conventional politics a significant factor in terms of forming resistance against capitalism? Similarly, what is the place and purpose today of forms of social protest and political organisation linked to trade unions, which are organically located within and embedded in the structures of capitalist society? These are the sort of questions that will need answering in future research.

Social Classes as the Agents of Political Change?

Finally, it is important to question the extent to which one needs to be reticent about the primary role attributed by Gramsci to social classes as the agents of political change (Bellamy and Schecter 1993: 166). Is there a productivist bias at the heart of such an approach that remains blinkered to the variety of identities that form in the consciousness of individual and collective actors? Is there a predetermined essentialist conception of human nature underpinning the analysis?

It is possible to answer such questions by noting how the term 'class' has been developed during the course of this book. An exploitation-centred conception of class was developed, rooted in the social relations of production and the antagonistic interests between exploiter and exploited that flow from such social relations (see Chapters 5, 6 and 7). To cite E.P. Thompson (1978: 149) on this process:

> People find themselves in a society structured in determined ways (crucially, but not exclusively, in productive relations), they experience exploitation (or the need to maintain power over those whom they exploit), they identify points of antagonistic interest, they commence to struggle around these issues and in the process of struggling they discover themselves as classes, they come to know this discovery as class-consciousness.

It was in this way that the concept of class, deriving from the notion of exploitation, was developed, in a discussion of the changing forms of productive relations and uneven development in Mexico (see Chapters 6 and 7). Yet this discussion did not overlook other forms of identity. Instead the concept of class captured a broad array of subaltern identities that have points of common convergence within the logic of exploitation. As a result, it was possible to avoid a class-reductionist argument, by appreciating that a variety of 'non-class' forms of identity arise as aspects related to the combined exploitation of the social and natural environment.

By extension, the focus on contexts of exploitation reveals an *emergentist* theory of class struggle situated in particular historical contexts of hegemony, passive revolution, and relations of uneven development, rather than mechanically deriving from objective determinations that have an automatic place in production relations (see Morton 2006a; 2007). This is preferential to the ideological hypostatisation of social conflict, formalised within the category of an antagonistic but totally contingent society, where history is considered as a succession of articulatory practices discursively produced and formed (Morton 2005a). As Maurice Finocchiaro (1992/2005: 230) has indicated, Gramsci holds an *anti-reductionist* approach to the question of theory and practice as an overall feature of his dialectical approach to the philosophy of praxis, to the degree that the Italian Marxist provides 'an account of the unity of theory and practice which advocates a nonreductionist and interactionist approach to the question of the relation of logic and politics'. Once again, by raising potential problems *against* the *Prison Notebooks* and by thinking in a Gramscian way about adaptations to changing circumstances, it is possible to think critically about such issues and outline how future debate might then proceed.

Conclusion: 'the Revolutionary Tide'

When introducing Gramsci at the beginning of this book, reference was made to one of his commonly used seafaring metaphors. 'We are in the flow of the historical current', stated Gramsci in 1923, 'and will succeed, provided we "row" well and keep a firm grasp on the rudder' (Gramsci 1978: 140). Perhaps such metaphors were used by Gramsci to convey the sense of intense social struggle involved in navigating a way through the stormy waters of capitalism. Even in prison, Gramsci wrote of his duty as captain not to abandon the sinking ship – meaning the PCd'I – unless all others could be saved in the effort to avoid shipwreck (Gramsci 1995: lxxxiv-lxxxvii, Q15§9). Similarly, in a journalistic article that was charged with earlier optimism, Gramsci referred to the 'revolutionary tide' that was breaking on a world scale between the period 1917 and 1919 (Gramsci 1977: 61). Although the nature of capitalism has certainly changed since this period it is still arguably no less threatening to those carried by and fighting against the tides of social and political upheaval today.

The purpose of this book was to examine such issues, by unravelling the historical and contemporary relevance of the thought and practice of Antonio Gramsci to factors of hegemony and passive revolution in the global political economy. By following the premise that Gramsci's approach to uneven development reveals pertinent concerns about conditions of hegemony and passive revolution, it was possible to explore new questions about his thought and action. It has therefore been argued that Gramsci can still help us to chart some kind of course through the stormy waters of capitalism, to examine the 'revolutionary' tides of social and political upheaval, even if at times he appears to be a little more rudderless or less helpful than one would like. Hence, throughout the book, there has been an emphasis on thinking in a Gramscian way about hegemony, passive revolution and uneven development, rather than rigidly 'applying' Gramsci's concepts, or believing that Gramsci has all the answers to present-day problems. It is the way in which he poses old questions and promotes one to ask new questions about capitalism and the problem of hegemony that maintains Gramsci's enduring resonance. As a result, it was possible to develop a Gramscian way of thinking, centred on the problematic of hegemony and passive revolution, about alternative social conditions. The objective was to do this in a manner that internalised Gramsci's method of thinking – the leitmotiv or rhythm of his thought – in considering the struggle over hegemony and passive revolution. As a result, a concrete account was given of the antagonisms, conflicts and contradictions of capital as well as the intensifying resistance against such forces within a specific context of uneven development in the case of Mexico. Through the motif of 'unravelling Gramsci', the book itself thus becomes an invitation to understand processes of hegemony and passive revolution within the conditions of uneven development shaping the global political economy. At the same time, it is also an invitation to think about practices that might rise above the circumstances of uneven development in world order. 'Tomorrow we will not declare the world we have built to be final', Gramsci stated, 'but rather we will always leave the road open toward betterment.'[5] This book has argued that both Gramsci's theory and his practice stand as essential components in critical argument about the past and present structured agencies shaping uneven development in world order.

Notes

Chapter 1

1. Also see the emphasis on moving beyond Gramsci as a necessary reflection on present political conditions in Landy (1994).
2. For further important references made by Gramsci to an 'intellectual plan' based on a 'cultural framework', see the letter to Tatiana Schucht (25 March 1929) in Gramsci (1994a: 256–9) and the letter to Tatiana Schucht (17 November 1930) in Gramsci (1994a: 360–1).
3. A specific convention associated with citing the *Prison Notebooks* is adopted in this book. In addition to giving the reference to the selected anthologies, the notebook number (Q) and section (§) accompanies all citations, to enable the reader to trace their specific collocation. The concordance table used is that compiled by Marcus Green and is available at the website of the International Gramsci Society, http://www.italnet.nd.edu/gramsci.
4. My translation here differs slightly from that found in Joll (1977: 109).
5. The following have made pointers in this direction: Kiernan (1974: 19–24); Mouffe and Showstack Sassoon (1977: 59); Hobsbawm (1977: 206); Davidson (1984: 139–54); Brennan (1988–89: 87–114); and Watson (1993).
6. The literature on this is extensive. Guha and Spivak (1988) or Arnold (1984) would be useful starting-points.
7. As cited in the profile by Madeleine Bunting in the *Guardian* (London), 'Passion and pessimism' (5 April 2003).
8. My translation. This passage appears out of context in its original placement in the English translation of the anthologies of the *Prison Notebooks*; see Gramsci (1975n.75). My attention was drawn to it by Gill (2004: 38).

Chapter 2

1. These demands were originally presaged by Hazel Smith's (1994: 147) warning that the incorporation within international studies of insights derived from Antonio Gramsci ran 'the risk of denuding the borrowed concepts of the theoretical significance in which they cohere'. Walker (1993: 93) also forewarned that 'Thucydides, Machiavelli, Hobbes, Rousseau and the rest [Gramsci? A.D.M.] appear to us as quite unproblematic figures, often in disguises that make them quite unrecognisable to anyone who examines the textual evidence we have of them'. Hence his concern about the 'interpretive violence' committed in the treatment of political theorists that have become mere cyphers for the necessities of power politics (Walker 1993: 23, 41).

2. This was noted in Chapter 1 as a tendency to indulge in the 'soft-focusing of Gramsci', see Lester (2000: 143).
3. It is worth noting that Gramsci himself expressed similar dissatisfaction with those who thought they could possess the keys to open all intellectual problems; see Gramsci (1985: 93, 23§3).
4. See also Gramsci (1994a: 40, 160, 161) and Gramsci (1994b: 365).
5. The significance of this piece and the role it played in Gramsci's thought should not be underestimated. In Gramsci's own writings this can be traced through the *Prison Notebooks* (Gramsci 1985: 147–63, Q4§78–§87). Crucial points are also raised in the prison letters, see Gramsci (1994a: 237–8, 284–5; Gramsci 1994b: 13–16, 56, 67–8, 140–1, 151–4). For commentaries, see Rosengarten (1986) and Bové (1991).
6. For an analysis of Gramsci's wider theatre criticism and the importance of Pirandello, see Dombroski (1986).
7. Useful works here would include Cammet (1967), Clark (1977), Davidson (1977), Fiori (1970), Spriano (1975), and Williams (1975).
8. I would like to thank both Trevor Griffiths and Gill Griffiths for providing me with copies of these articles.
9. For an important endeavour to critically explore Gramsci's criticisms of Croce, see Bellamy (2001).
10. This method is also echoed within wider currents of critical theory. Herbert Marcuse in *One-Dimensional Man* similarly tackles the 'spectre of historicism' by questioning the 'objective' basis on which to distinguish between different and conflicting ways of conceiving history. For Marcuse, the quest of judging between different philosophic and historic projects has a basis in two aspects of social reality:

    1. by virtue of the 'matter' opposed to the apprehending and comprehending subject which is not dissolvable into subjectivity; and
    2. by virtue of the structure of the specific society in which the development of concepts takes place.

    These two aspects of 'objectivity' pertain, respectively, to the physical structure of matter and to the form which matter has acquired in the collective historical practice that has made it into objects for a subject. The criteria for the 'truth value' of different historical projects thus lie in the manner in which a historical project realises given possibilities through practice. As Marcuse states, in capitalism, 'society has already demonstrated its truth value as historical project' (or has established a practical efficacy through the form of 'truth' in human action), which itself generates a transcendent sense of alternative historical projects attempting to establish efficacy in the concrete reality of social relations (Marcuse 1964/1999: 217–22).

Chapter 3

1. Although Isaiah Berlin (1979: 31n.1) demurs, stating that '[t]he Renaissance did not view itself in historical perspective . . . Machiavelli did not do, and could not have done, what he set out to do.'

2. From 'the robbery of common lands' to 'the usurpation of feudal and clan property' there were 'many idyllic methods of primitive accumulation' that 'conquered the field for capitalistic agriculture, made the soil part and parcel of capital, and created for the town industries the necessary supply of a "free" and outlawed proletariat' (Marx 1887/1996: 723).

3. Generally the notion of a 'bourgeois revolution' implies a revolutionary upheaval that advances the rise of capitalism, by changing property forms or the nature of the state, 'but such an all-embracing notion obscures as much as it reveals' (Wood 2002a: 118). This is because it is difficult to distinguish what was cause or consequence in the transition to capitalism, often imputing a self-conscious 'bourgeoisie' as central to the process before such a class has consciously emerged and cohered (Hobsbawm 1986: 22; Wood 2002a: 116–21). This position is raised as particularly problematic if the archetypal case of 'bourgeois revolution', the French Revolution, is better understood as a more complex product of intra-class conflict between aristocracy and monarchy, as 'a sort of civil war within the dominant class' (Comninel 1987: 200; Comninel 2003: 94).

4. Note here Rosenberg's important recasting of the causal mechanism of unevenness, so that, '"combined and uneven development" describes (without itself theorising) a general situation, while "uneven and combined development" denotes a specific causal sequence (unevenness leading to combined development), which it postulates as central to the overall shape of the modern historical process' (Rosenberg 2005: 68–9n.28). But also note the earlier commentary on this issue by George Novack, who states that 'the unevenness of development must precede any combinations of the disproportionately developed factors', so that uneven development provides the basis for the correlation of combined development (Novack 1972: 98).

5. My attention to this quotation was prompted by Wood's (2002b: 54) citation of the same passage.

6. The appellation derives from the title of a sequence of poems by Gabriele D'Annunzio.

7. Although it has to be noted that the term passive revolution itself is a thoroughly modified borrowing from Vincenzo Cuoco (1770–1823) and his account of the 1799 revolution, or Parthenopean Republic, in Naples.

8. It is worth noting that the concept of passive revolution was developed by Gramsci as an explicit elaboration of Marx's 'Preface' to *A Contribution to the Critique of Political Economy*, see Marx (1859/1987: 261–5).

9. Significantly, Roger Simon (1991: 34) has noted that 'Gramsci's account of the French Revolution verges on the idealistic' and signal differences can be witnessed between this reading and additional Marxist accounts (see Hobsbawm 1990 and Comninel 1987).

10. This quotation is referred to in Slater's (2004: 160) study of the geopolitical unevenness of development intrinsic to colonial and postcolonial power relations.

Chapter 4

1. For a general discussion of this approach to trade unions, see Frank Annunziato (1988: 142–64).

2. As Joseph Buttigieg (2005: 39) argues, Gramsci's use of the word 'state' only gives rise to confusion if his *Prison Notebooks* are read selectively and individual notes are removed from their content.

3. Eric Hobsbawm (1987: 286) aptly describes Croce as the first 'post-Marxist'.

4. Whilst backed up with the full force of military neoliberalism, it is significant that the destruction of infrastructure, ministries, museums, the national library, and archives during the 2003 invasion of Iraq was also partly 'a mask for the destruction of the collective memory and modern state of a key Arab nation, and the manufacture of disorder to create a hunger for the occupier's supervision'; see R. Drayton, 'Shock, awe and Hobbes have backfired on America's neocons', *Guardian* (28 December 2005): 26.

5. Whilst space restrictions preclude full elaboration, this conception differs in marked ways from the focus on discursive formations in *The Archaeology of Knowledge* (Foucault 1972), essentially because of the non-determinism linked to Foucault's notion of capillary power. For a more detailed critique of the deficits of discourse, see Bieler and Morton (forthcoming).

6. As Lenin put it, 'From the standpoint of Marxism, the class, so long as it renounces the idea of hegemony or fails to appreciate it, is not a class, or not yet a class, but a *guild*, or the sum total of various guilds. . . . It is the consciousness of the idea of hegemony and its implementation through their own activities that converts the guilds as a whole into a class' (Lenin 1963: 57–8, as cited by Anderson 1976/1977: 17).

7. This is the fundamental issue for Stuart Hall in undermining the intertextual constitution of subjectivities within discourse theory. There is no conception of the historical forces that structure concrete individuals and the interpellation of identities, so that tendencies such as the implantation of capital disappear. Hence, Foucault 'saves for himself "the political" within his insistence on power, but he denies himself *a politics* because he has no idea of the "relations of force"' (Hall 1996: 136).

8. Whilst this concept can be referred to as 'historic bloc' this convention is not followed because it can be misleading to place too much emphasis on the momentous, one-off, or literally 'historic' formation of such a bloc. This can give a static or 'snapshot-like' depiction rather than draw attention to dynamic processes that unfold, through the aspect of hegemony, within the *historical process*, and thus through the making of history; see Derek Boothman (1995: xi–xii) and Wolfgang Fritz Haug (1999: 111).

9. On this issue, see also Daniel O'Connell's (1993) view on Sinclair Lewis.

10. Issues that similarly touched Walter Benjamin, in his concern over the reproduction of works of art and the loss of authenticity, aura,

and uniqueness in the technical reproduction of reality; see Benjamin (1936/1970: 211–44).

11. On the positive side of this approach to the 'sexual question', see the letter to Teresina Gramsci Paulesu (4 May 1931) in Gramsci (1994b: 31–2); the remarks on Ibsen in Gramsci (1985: 70–3, 359–62, Q21§6); or Fiori (1970: 104–5). On the negative side, see the disparaging remarks in the letters to Tatiana Schucht (25 April 1927) in Gramsci (1994a: 103–7); to Tatiana Schucht (23 March 1931); and the letters to Giulia Schucht (28 November 1932, December 1936) in Gramsci (1994b: 19–21, 234–6, 367–8). The relationship between Gramsci, his wife Giulia Schucht, and his sister-in-law Tatiana are discussed in Teresa de Lauretis (1987) and Renate Holub (1992: Chap.7).

12. I am grateful to Bob Jessop for bringing this *aperçu* to my attention.

Chapter 5

1. Although overlaps may exist, the critical impetus bears an indirect affiliation with the constellation of social thought known as the Frankfurt School represented by, among others, the work of Max Horkheimer, Theodor Adorno or, more recently Jürgen Habermas (Cox 1995a: 32). Hence, Cox may not explicitly understand himself to be working within the fold of the Frankfurt School, although some of his positions may correlate (Schechter 2002: 4). For a useful discussion of the contradictory strands and influences between Frankfurt School critical theory and critical IR theory, see Wyn Jones (2000).

2. In this letter to his sister-in-law, Tatiana Schucht, dated 27 February 1928, Gramsci's ridicule is directed towards an anonymous prisoner – an Evangelist, Methodist, or Presbyterian – who has become obsessed not only with the impact of Buddhism on European Christianity but also with questions of race. Gramsci's aim was to therefore 'trap him in a briar patch of ideas with no way out' and to point out to him the absurdity of having to 'look at himself more attentively in the mirror in order to catch a glimpse of the coloured pigments in his blood' as a result of changes in cultural influence from Asian and African-American backgrounds (Gramsci 1994a: 178–80).

3. It is worth noting that, whilst the Keynesian welfare state form is referred to by Cox as the 'neoliberal state', this precedent is not followed here. This is because confusion can result when using his term and distinguishing it from the more conventional understanding of neoliberalism related to processes in the late 1970s and 1980s, which he calls 'hyperliberalism'.

4. It is noteworthy, though, that the metaphor of a transmission belt has been withdrawn from more recent work (Cox 2002: 33). On contentions surrounding the notion of the state as a 'transmission belt', see Bieler et al., (2006).

5. James Scott (1998) has extended this awareness in an interesting way by encompassing a variety of state naming practices, or 'state simplifications', that enhance the legibility of society.

6. Many of Gramsci's own insights, discussed in Chapter 4, on the conflict between capital and labour – arising from political action within new

workers' organisations known as 'Factory Councils' in Turin during the *biennio rosso* (1919–20) – have relevance here.

Chapter 6

1. It is noteworthy, though, that the metaphor of a transmission belt has been withdrawn from his more recent work (see Cox 2002: 33).
2. As representative works, see Morton (2002) on the EZLN or Petras and Veltmeyer (2002) and Rocha and Branford (2002) on the MST.
3. My attention to this quotation is owed to the citation by Kiely (2005: 44).
4. The phrase arises in Anderson (1983: 100).
5. See Morton (2006b) for an initial contribution to this project.
6. This citation owes a debt to the reading of Harvey (1982: 450).
7. For a more detailed examination of this intellectual's role in Mexico, see Morton (2003b).

Chapter 7

1. Recall that the phrase is Buci-Glucksmann's (1979: 232).
2. For a more critical analysis of Ruiz, see Krauze (1999: 65–73).
3. Amnesty International, 'Mexico: Torture with Impunity' (London: Amnesty International, AMR 41/04/91) and Amnesty International, 'Mexico: The Persistence of Torture and Impunity' (London: Amnesty International, AMR 41/01/93).
4. Report by an Independent Delegation to Mexico, *Chiapas, Before It's too Late...* (March 1998), 20. This consisted of an eight-person team formed with the help and advice of the aid agencies CAFOD, Trocaire, Save the Children Fund/UK, SCIAF and the Polden Puckham Charitable Trust, which visited Chiapas, 13–23 March 1998. I would like to thank Nikki Craske, who was a member of the delegation, for a copy of the report.
5. Coordinación de Organismos no Gubernamentales por la Paz de Chiapas (CONPAZ), Centro de Derechos Humanos Fray Bartolomé de las Casas, y Convergencia de Organismos Civiles por la Democracia, *Militarisation and Violence in Chiapas* (Servicios Procesados, A.C., 1997).
6. See Report by an Independent Delegation to Mexico, *Chiapas, Before It's too Late...*, 19.
7. For a more detailed examination of this intellectual's role as a *passive revolutionary* in Mexico, see Morton (2003b).
8. *The Times* [London], 'Doomed uprising rips veil from Mexican "miracle"' (7 January 1994).
9. *The Economist* [London], 'Back to square one in Chiapas' (5 May 2001).
10. Subcomandante Marcos, 'The Fourth World War Has Begun', *Le Monde diplomatique* (September 1997), English print edition, http://www.monde-diplomatique.fr/en; accessed 16 April 2000.
11. *The Economist* (London), 'A Fresh Start for Chiapas' (12 August 2000), 53–4.

12. Subcomandante Marcos, 'Letter to Vicente Fox' (2 December 2000), http://www.ezln.org; accessed 30 January 2001.
13. Carlos Monsiváis and Hermann Belinghausen, 'Interview with Subcomandante Marcos', *La Jornada* (Mexico City) (8 January 2001), http://www.ezln.org; accessed 30 January 2001.

Chapter 8

1. Following Anne Showstack Sassoon's (1987: 205) translation of this passage.
2. The phrase is Jessop's (2006b: 163).
3. In a geographical sense the Pillars of Hercules refer to the promontories flanking the Strait of Gibraltar, identified with Gibraltar in Europe and Cueta in Africa. In Greek mythology, the tenth labour conferred on Hercules entailed fetching the Cattle of Geryon, during which he created the mountains known as the Pillars of Hercules. The pillars came to demarcate the utmost limits of seafaring. One can therefore take the analogy to refer to the utmost limits in the accumulation of capital, or the stage at which contradictions in the mobile frontier of capital can no longer be surmounted. In Rosa Luxemburg's (1913/2003: 397) terms, a moment when granting a fresh lease of life, to avoid 'the standstill of accumulation', cannot be accomplished. Clearly, this is a moment that is still historically pending.
4. As noted by Bellamy, in a separate piece, the term 'totalitarianism' was coined during Gramsci's time to refer to the aspiration of uniting Italy around a 'total' vision (Communist or Fascist), therefore care must be taken in the use of the term. However, Bellamy concludes that Gramsci's own project would still have ended up being as coercive as Stalin's; see Richard Bellamy, 'How not to make Italians', *Times Literary Supplement* (22 December 1995): 12.
5. As cited by Finnochiaro (1992/2005: 211).

Bibliography

Adamson, W. L. (1980) *Hegemony and Revolution: A Study of Antonio Gramsci's Political and Cultural Theory*. Berkeley: University of California Press.

Adorno, T. W. (1974) *Minima Moralia: Reflections from Damaged Life*, trans. E. F. N. Jephcott. London: Verso.

Agnew, J. (1994) 'The Territorial Trap: The Geographical Assumptions of International Relations Theory', *Review of International Political Economy*, 1(1): 53–80.

—— (2001) *Reinventing Geopolitics: Geographies of Modern Statehood* (Hettner-Lecture 2000). Heidelberg: University of Heidelberg.

—— (2003) *Geopolitics: Re-Visioning World Politics*, 2nd edn. London: Routledge.

—— (2005) *Hegemony: The New Shape of Global Power*. Philadelphia: Temple University Press.

Althusser, L. (1993) *The Future Lasts a Long Time*, trans. R. Veasey. London: Chatto & Windus.

—— (1999) *Machiavelli and Us*, trans. and intro. G. Elliot. London: Verso.

Amin, S. (1974) *Accumulation on a World Scale: A Critique of the Theory of Underdevelopment*, trans. B. Pearce. New York: Monthly Review Press.

Amoore, L. (ed.) (2005a) *The Global Resistance Reader*. London: Routledge.

—— (2005b) 'Introduction: Global Resistance – Global Politics', in L. Amoore (ed.) *The Global Resistance Reader*. London: Routledge.

Amoore, L., R. Dodgson, R. Germain, B. Gills, P. Langley, and I. Watson (2000) 'Paths to a Historicised International Political Economy', *Review of International Political Economy*, 7(1): 53–71.

Anderson, P. (1974a) *Passages from Antiquity to Feudalism*. London: Verso.

—— (1974b) *Lineages of the Absolutist State*. London: Verso.

—— (1976/1977) 'The Antinomies of Antonio Gramsci', *New Left Review* (I), 100: 5–78.

—— (1992) *English Questions*. London: Verso.

—— (1983) *In the Tracks of Historical Materialism*. London: Verso.

—— (2002) 'Force and Consent', *New Left Review* (II), 17: 5–30.

—— (2005) *Spectrum: From Right to Left in the World of Ideas*. London: Verso.

Annuziato, F.R. (1988) 'Gramsci's Theory of Trade Unionism', *Rethinking Marxism*, 1(2): 142–64.

Apeldoorn, B. van (2002) *Transnational Capitalism and the Struggle over European Integration*. London: Routledge.

—— (2004) 'Theorising the Transnational: A Historical Materialist Approach', *Journal of International Relations and Development*, 7(2): 142–76.

Arnold, D. (1984) 'Gramsci and Peasant Subalternity in India', *The Journal of Peasant Studies*, 11(4): 155–77.

Arrighi, G. (2005a) 'Hegemony Unravelling – 1', *New Left Review* (II), 32: 23–80.

—— (2005b) 'Hegemony Unravelling – 2', *New Left Review* (II), 33: 83–116.

Ashley, R. K. (1984) 'The Poverty of Neorealism', *International Organization*, 38(2): 225–86.

—— (1989) 'Living on Border Lines: Man, Poststructuralism and War', in J. Der Derian and M. Shapiro (eds) *International/Intertextual Relations: Postmodern Readings of World Politics*. Toronto: Lexington Books.

Aubry, A. and A. Inda (1998) 'Who Are the Paramilitaries in Chiapas?', *NACLA Report on the Americas*, 31(5): 8–10.

Augelli, E. and Murphy, C.N. (1988) *America's Quest for Supremacy and the Third World: A Gramscian Analysis*. London: Pinter.

—— (1997) 'Consciousness, Myth and Collective Action: Gramsci, Sorel and the Ethical State', in S. Gill and J.H. Mittelman (eds) *Innovation and Transformation in International Studies*. Cambridge: Cambridge University Press.

Badie, B. and P. Birnbaum (1983) *The Sociology of the State*, trans. A. Goldhammer. Chicago: University of Chicago Press.

Baker, A. (1999) '*Nébuleuse* and the "Internationalisation of the State" in the UK?', *Review of International Political Economy*, 6(1): 79–100.

Balakrishnan, G. (2005) 'States of War', *New Left Review* (II), 36: 5–32.

Baránski, Z. G. (1990) 'Pier Paolo Pasolini: Culture, Croce, Gramsci', in Z. G. Baránski and R. Lumley (eds) *Culture and Conflict in Postwar Italy: Essays on Mass and Popular Culture*. London: Macmillan.

Barmeyer, N. (2003) 'The Guerrilla Movement as a Project: An Assessment of Community Involvement in the EZLN', *Latin American Perspectives*, 30(1): 122–38.

Bates, T. R. (1976) 'Antonio Gramsci and the Bolshevisation of the PCI', *Journal of Contemporary History*, 11(2–3): 115–31.

Barry, T. (1995) *Zapata's Revenge: Free Trade and the Farm Crisis*. Boston, Mass.: South End Press.

Bellamy, R. (1987) *Modern Italian Social Theory: Ideology and Politics from Pareto to the Present*. Cambridge: Polity Press.

—— (1990) 'Gramsci, Croce and the Italian Political Tradition', *History of Political Thought*, 11(2): 313–37.

—— (1992) 'Gramsci for the Italians', *Times Literary Supplement* (14 August): 5.

—— (1994) 'Introduction', in A. Gramsci, *Pre-Prison Writings*, ed. R. Bellamy, trans. V. Cox. Cambridge: Cambridge University Press.

—— (1995) 'How Not to Make Italians', *Times Literary Supplement* (22 December): 12.

—— (1997) 'The Intellectual as Social Critic: Antonio Gramsci and Michael Walzer', in J. Jennings and A. Kemp-Welch (eds) *Intellectuals in Politics: From the Dreyfus Affair to Salman Rushdie*. London: Routledge.

—— (2001) 'A Crocean Critique of Gramsci on Historicism, Hegemony and Intellectuals', *Journal of Modern Italian Studies*, 6(2): 209–29.

—— and Schecter, D. (1993) *Gramsci and the Italian State*. Manchester: Manchester University Press.

Beloff, M. (1954) *The Age of Absolutism, 1660–1815*. London: Hutchinson.

Benjamin, T. (1996) *A Rich Land, A Poor People: Politics and Society in Modern Chiapas*, with a foreword by L. Meyer. Albuquerque: University of New Mexico Press.

Benjamin, W. (1936/1970) 'The Work of Art in the Age of Mechanical Reproduction', in W. Benjamin, *Illuminations*, trans. H. Zohn. London: Jonathan Cape.

—— (1940/1970) 'Theses on the Philosophy of History', in W. Benjamin, *Illuminations*, trans. H. Zohn. London: Jonathan Cape.

Berins Collier, R. (1992) *The Contradictory Alliance: State–Labour Relations and Regime Change in Mexico*. Berkeley: University of Berkeley Press.

Berlin, I. (1979) 'The Originality of Machiavelli', in I. Berlin, *Against the Current: Essays in the History of Ideas*. London: Hogarth Press.

Bernstein, H. (2000) '"The Peasantry" in Global Capitalism: Who, Where and Why?' in L. Panitch and C. Leys (eds) *Socialist Register: Working Classes, Global Realities*. London: Merlin Press.

—— (2002) 'Land Reform: Taking a Long(er) View', *Journal of Agrarian Change*, 2(4): 433–63.

Bieler, A. (2000) *Globalisation and Enlargement of the EU: Austrian and Swedish Social Forces in the Struggle over Membership*. London: Routledge.

—— (2001) 'Questioning Cognitivism and Constructivism in IR Theory: Reflections on the Material Structure of Ideas', *Politics*, 21(2): 93–100.

—— (2003) 'Labour, Neoliberalism and the Conflict over Economic and Monetary Union: A Comparative Analysis of British and German Trade Unions', *German Politics*, 12(2): 24–44.

—— (2005) 'European Integration and the Transnational Restructuring of Social Relations: The Emergence of Labour as a Regional Actor?' *Journal of Common Market Studies*, 43(3): 461–84.

—— (2006) *Struggle for a Social Europe: Trade Unions and EMU in Times of Global Restructuring*. Manchester: Manchester University Press.

Bieler, A. and A. D. Morton (eds) (2001a) *Social Forces in the Making of the New Europe: The Restructuring of European Social Relations in the Global Political Economy*. London: Palgrave.

—— (2001b) 'The Gordian Knot of Agency-Structure in International Relations: A Neo-Gramscian Perspective', *European Journal of International Relations*, 7(1): 5–35.

—— (2003) 'Globalisation, the State and Class Struggle: A "Critical Economy" Engagement with Open Marxism', *British Journal of Politics and International Relations*, 5(4): 467–99.

—— (2004) '"Another Europe is Possible?": Labour and Social Movements at the European Social Forum', *Globalizations*, 1(2): 305–27.

—— (forthcoming) 'The Deficits of Discourse in IPE: Turning Base Metal into Gold?', *International Studies Quarterly*.

—— (eds) (2006) *Images of Gramsci: Connections and Contentions in Political Theory and International Relations*. London: Routledge.

Bieler, A., W. Bonefeld, P. Burnham, and A. D. Morton (2006) *Global Restructuring, State, Capital and Labour: Contesting Neo-Gramscian Perspectives*. London: Palgrave.

Bilgin, P. and A. D. Morton (2002) 'Historicising Representations of "Failed States": Beyond the Cold War Annexation of the Social Sciences?' *Third World Quarterly*, 23(1): 55–80.

Blaut, J. M. (1993) *The Colonizer's Model of the World: Geographical Diffusionism and Eurocentric History*. New York: The Guilford Press.

—— (1999) 'Marxism and Eurocentric Diffusionism', in R. Chilcote (ed.) *The Political Economy of Imperialism: Critical Appraisals*. Dordrecht: Kluwer.

Boggs, C. (1976) *Gramsci's Marxism*. London: Pluto Press.

Bohle, D. (2006) 'Neoliberal Hegemony, Transnational Capital and the Terms of the EU's Eastward Enlargement', *Capital and Class*, 88: 57–86.

Booth, D. (1985) 'Marxism and Development Sociology: Interpreting the Impasse', *World Development*, 13(7): 761–87.

—— (ed.) (1994) *Rethinking Social Development: Theory, Research and Practice*. Harlow: Longman.

Boothman, D. (1995) 'Introduction', in A. Gramsci, *Further Selections from the Prison Notebooks*, ed. and trans. D. Boothman. London: Lawrence & Wishart.

Bové, P. (1991) 'Dante, Gramsci and Cultural Criticism', *Rethinking Marxism*, 4(1): 74–86.

Brass, T. (2002) 'Latin American Peasants: New Paradigms for Old?' *Journal of Peasant Studies*, 29(3/4): 1–40.

—— (2005) 'Neoliberalism and the Rise of (Peasant) Nations within the Nation: Chiapas in Comparative and Theoretical Perspective', *Journal of Peasant Studies*, 32(3/4): 651–91.

Brennan, T. (1988–89) 'Literary Criticism and the Southern Question', *Cultural Critique*, 11: 87–114.

—— (2001) 'Antonio Gramsci and Postcolonial Theory: "Southernism"', *Diaspora*, 10(2): 143–87.

—— (2006) *Wars of Position: The Cultural Politics of Left and Right*. Columbia: Columbia University Press.

Brenner, R. (1977) 'The Origins of Capitalist Development: A Critique of Neo-Smithian Marxism', *New Left Review* (I), 104: 25–92.

—— (1985a) 'Agrarian Class Structure and Economic Development in Pre-Industrial Europe', in T.H. Aston and C.H.E. Philpin (eds) *The Brenner Debate: Agrarian Class Structure and Economic Development in Pre-Industrial Europe*. Cambridge: Cambridge University Press.

—— (1985b) 'The Agrarian Roots of European Capitalism', in T.H. Aston and C.H.E. Philpin (eds) *The Brenner Debate: Agrarian Class Structure and Economic Development in Pre-Industrial Europe*. Cambridge: Cambridge University Press.

—— (1986) 'The Social Basis of Economic Development', in J. Roemer (ed.) *Analytical Marxism*. Cambridge: Cambridge University Press.

—— (1993) *Merchants and Revolution: Commercial Change, Political Conflict and London's Overseas Traders, 1550–1653*. Cambridge: Cambridge University Press.

—— (2003) *The Boom and the Bubble: The US in the World Economy*. London: Verso.

Bruhn, K. (1999) 'Antonio Gramsci and the *Palabra Verdadera*: The Political Discourse of Mexico's Guerrilla Forces', *Journal of InterAmerican Studies and World Affairs*, 41(2): 29–55.

Buci-Glucksmann, C. (1979) 'State, Transition and Passive Revolution', in C. Mouffe (ed.) *Gramsci and Marxist Theory*. London: Routledge.

—— (1980) *Gramsci and the State*, trans. D. Fernbach. London: Lawrence & Wishart.

Burgos, R. (2002) 'The Gramscian Intervention in the Theoretical and Political Production of the Latin American Left', *Latin American Perspectives*, 29(1): 9–37.

Burnham, P. (1991) 'Neo-Gramscian Hegemony and the International Order', *Capital and Class*, 45: 73–93.

—— (1994) 'Open Marxism and Vulgar International Political Economy', *Review of International Political Economy*, 1(2): 221–31.

—— (2000) 'Globalisation, Depoliticisation and "Modern" Economic Management', in W. Bonefeld and K. Psychopedis (eds) *The Politics of Change: Globalisation, Ideology and Critique*. London: Palgrave.

Buttigieg, J.A. (1986) 'The Legacy of Antonio Gramsci', *Boundary 2*, 14(3): 1–17.

—— (1990) 'Gramsci's Method', *Boundary 2*, 17(2): 60–81.

—— (1994) 'Philology and Politics: Returning to the Text of Antonio Gramsci's *Prison Notebooks*', *Boundary 2*, 21(2): 98–138.

—— (1995) 'Gramsci on Civil Society', *Boundary 2*, 22(3): 1–32.

—— (2005) 'The Contemporary Discourse on Civil Society: A Gramscian Critique', *Boundary 2*, 32(1): 33–52.

Cafruny, A. and M. Ryner (eds) (2003) *A Ruined Fortress? Neoliberal Hegemony and Transformation in Europe*. Lanham: Rowman & Littlefield.

Cammack, P. (1999) 'Interpreting ASEM: Interregionalism and the New Materialism', *Journal of the Asia Pacific Economy*, 4(1): 13–32.

—— (2002) 'Attacking the Poor', *New Left* Review (II), 13: 125–34.

Cammet, J.M. (1967) *Antonio Gramsci and the Origins of Italian Communism*. Stanford: Stanford University Press.

Cancian, F. and P. Brown (1994) 'Who is Rebelling in Chiapas?' *Cultural Survival Quarterly*, 18(1): 22–5.

Carr, B. (1985) *Mexican Communism, 1968–1983: Eurocommunism in the Americas?* San Diego, CA.: Centre for US–Mexican Studies.

—— (1991) 'Labour and the Political Left in Mexico', in K. J. Middlebrook (ed.) *Unions, Workers and the State in Mexico*. San Diego, Calif.: Centre for US–Mexican Studies.

Castañeda, J. G. (1994) *Utopia Unarmed: The Latin American Left after the Cold War*. New York: Vintage.

—— (1995) *The Mexican Shock: Its Meaning for the US*. New York: The New Press.

Centeno, M.A. (1994) *Democracy Within Reason: Technocratic Revolution in Mexico*. Pennsylvania: Pennsylvania State University Press.

Centeno, M.A. and S. Maxfield (1992) 'The Marriage of Finance and Order: Changes in the Mexican Political Elite', *Journal of Latin American Studies*, 24(1): 57–85.

Charnock, G. (2006) 'Improving the Mechanisms of Global Governance? The Ideational Impact of the World Bank on National Reform Agendas in Mexico', *New Political Economy*, 11(1): 73–98.

Chatterjee, P. (1986) *Nationalist Thought and the Colonial World*. London: Zed Books.

Chilcote, R. (2000) *Theories of Comparative Political Economy*. Boulder, Colo.: Westview Press.

Christiansen, T., K. E. Jørgensen, and A. Wiener (eds) (2001) *The Social Construction of Europe*. London: Sage.

Clark, M. (1972) Review of *Selections from the Prison Notebooks*, by Antonio Gramsci, *Political Studies*, 20(4): 492–6.

—— (1977) *Antonio Gramsci and the Revolution that Failed*. New Haven: Yale University Press.

Clifton, J. (2000) *The Politics of Telecommunications in Mexico: Privatisation and State–Labour Relations, 1982–1995*. London: Macmillan.

Cockcroft, J. D. (1983) *Mexico: Class Formation, Capital Accumulation and the State*. New York: Monthly Review Press.

—— (1998) *Mexico's Hope: An Encounter with Politics and History*. New York: Monthly Review Press.

Collier, G. A. (1987) 'Peasant Politics and the Mexican State: Indigenous Compliance in Highland Chiapas', *Mexican Studies/Estudios Mexicanos*, 3(1): 71–98.

—— (1990) 'Seeking Food and Seeking Money: Changing Productive Relations in a Highland Mexican Community'. Geneva: United Nations Research Institute for Social Development.

—— (1994a) 'The Rebellion in Chiapas and the Legacy of Energy Development', *Mexican Studies/Estudios Mexicanos*, 10(2): 371–82.

—— (1994b) 'Reforms of Mexico's Agrarian Code: Impact on the Peasantry', *Research in Economic Anthropology*, 15: 105–27.

—— (1994c) 'Roots of the Rebellion', *Cultural Survival Quarterly*, 18(1): 14–18.

—— (1994d) 'The New Politics of Exclusion: Antecedents to the Rebellion in Mexico', *Dialectical Anthropology*, 19(1): 1–44.

—— D. C. Mountjoy and R. B. Nigh (1994) 'Peasant Agriculture and Global Change: A Maya Response to Energy Development in Southeastern Mexico', *BioScience*, 44(6): 398–407.

—— with E. L. Quaratiello (1994). *BASTA! Land and the Zapatista Rebellion in Chiapas*, with a foreword by Peter Rossett. Oakland, Calif.: Institute for Food and Development Policy.

Comninel, G.C. (1987) *Rethinking the French Revolution: Marxism and the Revisionist Challenge*. London: Verso.

—— (2000) 'English Feudalism and the Origins of Capitalism', *The Journal of Peasant Studies*, 27(4): 1–53.

—— (2003) 'Historical Materialist Sociology and Revolutions', in G. Delanty and E.F. Isin (eds) *Handbook of Historical Sociology*. London: Sage.

Cook, M.L. (1995) 'Mexican State–Labour Relations and the Political Implications of Free Trade', *Latin American Perspectives*, 22(1): 77–94.

—— K. J. Middlebrook, and J. M. Horcasitas (1994) 'The Politics of Economic Restructuring in Mexico: Actors, Sequencing, and Coalition Change', in M. L. Cook, K. J. Middlebrook, and J. M. Horcasitas (eds) *The Politics of Economic Restructuring: State–Society Relations and Regime Change in Mexico*. San Diego, Calif.: Centre for US–Mexican Studies.

Cornelius, W. A. (1985) 'The Political Economy of Mexico under de la Madrid: Austerity, Routinised Crisis and Nascent Recovery', *Mexican Studies/Estudios Mexicanos*, 1(1): 83–123.

—— (1995) 'Designing Social Policy for Mexico's Liberalised Economy: From Social Services and Infrastructure to Job Creation', in R. Roett (ed.) *The Challenge of Institutional Reform in Mexico*. Boulder: Lynne Rienner.

—— (1996) *Mexican Politics in Transition: The Breakdown of a One-Party Dominant Regime*. San Diego, Calif.: Centre for US–Mexican Studies.

—— (1999) 'Subnational Politics and Democratisation: Tensions Between Centre and Periphery in the Mexican Political System', in W. A. Cornelius, T. A. Eisenstadt, and J. Hindley (eds) *Subnational Politics and Democratisation in Mexico*. San Diego, Calif.: Centre for US–Mexican Studies.

—— A. L. Craig and J. Fox (1994) 'Mexico's National Solidarity Program: An Overview', in W. A. Cornelius, A. L. Craig and J. Fox (eds) *Transforming State–Society Relations in Mexico: The National Solidarity Strategy*. San Diego, Calif.: Centre for US–Mexican Studies.

Cox, R.W. (1981) 'Social Forces, States and World Orders: Beyond International Relations Theory', *Millennium: Journal of International Studies*, 10(2): 126–55.

—— (1982) 'Production and Hegemony: Toward a Political Economy of World Order', in H.K. Jacobson and D. Sidjanski (eds) *The Emerging International Economic Order: Dynamic Processes, Constraints and Opportunities*. London: Sage.

—— (1983) 'Gramsci, Hegemony and International Relations: An Essay in Method', *Millennium: Journal of International Studies*, 12(2): 162–75.

—— (1985/1996) 'Realism, Positivism and Historicism', in R.W. Cox with T.J. Sinclair, *Approaches to World Order*. Cambridge: Cambridge University Press.

—— (1987) *Production, Power and World Order: Social Forces in the Making of History*. New York: Columbia University Press.

—— (1989) 'Production, the State and Change in World Order', in E-O Czempiel and J. N. Rosenau (eds) *Global Changes and Theoretical Challenges: Approaches to World Politics for the 1990s*. Toronto: Lexington Books.

—— (1992) 'Global *perestroika*', in R. Miliband and L. Panitch (eds) *The Socialist Register: New World Order?* London: Merlin Press.

—— (1992/1996) 'Towards a Posthegemonic Conceptualisation of World Order: Reflections on the Relevancy of Ibn Khaldun', in R. W. Cox and T. J. Sinclair, *Approaches to World Order*. Cambridge: Cambridge University Press.

—— (1993/1996) 'Production and Security', in R. W. Cox and T. J. Sinclair, *Approaches to World Order*. Cambridge: Cambridge University Press.

—— (1994) 'The Forum: Hegemony and Social Change', *Mershon International Studies Review*, 38(2): 366–7.

—— (1995a) 'Critical Political Economy', in B. Hettne (ed.) *International Political Economy: Understanding Global Disorder*. London: Zed Books.

—— (1995b) 'Civilisations: Encounters and Transformations', *Studies in Political Economy*, 27: 7–31.

—— (1997) 'Reconsiderations', in R. W. Cox (ed.) *The New Realism: Perspectives on Multilateralism and World Order*. London: Macmillan.

—— (1999) 'Civil Society at the Turn of the Millennium: Prospects for an Alternative World Order', *Review of International Studies*, 25(1): 3–28.

—— (2000) 'The Way Ahead: Towards a New Ontology of World Order', in R. W. Jones (ed.) *Critical Theory and World Politics*. Boulder: Lynne Rienner.

—— (2002) 'Reflections and Transitions', in R. W. Cox with M. G. Schecter, *The Political Economy of a Plural World: Critical Reflections on Power, Morals and Civilisation*. London: Routledge.

Craske, N. (1994) *Corporatism Revisited: Salinas and the Reform of the Popular Sector*. London: Institute of Latin American Studies.

—— and V. Bulmer-Thomas (eds) (1994) *Mexico and the North American Free Trade Agreement: Who Will Benefit?* London: Macmillan.

Crehan, K. (2002) *Gramsci, Culture and Anthropology*. London: Pluto Press.

Davidson, A. (1972) 'The Varying Seasons of Gramscian Studies', *Political Studies*, 20(4): 448–61.

—— (1974) 'Gramsci and Lenin, 1917–1922', in R. Miliband and J. Saville (eds) *The Socialist Register: A Survey of Movements and Ideas*. London: Merlin Press.

—— (1977) *Antonio Gramsci: Towards an Intellectual Biography*. London: Merlin Press.

—— (1984) 'Gramsci, the Peasantry and Popular Culture', *Journal of Peasant Studies*, 11(4): 139–54.

Davidson, N. (2005a) 'How Revolutionary Were the Bourgeois Revolutions?—1', *Historical Materialism*, 13(3): 3–33.

—— (2005b) 'How Revolutionary Were the Bourgeois Revolutions?—2', *Historical Materialism*, 13(4): 3–54.

Davies, M. (1999) *International Political Economy and Mass Communication in Chile: National Intellectuals and Transnational Hegemony*. London: Macmillan.

Davis, D. E. (1993) 'The Dialectic of Autonomy: State, Class and Economic Crisis in Mexico, 1958–1982', *Latin American Perspectives*, 20(3): 46–75.

Davis, J. A. (ed.) (1979) *Gramsci and Italy's Passive Revolution*. London: Croom Helm.

—— (1994) 'Remapping Italy's Path to the Twentieth Century', *Journal of Modern History*, 66(2): 291–320.

Day, R. J. F. (2005) *Gramsci Is Dead: Anarchist Currents in the Newest Social Movements*. London: Pluto Press.

Dewalt, B. R. and M. W. Ress with A. D. Murphy (1994) *The End of Agrarian Reform in Mexico: Past Lessons and Future Prospects*. San Diego, Calif.: Centre for US–Mexican Studies.

Diggins, J.P. (1988) 'The Misuses of Gramsci', *The Journal of American History*, 75(1): 141–5.

Dombroski, D. (1986) 'On Gramsci's Theatre Criticism', *Boundary 2*, 14 (3): 91–117.

Drainville, A. (1994) 'International Political Economy in the Age of Open Marxism', *Review of International Political Economy*, 1(1): 105–32.

—— (1995) 'Of Social Spaces, Citizenship and the Nature of Power in the World Economy', *Alternatives*, 20(1): 51–79.

Dresser, D. (1991) *Neopopulist Solutions to Neoliberal Problems: Mexico's National Solidarity Program*. San Diego, Calif.: Centre for US–Mexican Studies.

—— (1994) 'Bringing the Poor Back In: National Solidarity as a Strategy of Regime Legitimation', in W. A. Cornelius, A. L. Craig and J. Fox (eds)

Transforming State–Society Relations in Mexico: The National Solidarity Strategy. San Diego, Calif.: Centre for US–Mexican Studies.

Dussel Peters, E. (2000) *Polarizing Mexico: The Impact of Liberalisation Strategy.* Boulder: Lynne Rienner.

Earle, D. (1994) 'Indigenous Identity at the Margin: Zapatismo and Nationalism', *Cultural Survival Quarterly*, 18(1): 26–30.

Eber, C. and C. Kovic (eds) (2003) *Women of Chiapas: Making History in Times of Struggle and Hope.* London: Routledge.

Eley, G. (1984) 'Reading Gramsci in English: Observations on the Reception of Antonio Gramsci in the English-Speaking World, 1957–1982', *European History Quarterly*, 14(4): 441–78.

Femia, J. V. (1975) 'Hegemony and Consciousness in the Thought of Antonio Gramsci', *Political Studies*, 23(1): 29–48.

—— (1979) 'The Gramsci Phenomenon: Some Reflections', *Political Studies*, 26(3): 472–83.

—— (1981a) 'An Historicist Critique of "Revisionist" Methods for Studying the History of Ideas', *History and Theory*, 20(2): 113–34.

—— (1981b) *Gramsci's Political Thought: Hegemony, Consciousness and the Revolutionary Process.* Oxford: Clarendon Press.

—— (1998) *The Machiavellian Legacy: Essays in Italian Political Thought.* London: Macmillan.

—— (2004) *Machiavelli Revisited.* Cardiff: University of Wales Press.

Finocchiaro, M. A. (1988) *Gramsci and the History of Dialectical Thought.* Cambridge: Cambridge University Press.

—— (1992/2005) 'Logic, Politics and Gramsci: Intellectuals, Dialectics and Philosophy in the *Prison Notebooks*', in M. Finocchiaro, *Arguments About Arguments: Systematic, Critical and Historical Essays in Logical Theory.* Cambridge: Cambridge University Press.

—— (1999) *Beyond Right and Left: Democratic Elitism in Mosca and Gramsci.* New Haven: Yale University Press.

Fiori, G. (1970) *Antonio Gramsci: Life of a Revolutionary*, trans. T. Nairn. London: Verso.

Fontana, B. (1993) *Hegemony and Power: On the Relation between Gramsci and Machiavelli.* Minneapolis: University of Minnesota Press.

—— (1999) 'Politics, Philosophy and Modernity in Gramsci', *The Philosophical Forum*, 29(3–4): 104–18.

Forgacs, D. (1984) 'National–Popular: Genealogy of a Concept', in T. Bennet (ed.) *Formations of Nation and People.* London: Routledge.

—— (1989) 'Gramsci and Marxism in Britain', *New Left Review* (I), 176: 70–88.

—— and G. Nowell-Smith (1985) 'Introduction', in Antonio Gramsci, *Selections from Cultural Writings*, ed. and intro. D. Forgacs and G. Nowell-Smith, trans. W. Boelhower. London: Lawrence & Wishart.

Foster-Carter, A. (1977) 'The Modes of Production Controversy', *New Left Review* (I), 107: 47–77.

Foucault, M. (1972) *The Archaeology of Knowledge*, trans. A.M. Sheridan Smith. New York: Pantheon Books.

Foweraker, J. (1993) *Popular Mobilisation in Mexico: The Teachers' Movement, 1977–87.* Cambridge: Cambridge University Press.

—— (1995) *Theorising Social Movements*. London: Pluto Press.

Fox, J. (1993) *The Politics of Food in Mexico: State Power and Social Mobilisation*. Ithaca: Cornell University Press.

Francese, J. (1999) 'The Latent Presence of Crocean Aesthetics in Pasolini's "Critical Marxism"', in Z.G. Baránski (ed.) *Pasolini Old and New: Surveys and Studies*. Oxford: Four Courts Press.

Fuentes, C. (1990) *Christopher Unborn*, trans. Alfred MacAdam and the author. London: Picador.

Gall, O. (1998) 'Racism, Interethnic War and Peace in Chiapas', *Peace and Change*, 23(4): 531–44.

García de Leon, A. (1995) 'Chiapas and the Mexican Crisis', *NACLA Report on the Americas*, 29(1): 10–13.

—— (2005) 'From Revolution to Transition: The Chiapas Rebellion and the Path to Democracy in Mexico', *The Journal of Peasant Studies*, 32(3/4): 508–27.

Gareau, F. H. (1993) 'A Gramscian Analysis of the Social Sciences', *International Social Science Journal*, 45(136): 301–10.

Garibaldi, G. (2004) *My Life*, trans. S. Parkin. London: Hesperus Books.

Germain, R. and M. Kenny (1998) 'Engaging Gramsci: International Relations Theory and the New Gramscians', *Review of International Studies*, 24(1): 3–21.

Germino, D. (1990) *Antonio Gramsci: Architect of a New Politics*. Baton Rouge: Louisiana State University Press.

Ghosh, P. (2001) 'Gramscian Hegemony: An Absolutely Historicist Approach', *History of European Ideas*, 27(1): 1–43.

Gilbreth, C. and G. Otero (2001) 'Democratisation in Mexico: The Zapatista Uprising and Civil Society', *Latin American Perspectives*, 28(4): 7–29.

Gill, S. (1990) *American Hegemony and the Trilateral Commission*. Cambridge: Cambridge University Press.

—— (1991) 'Reflections on Global Order and Sociohistorical Time', *Alternatives*, 16(3): 275–314.

—— (1992) 'The Emerging World Order and European Change: The Political Economy of European Union', in R. Miliband and L. Panitch (eds) *The Socialist Register: New World Order?* London: Merlin Press.

—— (ed.) (1993a) *Gramsci, Historical Materialism and International Relations*. Cambridge: Cambridge University Press.

—— (1993b) 'Epistemology, Ontology and the "Italian School"', in S. Gill (ed.) *Gramsci, Historical Materialism and International Relations*. Cambridge: Cambridge University Press.

—— (1995a) 'Globalisation, Market Civilisation and Disciplinary Neoliberalism', *Millennium: Journal of International Studies*, 24(3): 399–423.

—— (1995b) 'The Global Panopticon? The Neoliberal State, Economic Life and Democratic Surveillance', *Alternatives*, 20(1): 1–49.

—— (2000) 'Toward a Postmodern Prince? The Battle in Seattle as a Moment in the New Politics of Globalisation', *Millennium: Journal of International Studies*, 29(1): 131–40.

—— (2001) 'Constitutionalising Capital: EMU and Disciplinary Neoliberalism', in A. Bieler and A. D. Morton (eds) *Social Forces in the Making of the New*

Europe: The Restructuring of European Social Relations in the Global Political Economy. London: Palgrave.

—— (2004) 'The Contradictions of US Supremacy', in L. Panitch and C. Leys (eds) *The Socialist Register: The Empire Reloaded*. London: Merlin Press.

—— and D. Law (1988) *The Global Political Economy: Perspectives, Problems and Policies*. London: Harvester & Wheatsheaf.

—— (1989) 'Global Hegemony and the Structural Power of Capital', *International Studies Quarterly*, 33(4): 475–99.

Gills, B. K. (1993) 'The Hegemonic Transition in East Asia: A Historical Perspective', in S. Gill (ed.) *Gramsci, Historical Materialism and International Relations*. Cambridge: Cambridge University Press.

Gilly, A. (1998) 'Chiapas and the Rebellion of the Enchanted World', in D. Nugent (ed.) *Rural Revolt in Mexico: US Intervention and the Domain of Subaltern Politics*, expanded edition. Durham: Duke University Press.

Gledhill, J. (1996) 'The State, the Countryside . . . and Capitalism', in R. Aitken et al., (eds) *Dismantling the Mexican State?* London: Macmillan.

Gobetti, P. (1924/2000) 'Uomini e idee [x]. Gramsci', *La Revoluzione Liberale*, 3:17 (22 April 1924) in P. Gobetti, *On Liberal Revolution*, ed. and intro. N. Urbinati, trans. W. McCuaig. New Haven: Yale University Press.

Golding, S. (1992) *Gramsci's Democratic Theory: Contributions to Post-Liberal Democracy*. Toronto: University of Toronto Press.

Gramsci, A. (1971) *Selections from the Prison Notebooks*, ed. and trans. Q. Hoare and G. Nowell-Smith. London: Lawrence & Wishart.

—— (1975) *History, Philosophy and Culture in the Young Gramsci*, ed. P. Cavalcanti and P. Piccone. Saint Louis: Telos Press.

—— (1977) *Selections from Political Writings, 1910–1920*, ed. Q. Hoare, trans. J. Matthews. London: Lawrence & Wishart.

—— (1978) *Selections from Political Writings, 1921–1926*, ed. and trans. Q. Hoare. London: Lawrence & Wishart.

—— (1985) *Selections from Cultural Writings*, ed. D. Forgacs and G. Nowell-Smith, trans. W. Boelhower. London: Lawrence & Wishart.

—— (1988) *A Gramsci Reader: Selected Writings, 1916–1935*, ed. D. Forgacs. London: Lawrence & Wishart.

—— (1992) *The Prison Notebooks*, vol.1, ed. and intro. J.A. Buttigieg, trans. J.A. Buttigieg and A. Callari. New York: Columbia University Press.

—— (1994a) *Letters from Prison*, vol.1, ed. F. Rosengarten, trans. R. Rosenthal. New York: Columbia University Press.

—— (1994b) *Letters from Prison*, Vol.2, ed. F. Rosengarten, trans. R. Rosenthal. New York: Columbia University Press.

—— (1994c) *Pre-Prison Writings*, ed. R. Bellamy, trans. V. Cox. Cambridge: Cambridge University Press.

—— (1995) *Further Selections from the Prison Notebooks*, ed. and trans. D. Boothman. London: Lawrence & Wishart.

—— (1996) *The Prison Notebooks*, vol.2, ed. and trans. J.A. Buttigieg. New York: Columbia University Press.

—— (2001) *Cuadernos de la cárcel*, 6 vols. Mexico City: Ediciones Era.

Green, M. (2002) 'Gramsci Cannot Speak: Presentations and Interpretations of Gramsci's Concept of the Subaltern', *Rethinking Marxism*, 14(3): 1–24.

Griffiths, T. (1971) 'In Defence of Occupations', *7 Days* (8 December): 22.

—— (1996) *Plays 1*, London: Faber and Faber.

Guha, R. and G. C. Spivak (eds) (1988) *Selected Subaltern Studies*, with a foreword by E. Said. Ocford: Oxford University Press.

Gundle, S. (1995) 'The Legacy of the Prison Notebooks: Gramsci, the PCI and Italian Culture in the Cold War Period', in C. Duggan and C. Wagstaff (eds) *Italy in the Cold War: Politics, Culture and Society, 1948–58*. Oxford: Berg.

Hall, S. (1986) 'Gramsci's Relevance for the Study of Race and Ethnicity', *Journal of Communication Inquiry*, 10(2): 5–27.

—— (1988) *The Hard Road to Renewal: Thatcherism and the Crisis of the Left*. London: Verso.

—— (1991a) 'Introductory Essay: Reading Gramsci', in R. Simon, *Gramsci's Political Thought: An Introduction*, London: Lawrence & Wishart.

—— (1991b) 'Gramsci and Us', in R. Simon, *Gramsci's Political Thought: An Introduction*, London: Lawrence & Wishart.

—— (1996) 'On Postmodernism and Articulation' (an interview edited by L. Grossberg), in D. Morley and K-H Chen (eds) *Stuart Hall: Critical Dialogues in Cultural Studies* (London: Routledge).

—— (1997) 'Culture and Power', interview by P. Osbourne and L. Segal (London, June 1997), *Radical Philosophy*, 86: 24–41.

Halliday, F. (1987) 'State and Society in International Relations: A Second Agenda', *Millennium: Journal of International Studies*, 16(2): 215–29.

—— (1992) 'International Society as Homogeneity: Burke, Marx and Fukuyama', *Millennium: Journal of International Studies*, 21(3): 435–61.

—— (1999) *Revolution and World Politics: The Rise and Fall of the Sixth Great Power*. London: Macmillan.

Hampton, M. (2006) 'Hegemony, Class Struggle and the Radical Historiography of Global Monetary Standards', *Capital and Class*, 89: 131–64.

Hardt, M. and A. Negri (2000) *Empire*. Cambridge, Mass.: Harvard University Press.

Harris, D. (1992) *From Class Struggle to the Politics of Pleasure: The Effects of Gramscianism on Cultural Politics*. London: Routledge.

Harvey, D. (1982) *Limits to Capital*. Oxford: Basil Blackwell.

—— (2003) *The New Imperialism*. Oxford: Oxford University Press.

—— (2006) *Spaces of Global Capitalism: Towards a Theory of Uneven Geographical Development* (Hettner-Lecture 2004). London: Verso.

Harvey, N. (1988) 'Personal Networks and Strategic Choices in the Formation of an Independent Peasant Organisation: The OCEZ of Chiapas, Mexico', *Bulletin of Latin American Research*, 7(2): 299–312.

—— (1990) *The New Agrarian Movement in Mexico, 1979–1990*. London: Institute of Latin American Studies.

—— (1995) 'Rebellion in Chiapas: Rural Reforms and Popular Struggle', *Third World Quarterly*, 16(1): 39–73.

—— (1996) 'Rural Reforms and the Zapatista Rebellion: Chiapas, 1988–1995', in G. Otero (ed.) *Neoliberalism Revisited: Economic Restructuring and Mexico's Political Future*. Boulder: Westview Press.

—— (1998) *The Chiapas Rebellion: The Struggle for Land and Democracy*. Durham: Duke University Press.

—— (2000) 'The Zapatistas, Radical Democratic Citizenship and Women's Struggle', *Social Politics*, 5(2): 158–87.

Haug, W. F. (1999) 'Rethinking Gramsci's Philosophy of Praxis from One Century to the Next', *Boundary 2*, 26(2): 101–17.

—— (2001) 'From Marx to Gramsci, From Gramsci to Marx: Historical Materialism and the Philosophy of Praxis', *Rethinking Marxism*, 13(1): 69–82.

Havel, V. (1985) 'The Power of the Powerless', in V. Havel et al., *The Power of the Powerless: Citizens Against the State in Central-Eastern Europe*. New York: M.E. Sharpe.

Hellman, J. A. (1995) 'The Riddle of New Social Movements: Who They Are and What They Do', in S. Halebsky and R. L. Harris (eds) *Capital, Power and Inequality in Latin America*. Boulder: Westview Press.

Heredia, B. (1996) 'State–Business Relations in Contemporary Mexico', in M. Serrano and V. Bulmer-Thomas (eds) *Rebuilding the State: Mexico After Salinas*. London: Institute of Latin American Studies.

Hernández Castillo, R. A. (1995) 'Reinventing Tradition', *Cultural Survival Quarterly*, 19(1): 24–5.

—— (ed.) (2001) *The Other Word: Women and Violence in Chiapas Before and After ACTEAL*. Copenhagen: International Working Group for Indigenous Affairs.

Hernández Navarro, L. (1998) 'The Escalation of the War in Chiapas', *NACLA Report on the Americas*, 31(5): 7–10.

—— (2004) 'The Global Zapatista Movement', America Program. Silver City, N.MEX.: Interhemispheric Resource Centre.

Hewitt de Alcántara, C. (1994) 'Introduction: Economic Restructuring and Rural Subsistence in Mexico', in C. Hewitt de Alcántara (ed.) *Economic Restructuring and Rural Subsistence in Mexico: Corn and the Crisis of the 1980s*. San Diego, Calif.: Centre for US–Mexican Studies.

Hirst, P. and G. Thompson (1999) *Globalisation in Question: The International Economy and the Possibilities of Governance*, 2dn edn. Cambridge: Polity Press.

Hoare, Q. (1978) 'Introduction', in A. Gramsci, *Selections from Political Writings, 1921–1926*, trans. and ed. Q. Hoare. London: Lawrence & Wishart.

—— and G. Nowell-Smith (1971) 'Notes on Italian History: Introduction', in A. Gramsci, *Selections from the Prison Notebooks*, ed. and trans. Q. Hoare and G. Nowell-Smith. London: Lawrence & Wishart.

Hobsbawm, E. (1960) 'The Seventeenth Century in the Development of Capitalism', *Science and Society*, 24(2): 97–112.

—— (1962) *The Age of Revolution, 1789–1848*. London: Weidenfeld & Nicolson.

—— (1962/1976) 'From Feudalism to Capitalism', in R. Hilton (ed.) *The Transition from Feudalism to Capitalism*. London: Verso.

—— (1965) 'The Crisis of the Seventeenth Century', in T. Aston (ed.) *Crisis in Europe, 1560–1660: Essays from Past and Present*. London: Routledge.

—— (1975) *The Age of Capital, 1848–1875*. London: Weidenfeld & Nicolson.

—— (1977) 'Gramsci and Political Theory', *Marxism Today*, 21(7): 205–13.

—— (1986) 'Revolution', in T. Porter and M. Teich (eds) *Revolution in History*. Cambridge: Cambridge University Press.

—— (1987) *The Age of Empire, 1875–1914*. London: Weidenfeld & Nicolson.

—— (1990) *Echoes of the Marsellaise: Two Centuries Look Back on the French Revolution*. London: Verso.

—— (1994) *Age of Extremes: The Short Twentieth Century, 1914–1991*. London: Penguin.

—— (1999) 'Peasants and Politics' [1973] in E. Hobsbawm, *Uncommon People: Resistance, Rebellion and Jazz*. London: Abacus.

Hodges, D. and R. Gandy (2002a) *Mexico Under Siege: Popular Resistance to Presidential Despotism*. London: Zed Books.

—— (2002b) *Mexico, the End of the Revolution*. Westport, Conn.: Praeger Publishers.

Holloway, J. (2002) *Change the World Without Taking Power: The Meaning of Revolution Today*. London: Pluto Press.

Holman, O. (1996) *Integrating Southern Europe: EC Expansion and the Transnationalisation of Spain*. London: Routledge.

—— H. Overbeek and M. Ryner (ed.) (1998) 'Neoliberal Hegemony and European Restructuring', *International Journal of Political Economy*, 28(1–2) (special issues).

Holub, R. (1992) *Antonio Gramsci: Beyond Marxism and Postmodernism*. London: Routledge.

Ives, P. (2004a) *Gramsci's Politics of Language: Engaging the Bakhtin Circle and the Frankfurt School*. Toronto: University of Toronto Press.

—— (2004b) *Language and Hegemony in Gramsci*. London: Pluto Press.

Jacobitti, E. (1980) 'Hegemony before Gramsci: The Case of Benedetto Croce', *Journal of Modern History*, 52(1): 66–84.

—— (1983) 'From Vico's Common Sense to Gramsci's Hegemony', in G. Tagliacozzo (ed.) *Vico and Marx: Affinities and Contrasts*. New Jersey: Humanities Press.

Janvry, A. de (1981) *The Agrarian Question and Reformism in Latin America*. Baltimore: Johns Hopkins University Press.

—— G. Gordillo and E. Sadoulet (1997) *Mexico's Second Agrarian Reform: Household and Community Responses, 1990–1994*. San Diego, Calif.: Centre for US–Mexican Studies.

Jessop, B. (1990) *State Theory: Putting the Capitalist State in its Place*. Cambridge: Polity Press.

—— (2002) *The Future of the Capitalist State*. Cambridge: Polity Press.

—— (2006a) 'Gramsci as a Spatial Theorist', in A. Bieler and A. D. Morton (eds) *Images of Gramsci: Connections and Contentions in Political Theory and International Relations*. London: Routledge.

—— (2006b) 'Spatial Fixes, Temporal Fixes and Spatio-Temporal Fixes', in N. Castree and D. Gregory (eds) *David Harvey: A Critical Reader*. Oxford: Blackwell Publishing.

Joll, J. (1977) *Gramsci*. Glasgow: Fontana Paperbacks.

Kampwirth, K. (1998) 'Peace Talks, But No Peace', *NACLA Report on the Americas*, 31(5): 15–19.

Katz, C. J. (1993/1999) 'Karl Marx on the Transition from Feudalism to Capitalism', in B. Jessop and R. Wheatley (eds) *Karl Marx's Social and Political Thought: Critical Assessments II*, vol.6. London: Routledge.

Keohane, R. O. (1984) *After Hegemony: Cooperation and Discord in the World Political Economy*. Princeton: Princeton University Press.

—— (1989) *International Institutions and State Power.* Boulder: Westview Press.

Kiely, R. (2005) 'Capitalist Expansion and the Imperialism–Globalisation Debate: Contemporary Marxist Explanations', *Journal of International Relations and Development,* 8(1): 27–57.

Kiernan, V. (1974) 'Gramsci and the Other Continents', *New Edinburgh Review,* 27: 19–24.

King, P. (2000) *Thinking Past a Problem: Essays on the History of Ideas.* London: Frank Cass.

Kolakowski, Leszek (2005) *Main Currents of Marxism,* trans. P. S. Falla. New York: W.W. Norton.

Kovic, C. (2003) 'The Struggle for Liberation and Reconciliation in Chiapas, Mexico', *Latin American Perspectives,* 30(3): 58–79.

Krauze, E. (1988) 'The Guerrilla Dandy', *New Republic* (27 June): 28–38.

—— (1999) 'Chiapas: The Indians' Prophet', *New York Review of Books,* 46(20): 65–73.

La Botz, D. (1995) *Democracy in Mexico: Peasant Rebellion and Political Reform.* Boston, Mass.: South End Press.

Lacher, H. (1999) 'Embedded Liberalism, Disembedded Markets: Reconceptualising the Pax Americana', *New Political Economy,* 4(3): 343–60.

—— (2002) 'Making Sense of the International System: The Promises and Pitfalls of Contemporary Marxist Theories of International Relations', in M. Rupert and H. Smith (eds) *Historical Materialism and Globalisation.* London: Routledge.

—— (2003) 'Putting the Capitalist State in Its Place: The Critique of State-Centrism and Its Limits', *Review of International Studies,* 29(4): 521–41.

—— (2005) 'International Transformation and the Persistence of Territoriality: Toward a New Political Geography of Capitalism', *Review of International Political Economy,* 12(1): 26–52.

Laclau, E. and C. Mouffe (2001) *Hegemony and Socialist Strategy: Towards a Radical Democratic Politics,* 2nd edn. London: Verso.

Lampedusa, G. T. di (1996) *The Leopard,* trans. A. Colquhoun. London: Harvill Press.

Landy, M. (1994) *Film, Politics and Gramsci.* Minneapolis: University of Minnesota Press.

Lauretis, T. de (1987) 'Gramsci Notwithstanding: Or, the Left Hand of History', in T. de Lauretis (ed.) *Technologies of Gender: Essays on Theory, Film and Fiction.* London: Macmillan.

Lawner, L. (1979) 'Introduction', in Antonio Gramsci, *Letters from Prison,* trans. L. Lawner. London: Quartet Books.

Lee, K. (1995) 'A neo-Gramscian Approach to International Organisation: An Expanded Analysis of Current Reforms to UN Development Activities', in J. Macmillan and A. Linklater (eds) *Boundaries in Question: New Directions in International Relations.* London: Pinter.

Lenin, V. I. (1963) *Collected Works* (December 1910-April 1912), vol. 17. London: Lawrence & Wishart.

Lester, J. (2000) *The Dialogue of Negation: Debates on Hegemony in Russia and the West.* London: Pluto Press.

Levy, C. (1999) *Gramsci and the Anarchists.* Oxford: Berg.

Leyva Solano, X. (1998) 'The New Zapatista Movement: Political Levels, Actors and Political Discourse in Contemporary Mexico', in V. Napolitano and X. Leyva Solano (eds) *Encuentros Antropológicos: Power, Identity and Mobility in Mexican Society*. London: Institute of Latin American Studies.

Ling, L.H.M (1996) 'Hegemony and the Internationalising State: A Post-colonial Analysis of China's Integration into Asian Corporatism', *Review of International Political Economy*, 3(1): 1–26.

Löwy, M. (1981) *The Politics of Combined and Uneven Development: The Theory of Permanent Revolution*. London: Verso.

Luna, M. (1995) 'Entrepreneurial Interests and Political Action in Mexico: Facing the Demands of Economic Modernisation', in R. Roett (ed.) *The Challenge of Institutional Reform in Mexico*. Boulder: Lynne Rienner.

Luxemburg, R. (1913/2003) *The Accumulation of Capital*, trans. A. Schwarzschild. London: Routledge.

MacEoin, G. (1996) *The People's Church: Bishop Samuel Ruiz of Mexican and Why He Matters*. New York: Crossroad Publishing Company.

Maclean, J. (1981) 'Political Theory, International Theory and Problems of Ideology', *Millennium: Journal of International Studies*, 10(2): 102–25.

McMichael, P. (1990) 'Incorporating Comparison within a World-Historical Perspective: An Alternative Comparative Method', *American Sociological Review*, 55(3): 385–97.

—— (2001) 'Revisiting the Question of the Transnational State: A Comment on William Robinson's "Social Theory of Globalisation"', *Theory and Society*, 30(2): 201–9.

Machiavelli, N. (1993) *The Prince*, ed. Q. Skinner and R. Price. Cambridge: Cambridge University Press.

—— (2003) *The Discourses*, ed. and intro. B. Crick, trans. L. J. Walker. London: Penguin.

Mandel, E. (1975) *Late Capitalism*, trans. J. De Bres. London: Verso.

Mansfield, S.R. (1993) 'Gramsci and the Dialectic: Resisting "encrocement"', *Rethinking Marxism*, 6(2): 81–103.

Marcos, Subcomandante (1995) *Shadows of Tender Fury: The Letters and Communiqués of Subcomandante Marcos and the Zapatista Army of National Liberation*, trans. Frank Bardacke et al. New York: Monthly Review Press.

Marcuse, H. (1937/1968) 'Philosophy and Critical Theory', in H. Marcuse, *Negations: Essays in Critical Theory*, trans. J. J. Shapiro. London: Allen Lane.

—— (1964/1999) *One-Dimensional Man*, 2nd edn. London: Routledge.

Martin, J. (1998) *Gramsci's Political Analysis: A Critical Introduction*. London: Macmillan.

—— (2006) 'Antonio Gramsci', in T. Carver and J. Martin (eds) *Continental Political Thought*. London: Palgrave.

Martinelli, A. (1968–69) 'In Defence of the Dialectic: Antonio Gramsci's Theory of Revolution', *Berkeley Journal of Sociology*, 13–14: 1–27.

Marx, K. (1843/1975a) 'Contribution to the Critique of Hegel's Philosophy of Law', in K. Marx and F. Engels, *Collected Works*, vol.3. London: Lawrence & Wishart.

—— (1843/1975b) 'On the Jewish Question', in K. Marx and F. Engels, *Collected Works*, Vol.3. London: Lawrence & Wishart.

—— (1844/1975) 'Economic and Philosophic Manuscripts of 1844', in K. Marx and F. Engels, *Collected Works*, vol.3. London: Lawrence & Wishart.

—— (1850/1978) *The Class Struggles in France, 1848–1850*, in K. Marx and F. Engels, *Collected Works*, vol. 10. London: Lawrence & Wishart.

—— (1859/1987) *A Contribution to the Critique of Political Economy*, in K. Marx and F. Engels, *Collected Works*, vol. 29. London: Lawrence & Wishart.

—— (1887/1996) *Capital*, vol. I, in K. Marx and F. Engels, *Collected Works*, vol. 35. London: Lawrence & Wishart.

—— (1894/1959) *Capital*, vol. III. London: Lawrence & Wishart.

—— (1970) *Theses on Feuerbach*, in K. Marx and F. Engels, *The German Ideology*, ed. and intro. C. J. Arthur. London: Lawrence & Wishart.

—— and F. Engels (1845–46/1976) *The German Ideology*, in K. Marx and F. Engels, *Collected Works*, Vol.5. London: Lawrence & Wishart.

—— (1848/1998) *The Communist Manifesto*, intro. E. Hobsbawm. London: Verso.

Mészáros, I. (2001) *Socialism or Barbarism: From the 'American Century' to the Crossroads*. New York: Monthly Review Press.

Middlebrook, K. J. (1993) 'Political Liberalisation in an Authoritarian Regime: The Case of Mexico', in G. O'Donnell, P. Schmitter, and L. Whitehead (eds) *Transitions From Authoritarian Rule: Latin America*. Baltimore: Johns Hopkins University Press.

—— (1995) *The Paradox of Revolution: Labour, the State and Authoritarianism in Mexico*. Baltimore: Johns Hopkins University Press.

—— (ed.) (2004) *Dilemmas of Political Change in Mexico*. San Diego, Calif.: Centre for US–Mexican Studies.

Miliband, R. (1977) *Marxism and Politics*. Oxford: Clarendon Press.

Moe, N. (2002) *The View from Vesuvius: Italian Culture and the Southern Question*. Berkeley: University of California Press.

Moran, J. (1998) 'The Dynamics of Class Politics and National Economies in Globalisation: The Marginalisation of the Unacceptable', *Capital and Class*, 66: 53–83.

Morera, E. (1990) *Gramsci's Historicism: A Realist Interpretation*. London: Routledge.

—— (2000) 'Gramsci's Critical Modernity', *Rethinking Marxism*, 12(1): 16–46.

Morris, J. (1997) 'Challenging *Meridionalismo*: Constructing a New History for Southern Italy', in R. Lumley and J. Morris (eds) *The New History of the Italian South: The Mezzogiorno Revisited*. Devon: University of Exeter Press.

Morton, A. D. (2001) 'The Sociology of Theorising and Neo-Gramscian Perspectives: The Problems of "School" Formation in IPE', in A. Bieler and A. D. Morton (eds) *Social Forces in the Making of the New Europe: The Restructuring of European Social Relations in the Global Political Economy*. London: Palgrave.

—— (2002) '"La Resurrección del Maíz": Globalisation, Resistance and the Zapatistas', *Millennium: Journal of International Studies*, 31(1): 27–54.

—— (2003a) 'Historicising Gramsci: Situating Ideas in and Beyond their Context', *Review of International Political Economy*, 10(1): 118–46.

—— (2003b) 'The Social Function of Carlos Fuentes: A Critical Intellectual or in the "Shadow of the State"?' *Bulletin of Latin American Research*, 22(1): 27–51.

—— (2003c) 'Structural Change and Neoliberalism in Mexico: "Passive Revolution" in the Global Political Economy', *Third World Quarterly*, 24(4): 631–53.

—— (2005a) 'A Double Reading of Gramsci: Beyond the Logic of Contingency', *Critical Review of International Social and Political Philosophy*, 8(4): 439–53.

—— (2005b) 'The Age of Absolutism: Capitalism, the Modern States-System and International Relations', *Review of International Studies*, 31(3): 495–517.

—— (2005c) 'Change within Continuity: The Political Economy of Democratic Transition in Mexico', *New Political Economy*, 10(2): 181–202.

—— (2006a) 'The Grimly Comic Riddle of Hegemony in IPE: Where Is Class Struggle?' *Politics*, 26(1): 62–72.

—— (2006b) 'Mexican Revolution, Primitive Accumulation, Passive Revolution', paper presented at 31st Annual Conference of the British International Studies Association (BISA), University of Cork/Ireland (18–20 December).

—— (2007) 'Unquestioned answers/Unanswered questions in IPE: a rejoinder to "non-Marxist" historical materialism', *Politics*, 27(2): forthcoming.

Mouffe, C. and A. Showstack Sassoon (1977) 'Gramsci in France and Italy: A Review of the Literature', *Economy and Society*, 6(1): 31–68.

Murphy, C. N. (1994) *International Organisation and Industrial Change*. Cambridge: Polity Press.

—— (1998a) 'Understanding IR: Understanding Gramsci', *Review of International Studies*, 24(3): 417–25.

—— (1988b) 'Globalisation and Governance: A Historical Perspective', in R. Axtman (ed.) *Globalisation and Europe: Theoretical and Empirical Investigations*. London: Pinter.

—— (1999) 'Inequality, Turmoil and Democracy: Global Political–Economic Visions at the End of the Century', *New Political Economy*, 4(2): 289–304.

Nadal, A. (1998a) 'Terror in Chiapas', *The Bulletin of the Atomic Scientists*, 54(2) : 18–25.

—— (1998b) 'Political Cleansing in Chiapas', *The Bulletin of the Atomic Scientists*, 54(3): 20–2.

Nairn, T. (1971) 'Mucking About with Love and Revolution', *7 Days* (10 November): 18–19.

—— (1980a) 'Euro-Gramscism', *London Review of Books*, 2(13): 13–15.

—— (1980b) 'Euro-Gramscism (cont.)', *London Review of Books*, 2(14): 12–14.

—— (1982) 'Antonu su Gobbu', in A.S. Sassoon (ed.) *Approaches to Gramsci*. London: Readers and Writers.

Nash, J. (1994) 'Global Integration and Subsistence Insecurity', *American Anthropologist*, 96(1): 7–30.

—— (1995) 'The Reassertion of Indigenous Identity: Mayan Responses to State Intervention in Chiapas', *Latin American Research Review*, 30(3): 7–41.

—— and C. Kovic (1996) 'The Reconstitution of Hegemony: The Free Trade Act and the Transformation of Rural Mexico', in J. H. Mittelman (ed.) *Globalisation: Critical Reflections*. Boulder: Lynne Rienner.

Nations, J. D. (1994) 'The Ecology of the Zapatista Revolt', *Cultural Survival Quarterly*, 18(1): 31–3.

Neufeld, M. (2002) 'Democratic Socialism in a Global(-ising) Context: Towards a Collective Research Programme', paper presented at the 43rd Annual Convention of the International Studies Association, New Orleans (24–27 March).

Nield, K. and J. Seed (1981) 'Waiting for Gramsci', *Social History*, 6(2): 209–27.

Nimni, E. (1994) *Marxism and Nationalism: Theoretical Origins of a Political Crisis*, with a preface by E. Laclau. London: Pluto Press.

Novack, G. (1972) *Understanding History: Marxist Essays*. New York: Pathfinder Press.

O'Connell, D. (1993) 'Bloom and Babbitt: A Gramscian View', *Rethinking Marxism*, 6(1): 96–103.

Ohmae, K. (1990) *The Borderless World*. New York: Fontana.

—— (1996) *The End of the Nation State: The Rise of Regional Economies*. New York: Free Press.

Olesen, T. (2004) 'Globalising the Zapatistas: from Third World Solidarity to Global Solidarity?' *Third World Quarterly*, 25(1): 255–67.

—— (2005) *International Zapatismo: The Construction of Solidarity in the Age of Globalisation*. London: Zed Books.

Otero, G. (2004) 'Contesting Neoliberal Globalism from Below: The EZLN, Indian Rights, and Citizenship', in G. Otero (ed.) *Mexico in Transition: Neoliberal Globalism, the State and Civil Society*. London: Zed Books.

Overbeek, H. (1990) *Global Capitalism and National Decline: The Thatcher Decade in Historical Perspective*. London: Routledge.

—— (ed.) (1993) *Restructuring Hegemony in the Global Political Economy: The Rise of Transnational Neoliberalism in the 1980s*. London: Routledge.

—— (1994) 'The Forum: Hegemony and Social Change', *Mershon International Studies Review*, 38(2): 368–9.

—— (2004) 'Transnational Class Formation and Concepts of Control: Towards a Genealogy of the Amsterdam Project in International Political Economy', *Journal of International Relations and Development*, 7(2): 113–41.

Panitch, L. (1994) 'Globalisation and the State', in L. Panitch and R. Miliband (eds) *The Socialist Register: Between Globalism and Nationalism*. London: Merlin Press.

—— (2000) 'The New Imperial State', *New Left Review* (II), 2: 5–20.

—— and S. Ginden (2005) 'Superintending Global Capital', *New Left Review* (II), 35: 101–23.

Pansters, W. (1999) 'The Transition Under Fire: Rethinking Contemporary Mexican Politics', in K. Koonings and D. Krujit (eds) *Societies of Fear: The Legacy of Civil War and Terror in Latin America*. London: Zed Books.

Pasolini, P.P. (1996) *Poems*, trans. N. MacAfee with L. Martinengro, with a foreword by E. Siciliano. New York: Farrar, Straus, & Giroux.

Petras, J. and H. Veltmeyer (2002) 'The Peasantry and the State in Latin America: A Troubled Past, an Uncertain Future', *The Journal of Peasant Studies*, 29(3/4): 41–82.

Phillips, A. S. and A. G. Bedian (1990) 'Understanding Antonio Gramsci's Ambiguous Legacy', *International Journal of Social Economics*, 17(10): 36–41.

Piester, K. (1997) 'Targeting the Poor: The Politics of Social Policy Reforms in Mexico', in D.A. Chalmers et al. (eds) *The New Politics of Inequality in Latin America: Rethinking Participation and Representation*. Oxford: Oxford University Press.

Pijl, K. van der (1984) *The Making of an Atlantic Ruling Class*. London: Verso.

—— (1989) 'Ruling Classes, Hegemony and the State System: Theoretical and Historical Considerations', *International Journal of Political Economy*, 19(3): 7–35.

—— (1996) 'A Theory of Transnational Revolution: Universal History According to Eugen Rosenstock-Huessy and Its Implications', *Review of International Political Economy*, 3(2): 287–318.

—— (1998) *Transnational Classes and International Relations*. London: Routledge.

—— (2006) 'A Lockean Europe?' *New Left Review* (II), 37: 9–37.

Portelli, H. (1973) *Gramsci y el bloque histórico*. Mexico: Siglo XXI.

Poulantzas, N. (1973) *Political Power and Social Classes*, trans. T. O'Hagan. London: New Left Books.

—— (1975) *Classes in Contemporary Capitalism*, trans. D. Fernbach. London: New Left Books.

Powell, K. (1996) 'Neoliberalism and Nationalism', in R. Aitken et al. (eds) *Dismantling the Mexican State?* London: Macmillan.

Robinson, W. I. (1996) *Promoting Polyarchy: Globalisation, US Intervention and Hegemony*. Cambridge: Cambridge University Press.

—— (2000) 'Promoting Capitalist Polyarchy: The Case of Latin America', in M. Cox, G. J. Ikenberry and T. Inoguchi (eds) *American Democracy Promotion: Impulses, Strategies and Impacts*. Oxford: Oxford University Press.

—— (2001a) 'Transnational Processes, Development Studies and Changing Social Hierarchies in the World System: A Central American Case Study', *Third World Quarterly*, 22(4): 529–63.

—— (2001b) 'Social Theory and Globalisation: The Rise of a Transnational State', *Theory and Society*, 30(2): 157–200.

—— (2003) *Transnational Conflicts: Central America, Social Change and Globalisation*. London: Verso.

—— (2004a) *A Theory of Global Capitalism: Production, Class and State in a Transnational World*. Baltimore: Johns Hopkins University Press.

—— (2004b) 'Global Crisis and Latin America', *Bulletin of Latin American Research*, 23(2): 135–53.

—— (2006) 'Gramsci and Globalisation: From Nation-State to Transnational Hegemony', in A. Bieler and A. D. Morton (eds) *Images of Gramsci: Connections and Contentions in Political Theory and International Relations*. London: Routledge.

Rocha, J. and S. Branford (2002) *Cutting the Wire: The Story of the Landless Movement in Brazil*. London: Latin American Bureau.

Roman, R. and E. V. Arregui (1997) 'Zapatismo and the Workers' Movement in Mexico at the End of the Twentieth Century', *Monthly Review*, 49(3): 98–116.

Rosamond, B. (2000) *Theories of European Integration*. London: Macmillan.

Roseberry, W. (1994) 'Hegemony and the Language of Contention', in G. M. Joseph and D. Nugent (eds) *Everyday Forms of State Formation: Revolution and the Negotiation of Rule in Modern Mexico*. Durham: Duke University Press.

Rosen, F. and J-M. Burt (1997) '16 Activists Reflect on the Current Political Moment: Bishop Samuel Ruiz García', *NACLA: Report on the Americas*, 31(1): 38–43.

Rosenberg, J. (1994) *The Empire of Civil Society: A Critique of the Realist Theory of International Relations*. London: Verso.

—— (1996) 'Isaac Deutscher and the Lost History of International Relations', *New Left Review* (I), 215: 3–15.

—— (2000) *The Follies of Globalisation Theory*. London: Verso.

—— (2005) 'Globalisation Theory: A Post-Mortem', *International Politics*, 42(1): 2–74.

Rosengarten, F. (1986) 'Gramsci's "Little Discovery": Gramsci's Interpretation of Canto X of Dante's Inferno', *Boundary 2*, 14(3): 71–90.

—— (1994) 'Introduction', in Antonio Gramsci, *Letters from Prison*, vol. 1, ed. F. Rosengarten, trans. Raymond Rosenthal. New York: Columbia University Press.

Ross, J. (1995) *Rebellion from the Roots: Indian Uprising in Chiapas*. Monroe, Minn.: Common Courage Press.

Rovira, G. (2000) *Women of Maize: Indigenous Women and the Zapatista Rebellion*, trans. A. Keene. London: Latin America Bureau.

Ruggie, J. G. (1982) 'International Regimes, Transactions and Change: Embedded Liberalism in the Postwar Economic Order', *International Organization*, 36(2): 379–415.

Rupert, M. (1995a) *Producing Hegemony: The Politics of Mass Production and American Global Power*. Cambridge: Cambridge University Press.

—— (1995b) '(Re)Politicising the Global Economy: Liberal Common Sense and Ideological Struggle in the US NAFTA Debate', *Review of International Political Economy*, 2(4): 658–92.

—— (1998) '(Re-)Engaging Gramsci: A Response to Germain and Kenny', *Review of International Studies*, 24(3): 427–34.

—— (2000) *Ideologies of Globalisation: Contending Visions of a New World Order*. London: Routledge.

—— (2003) 'Globalising Common Sense: A Marxian–Gramscian (Re-)vision of the Politics of Governance/Resistance', *Review of International Studies*, 29 (special issue): 181–98.

Rus, J. (1994) 'The "Comunidad Revolucionario Institucional": The Subversion of Native Government in Highland Chiapas, 1936–1968', in G. Joseph and D. Nugent (eds) *Everyday Forms of State Formation: Revolution and the Negotiation of Rule in Modern Mexico*. Durham: Duke University Press.

—— (1995) 'Local Adaptation to Global Change: The Reordering of Native Society in Highland Chiapas, Mexico, 1974–1994', *European Review of Latin American and Caribbean Studies*, 58: 71–89.

Ryner, M. (2002) *Capitalist Restructuring, Globalisation and the Third Way: Lessons from the Swedish Model*. London: Routledge.

Said, E. W. (1984) *The World, the Text and the Critic*. London: Faber and Faber.

—— (1985) 'Orientalism Reconsidered', *Race and Class*, 27(2): 1–15.

—— (1990) 'Figures, Configurations, Transfigurations', *Race and Class*, 32(1): 1–16.

—— (2000) 'History. Literature and Geography', in Edward W. Said, *Reflections on Exile and Other Literary and Cultural Essays*. London: Granta.

Salinas de Gortari, C. (2002) *México: The Policy and Politics of Modernisation*, trans. P. Hearn and P. Rosas. Barcelona: Plaza & Janés Editores.

Sassoon, A. S. (1987) *Gramsci's Politics*, 2nd edn. Minneapolis: University of Minnesota Press.

—— (1995) 'Family, Civil Society and the State: The Actuality of Gramsci's Notion of "società civile"', *Dialektik*, 3: 67–82.

—— (2000) *Gramsci and Contemporary Politics: Beyond Pessimism of the Intellect*. London: Routledge.

—— (2001) 'Globalisation, Hegemony and Passive Revolution', *New Political Economy*, 6(1): 5–17.

Schecter, D. (1991) *Gramsci and the Theory of Industrial Democracy*. Aldershot: Avebury.

Schechter, M. G. (2002) 'Critiques of Coxian Theory: Background to a Conversation', in R. W. Cox with M. G. Schechter, *The Political Economy of a Plural World: Critical Reflections on Power, Morals and Civilisation*. London: Routledge.

Schneider, J. (ed.) (1998) *Italy's 'Southern Question': Orientalism in One Country*. Oxford: Berg.

Scott, J. C. (1998) *Seeing Like a State: How Certain Schemes to Improve the Human Condition Have Failed*. New Haven: Yale University Press.

Scott-Smith, G. (2002) *The Politics of Apolitical Culture: The Congress for Cultural Freedom and the CIA and Post-War American Hegemony*. London: Routledge.

Sennett, R. (1977) *The Fall of Public Man*. London: Penguin.

Serrano, M. (1997) 'Civil Violence in Chiapas: The Origins and the Causes of the Revolt', in M. Serrano (ed.) *Mexico: Assessing Neoliberal Reform*. London: Institute of Latin American Studies.

Shields, S. (2003) 'The Charge of the "Right Brigade": Transnational Social Forces and the Neoliberal Configuration of Poland's Transition', *New Political Economy*, 8(2): 225–44.

Shilliam, R. (2004) 'Hegemony and the Unfashionable Problematic of "Primitive Accumulation"', *Millennium: Journal of International Studies*, 33(1): 59–88.

Sillanpoa, W. P. (1981) 'Pasolini's Gramsci', *Modern Language Notes*, 96(1): 120–37.

Simon, R. (1991) *Gramsci's Political Thought: An Introduction*. London: Lawrence & Wishart.

Skinner, Q. (1969) 'Meaning and Understanding in the History of Ideas', *History and Theory*, 8(1): 3–53.

—— (1974a) 'Some Problems in the Analysis of Political Thought and Action', *Political Theory*, 2(3): 277–303.

—— (1974b) '"Social Meaning" and the Explanation of Social Action', in P. Gardiner (ed.) *The Philosophy of History*. Oxford: Oxford University Press.

Sklair, L. (2001) *The Transnational Capitalist Class*. Oxford: Blackwell.

Sklair, L. (1993) *Assembling for Development: The Maquila Industry in Mexico and the United States*, expanded edition. San Diego, Calif.: Centre for US–Mexican Studies.

Slater, D. (2004) *Geopolitics and the Post-Colonial: Rethinking North–South Relations*. Oxford: Blackwell.

Smith, H. (1994) 'Marxism and International Relations Theory', in A. J. R. Groom and M. Light (eds) *Contemporary International Relations: A Guide to Theory*. London: Pinter.

Soederberg, S. (2001) 'From Neoliberalism to Social Liberalism: Situating the National Solidarity Program within Mexico's Passive Revolutions', *Latin American Perspectives*, 28(3): 102–23.

Spriano, P. (1975) *The Occupation of the Factories: Italy 1920*, trans. G. A. Williams. London: Pluto Press.

—— (1979) *Antonio Gramsci and the Party: The Prison Years*, trans. J. Fraser. London: Lawrence & Wishart.

Stack, O. (1969) *Pasolini on Pasolini: Interviews with Oswald Stack*. London: Thames & Hudson.

Stahler-Stock, R. (1998) 'The Lessons of Acteal', *NACLA Report on the Americas*, 31(5): 11–14.

Stephen, L. (1995) 'The Zapatista Army of National Liberation and the National Democratic Convention', *Latin American Perspectives*, 22(4): 88–99.

—— (1997) 'Election Day in Chiapas: A Low-Intensity War', *NACLA Report on the Americas*, 31(2): 10–11.

—— (2002) *¡Zapata Lives! Histories and Cultural Politics in Southern Mexico*. Berkeley: University of California Press.

Ste. Croix, G.E.M. de (1981) *The Class Struggle in the Ancient Greek World from the Archaic Age to the Arab Conquests*. London: Duckworth.

Stienstra, D. (1994) *Women's Movements and International Organisations*. London: Macmillan.

Strange, G. (2002) 'Globalisation, Regionalism and Labour Interests in the new IPE', *New Political Economy*, 7(3): 343–65.

Strange, S. (1996) *The Retreat of the State: The Diffusion of Power in the World Economy*. Cambridge: Cambridge University Press.

Sullivan, K. (1995) 'Rural–Urban Restructuring Among the Chamula People in the Highlands of Chiapas', in J. Nash et al. *The Explosion of Communities in Chiapas*. Copenhagen: The International Working Group for Indigenous Affairs.

Taylor, I. (2001) *Stuck in Middle GEAR: South Africa's Post-Apartheid Foreign Relations*. Westport, Conn.: Praeger Publishers.

Teichman, J. A. (1996) 'Mexico: Economic Reform and Political Change', *Latin American Research Review*, 31(2): 252–62.

Teschke, B. (1998) 'Geopolitical Relations in the European Middle Ages: History and Theory', *International Organization*, 52(2): 325–58.

—— (2002) 'Theorising the Westphalian System of States: International Relations from Absolutism to Capitalism', *European Journal of International Relations*, 8(1): 5–48.

—— (2003) *The Myth of 1648: Class, Geopolitics and the Making of Modern International Relations*. London: Verso.

—— (2005) 'Bourgeois Revolution, State Formation and the Absence of the International', *Historical Materialism*, 13(2): 3–26.

Thompson, E.P. (1968) *The Making of the English Working Class*. London: Penguin.

—— (1971/1993) 'The Moral Economy of the English Crowd in the Eighteenth Century', in E.P. Thomson, *Customs in Common*. London: Penguin.

—— (1975) *Whigs and Hunters: The Origin of the Black Act*. London: Penguin.

—— (1978) 'Eighteenth Century English Society: Class Struggle Without Class?' *Social History*, 3(2): 133–65.

Togliatti, P. (1979) *On Gramsci and Other Writings*, ed. and intro. D. Sassoon. London: Lawrence & Wishart.

Tooze, R. (1990) 'Understanding the Global Political Economy: Applying Gramsci', *Millennium: Journal of International Studies*, 19(2): 273–80.

Trotsky, L. (1936) *The History of the Russian Revolution*, vol.1. London: Victor Gollancz.

Ugalde, F. V. (1994) 'From Bank Nationalisation to State Reform: Business and the New Mexican Order', in M. L. Cook, K. J. Middlebrook and J. M. Horcasitas (eds) *The Politics of Economic Restructuring: State–Society Relations and Regime Change in Mexico*. San Diego, Calif.: Centre for US–Mexican Studies.

—— (1996) 'The Private Sector and Political Regime Change in Mexico', in G. Otero (ed.) *Neoliberalism Revisited: Economic Restructuring and Mexico's Political Future*. Boulder: Westview Press.

Urbinati, N. (2002) 'From the Periphery of Modernity: Antonio Gramsci's Theory of Subordination and Hegemony', in James Martin (ed.) *Antonio Gramsci: Critical Assessments of Leading Political Philosophers*, vol. 3. London: Routledge.

Urquidi, V. L. (1994) 'The Outlook for Mexican Economic Development in the 1990s', in M. L. Cook, K. J. Middlebrook and J. M. Horcasitas (eds) *The Politics of Economic Restructuring: State–Society Relations and Regime Change in Mexico*. San Diego, Calif.: Centre for US–Mexican Studies.

Van der Haar, G. (2005) 'Land Reform, the State and the Zapatista Uprising in Chiapas', *The Journal of Peasant Studies*, 32(3/4): 484–507.

Veltmeyer, H. (1997) 'New Social Movements in Latin America: The Dynamics of Class and Identity', *The Journal of Peasant Studies*, 25(1): 139–69.

—— (2000) 'The Dynamics of Social Change and Mexico's EZLN', *Latin American Perspectives*, 27(5): 88–110.

Vico. G. (1984) *The New Science of Giambattista Vico*, trans. T. G. Bergin and M. H. Fisch from the third edition (1744) with the addition of 'Practic of the New Science'. Ithaca: Cornell University Press.

Vilas, C. M. (1996) 'Are There Left Alternatives? A Discussion from Latin America', in L. Panitch (ed.) *The Socialist Register: Are There Alternatives?* London: Merlin Press.

Villafuerte Solís, D. (2005) 'Rural Chiapas Ten Years after the Armed Uprising: An Economic Overview', *The Journal of Peasant Studies*, 32(3/4): 461–83.

Walker, R. B. J. (1993) *Inside/Outside: International Relations as Political Theory*. Cambridge: Cambridge University Press.

Waltz, K. N. (1979) *Theory of International Politics*. Reading, Mass.: Addison-Wesley.

Walzer, M. (1988) 'The Ambiguous Legacy of Antonio Gramsci', *Dissent*, 35: 444–56.

Watkins, E. (1986) 'Gramsci's Anti-Croce', *Boundary 2*, 14(3): 121–35.

Watson, T. (1993) 'Comrade Gramsci's Progeny', *Postmodern Culture*, 3(3). Available at http://www.iath.virginia.edu/pmc/text-only/issue.593/review-1.593; accessed 30 September 1999.

Weinberg, B. (2000) *Homage to Chiapas: The New Indigenous Struggles in Mexico*. London: Verso.

Weiss, L. (1998) *The Myth of the Powerless State: Governing the Economy in a Global Era*. Cambridge: Polity Press.

Whitehead, L. (1980) 'Mexico From Bust to Boom: A Political Evaluation of the 1976–1979 Stabilisation Program', *World Development*, 8(11): 843–64.

—— (1989) 'Political Change and Economic Stabilisation: The "Economic Solidarity Pact"', in W. A. Cornelius, J. Gentleman, and P. H. Smith (eds) *Mexico's Alternative Political Futures*. San Diego, Calif.: Centre for US–Mexican Studies.

Whitworth, S. (1994) *Feminism and International Relations: Towards a Political Economy of Gender in Interstate and Non-Governmental Institutions*. London: Macmillan.

Wiener, A. and T. Diez (eds) (2003) *European Integration Theory*. Oxford: Oxford University Press.

Williams, G. A. (1960) 'The Concept of "Egemonia" in the Thought of Antonio Gramsci: Some Notes on Interpretation', *Journal of the History of Ideas*, 21(4): 586–99.

—— (1974) 'The Making and Unmaking of Antonio Gramsci', *New Edinburgh Review*, 7–15. (Gramsci special edition 3).

—— (1975) *Proletarian Order: Antonio Gramsci, Factory Councils and the Origins of Communism in Italy 1911–1921*. London: Pluto Press.

Womack, J. (1968) *Zapata and the Mexican Revolution*. New York: Random House.

—— (1999) *Rebellion in Chiapas: An Historical Reader*. New York: New Press.

Wood, E. M. (1991) *The Pristine Culture of Capitalism: An Historical Essay on Old Regimes and Modern States*. London: Verso.

—— (1995) *Democracy Against Capitalism: Renewing Historical Materialism*. London: Verso.

—— (2002a) *The Origin of Capitalism: A Longer View*. London: Verso.

—— (2002b) 'Landlords and Peasants, Masters and Slaves: Class Relations in Greek and Roman Antiquity', *Historical Materialism*, 10(3): 17–69.

—— (2002c) 'Global Capital, National States', in M. Rupert and H. Smith (eds) *Historical Materialism and Globalisation*. London: Routledge.

Wyn Jones, R. (2000) *Critical Theory and World Politics*. Boulder: Lynne Rienner.

Zangheri, R. (1998) 'Notes on Gramsci and the Twentieth Century', *The Philosophical Forum*, 29(3–4): 93–103.

Zermeño, S. (1997) 'State, Society and Dependent Neoliberalism in Mexico: The Case of the Chiapas Uprising', in W. C. Smith and R. P. Korzeniewicz (eds) *Politics, Social Change and Economic Restructuring in Latin America*. Miami, Fla.: North–South Centre Press.

Index

Compiled by Fulya Memişoğlu

247

Griffiths, Trevor, 24–5, 216, 232

Habermas, Jürgen, 219
Hall, Stuart, 2, 6, 16, 18, 35–6, 218,
    233
  thinking in a Gramscian way, 18
Halliday, Fred, 65, 75, 152, 233
Harvey, David, 136, 149, 152, 168,
    181–3, 185–6, 194, 220, 233,
    235
hegemony,
  beyond theory of the state-as-
    force, 76–7, 88, 93, 135
  and class, 163, 169
  coercion, 203
  consent, as the organisation of,
    75, 93
  corruption/fraud, 95, 163
  'counter'hegemony, 95, 97–8,
    114, 132, 191, 193
  crisis of hegemony, 166, 169
  critical theory of, 111, 134–5
  cultural, 5, 129
  fractured, 189, 202–4
  Gramsci's definition, 206
  history of before Gramsci, 235
  and ideology, 95, 114
  integral, 89–90, 93
  as intersubjective, 93–4, 106,
    113–14
  minimal, 107
  normal, 94, 107, 163, 188–9, 203
  neo-Realist theory of, 111, 120
  social basis of, 8, 78, 93, 106, 135
  struggle for, 101, 120, 122
  variations of, 107
historical bloc, 78, 95–8, 106,
    118–19, 121–2, 126–7, 132–3
historical materialism/ist, 3, 21, 26,
    28, 40, 62, 65, 80, 88, 111, 118,
    128–9, 135, 175, 204, 206, 222,
    227, 229, 231–2, 234, 236, 244,
    246
  see also Marxism
  see also philosophy of praxis
historical sociology, 8, 40–2, 50, 59,
    67–8, 70, 75, 153, 203, 205, 227
  method of historical analogy, 58,
    68–9, 75, 202

method of historical
    interpretation, 41, 76
method of incorporated
    comparison, 70
method of subaltern class
    analysis, 175
historicism, 18, 34, 76, 216, 223,
    228, 238
  absolute historicism, 17, 24–5,
    29–30, 32, 37, 76
  austere historicism, 17, 24–5, 27,
    29, 32, 37
Hobsbawm, Eric, 45, 65, 75, 112,
    130–1, 143, 152, 176, 215,
    217–18, 234–5, 238
Holub, Renate, 36, 219, 235
Horkheimer, Max, 219
Humanism, 29, 56–8

Idealism/ist, 20, 34, 78, 90–1, 106,
    129, 217
identity, 22–3, 41, 48, 51, 55, 60,
    62, 80–1, 97, 103, 117, 130,
    172, 174–6, 180, 190, 193–4,
    199, 200, 211, 230, 237, 239,
    245
  class identity, 117, 174, 176
  gender, 104–5, 114, 117, 129,
    175, 180, 194, 236, 246
ideology, 28, 50, 71–3, 81, 87, 92,
    94–6, 103–4, 114, 127, 129–31,
    158, 223, 237–8
Il Grido del Popolo, 3
imperialism, 4–5, 70, 72, 112, 136,
    225, 233, 236
  see also colonialism
immanent critique, 18, 37
immanent reading, 23
Import Substitution
    Industrialisation (ISI), 154,
    158, 161, 163, 168, 169
individuals, 44, 46, 61, 79, 89, 118,
    151, 183, 209, 218
Institutional Revolutionary Party
    (PRI), 154–5, 157, 160–1,
    163–6, 169–70, 178, 181,
    183–90, 193, 195–6
intellectuals, 19, 22, 28, 82, 87
  and class, 60–1, 92, 150

Printed in Great Britain
by Amazon

49929540R00156